History of
Emporia
and
Lyon County
Kansas

WITH AN INTRODUCTION BY
William Allen White

Laura M. French

HERITAGE BOOKS
2008

HERITAGE BOOKS
AN IMPRINT OF HERITAGE BOOKS, INC.

Books, CDs, and more—Worldwide

For our listing of thousands of titles see our website
at
www.HeritageBooks.com

A Facsimile Reprint
Published 2008 by
HERITAGE BOOKS, INC.
Publishing Division
100 Railroad Ave. #104
Westminster, Maryland 21157

Originally published
Emporia, Kansas
Emporia Gazette Print
1929

— Publisher's Notice —
In reprints such as this, it is often not possible to remove blemishes from the original. We feel the contents of this book warrant its reissue despite these blemishes and hope you will agree and read it with pleasure.

International Standard Book Number: 978-0-7884-0346-0

To the scores of men and women who have contributed of their recollections to the making of this book; for the research of others into dusty records; for the frequent response, "I can't tell you that, but I can tell you who can"; for the interest and cooperation of all of these, and of many others, I wish to express my sincere gratitude and appreciation.

—L. M. F.

December, 1929.

To my Father and Mother; to Mr. and Mrs. George Plumb; and to all the other Dear Pioneers of Emporia and Lyon County.

INTRODUCTION

THE LOCAL TRADITION

Every community in the world differs from every other community. Getting down to the last, smallest unit of human activity, each particle is unique. And moreover, the traditions of each unit of human society are valuable. They make background upon which life and institutions are founded.

This history of Emporia and Lyon County is the most comprehensive history of the people of this community ever ma Several of the stories have been written, but nothing has be written for a generation and little had been written before comparable with this story. Here is set down the beginnings of Lyon County, the growth of her people, the story of three wars whose soldiers marched away from Sixth and Commercial in Emporia, the rise of a new, raw, prosperous community in the Sixties, Seventies and Eighties, the great accounting in the Nineties, when the mortgages fell due and the Populists rose and made politics out of pay-day, the big boom of the first two decades of the century—all are set down here. Names and dates and places are accurately recorded. The best thing about this book is its accuracy. The spelling of the names and the dates are as dependable as spelling and dates may be in any book. It is carefully and beautifully written.

It is most important that we should know our past, that we of Emporia and Lyon County should know why we are what we are; how inevitably today came out of yesterday. At the start we were of New England blood. Today more than 90 per cent of our people bear English names or Welsh, which is the same so far as nomenclature goes, if not blood. Out of this community, which for want of a better name we will call Anglo-Saxon, has been developed the town and county that abides today. It was inevitable that it should grow as it has grown. To understand it, to appreciate it, to love it all, we must know its seeds and the beginnings of its growth.

The need for that knowledge is the justification of this story, an interesting story well written.

W. A. WHITE.

CONTENTS

Chapter	Page
I—1857-1860: The Beginnings of Emporia—How the Town Was Named—Prohibition Incorporated in Charter—Newspaper An Important Factor—Ideal Location—Mail Facilities—Becomes County Seat —Drouth of 1860—First School—First Town Well Gristmills and Sawmills	1-20
II—1860-1865: The Civil War Period—Community's Contribution of Soldiers—The Making of the Flags—With Those Who Wait—Establishment of State Normal School	20-30
III—1865-1875: Town and County Start Anew Following Civil War—First School Building—Rush of Settlers—Livestock Industry—The First Bank	31-49
IV—1875-1880: A Period of Prosperity—Town Grows As Never Before—Preston B. Plumb Elected To United States Senate—The Exodus—Hayes, Sherman and Grant Visit Emporia—Waterworks Plant Established—The City Library	43-49
V—1880-1890: An Era of Building—New Grade Schools —High School—College of Emporia—Opera Houses and Hotels—Handsome Residences—First Gas For Lighting—Telephones—Street Cars—First Alfalfa In Kansas Grown At Emporia—Ottawa Branch of Santa Fe—Early Closing For Stores— Free Mail Delivery Established	51-61
VI—1890-1900: Enforcing Prohibitory Law—Sewer System Established—Death of Senator Plumb—Emporia Sends Company E To Spanish-American War—First National Bank Fails—First Automobile Comes To Emporia For Street Fair, 1899	62-72
VII—1900-1910: Rural Free Mail Delivery—Orient Railway Plans—Carnegie Presents Library Building To Town—Work Starts on Post Office Building— First Street Paving 1905—Emporia Observes Fiftieth Anniversary of Founding—G. W. Brown, President of Town Company, Guest of Honor	73-93

HISTORY OF EMPORIA AND LYON COUNTY

VIII—1910-1920: Emporia Adopts Commission Form of Government—Women Take Up Seriously Their New Duties of Citizenship—New High School Building—Emporia For Third Time Sends Her Boys To War—Red Cross and Liberty Loan Activities—First Influenza Epidemic—College of Emporia Burns _____ 94-115

IX—1920-1929: Southwestern Mortgage Company Closes Doors—Newman Memorial County Hospital Opened—Santa Fe Announces Five Million Dollar Improvement Program—Town Votes Bonds For Junior High School—Broadview Hotel Opened—Town Discards Street Cars In Favor of Busses—City Buys Soden's Grove—Official Emporia Flag Adopted—New St. Mary's Hospital Opened—J. S. Kenyon Leaves One Hundred Thousand Dollars to College of Emporia—Mrs. Cora Borton Ryder Makes Bequest of Two Hundred Thousand To Newman Memorial County Hospital—Citizens Bank Changes Hands—Death of F. C. Newman__116-128

LYON COUNTY TOWNS
Americus _____129
Hartford _____130
Plymouth _____132
Neosho Rapids _____134
Reading _____135
Olpe _____137
Allen _____137
Admire _____139
Bushong _____141
Miller _____141

A FEW OF THE FIRST THINGS
First Religious Services _____143
The First Wedding _____144
How Two Men Helped _____146
John Brown in Emporia _____147
First Night in Emporia _____148
Bleeding Kansas _____150
Early-day Table Delicacies _____154

RELIGIOUS BODIES
Protestant Churches _____158
Catholic Church and Congregation _____167

IN THE GOOD OLD DAYS
Early-day Hospitality _____171
Defunct Towns and Post Offices _____173
Outlaw Raids and Victims _____176
Carrying the Mail _____180

HISTORY OF EMPORIA AND LYON COUNTY

ORCHARDISTS AND OTHERS
- Early-day Orchardists --- 182
- Diversified Stock-raising --- 184
- Foreign Immigration --- 187
- Floods in Lyon County --- 189

MANNERS AND CUSTOMS
- The Horse-and-Buggy Days --- 194
- Rattlesnakes and "Rosum" Weeds --- 195
- Prairie Fires --- 197
- Playtime and Playgrounds --- 198
- Changing Conditions --- 204
- Early-day Funerals --- 212
- Floursack Days --- 213
- Emporia Bands --- 215

IN THE PUBLIC EYE
- Lyon County Newspapers --- 222
- Politics and Politicians --- 229

ORGANIZATIONS
- Women's City Club --- 235
- County Association of Clubs --- 237
- The First Study Clubs --- 239
- Business and Professional Women's Club --- 243

PATRIOTIC
- Grand Army of the Republic --- 244
- Women's Relief Corps --- 245
- Ladies of G. A. R. --- 245
- Sons of Veterans --- 245
- Sons of Veterans Auxiliary --- 245
- Daughters of Union Veterans --- 245
- Spanish War Veterans --- 245
- Spanish War Women's Auxiliary --- 245
- American Legion --- 245
- Daughters of American Revolution --- 245

FRATERNAL
- Masons and Eastern Star --- 246
- Odd Fellows and Rebekahs --- 246
- The Elks and Women's Auxiliary --- 246
- Other Fraternal Bodies --- 246

FARM
- Agricultural Society --- 247
- The Grange --- 247
- Farmers Union --- 248
- Lyon County Farm Bureau --- 248
- 4-H Clubs --- 249
- Home Demonstration Agent --- 249
- Farmers' Alliance --- 249
- Farmers' Association --- 250
- Chamber of Commerce --- 250
- Retailers' Association --- 250

HISTORY OF EMPORIA AND LYON COUNTY

SOME OF THE SCHOOLS
Teachers College Chronology ---253
Emporia Business College ---256
The District Schools ---257

TOWN AND COUNTY TODAY
City Water System ---260
Emporia's Physical Growth ---262
Public Health Service ---266
Roads and Bridges ---267

OUTSTANDING CITIZENS
Preston B. Plumb ---275
Other Distinguished Citizens ---278
Lyon County Officials—1929 ---282
Emporia City Officials—1929 ---283
Walt Mason ---284
The Honor Roll ---285
Citizens Bank Changes Hands ---286

HISTORY OF EMPORIA AND LYON COUNTY

CHAPTER I—1857-1860

Emporia, Kanzas Territory, was founded in 1857. George W. Brown, president of the Emporia Town Company, who came from Rockford, Illinois, to be guest of honor at the celebration of the town's fiftieth anniversary, in 1907, said of the date of the founding:

"The Emporia Town Company, with George W. Brown as president, and G. W. Deitzler as secretary, was christened by the Territorial Legislature February 20, 1857, on the very day and, perhaps, the identical hour the surveyor found the corners and gave the description for entry in the surveyor general's office, at Lecompton."

Mr. Brown told also of the naming of the town. He said: "The name, which I selected during the first days of February, 1857, gave to the Town Company and received its endorsement, is mentioned in Book 2, Part 2, Section 2, in a note by its author, Rollin's History of the Carthaginians. Emporia was a country in Africa on the Lesser Syrtis, in which Leptis stood. No part of the Carthaginian Dominion was more fruitful than this."

Continuing, Mr. Brown said:

"Polybius says in substance: 'The revenue that arose from Emporia was so considerable that nearly all of the Carthaginian hopes were founded on it. Because of its great wealth, they feared the Romans would attempt its conquest.' Lemprier, in his Classical Dictionary, mentions Emporia, situated where now is Tunis; and a West Emporia, on the west coast of the Mediterranean, a little north of where now is Barcelona, at the almost extreme northeast corner of Spain. Grote also mentions it in his Unabridged History of Greece."

So, Emporia was named for a great financial center, in the fond hope that the Kansas town one day would rival the ancient country.

The Emporia Town Company included, besides Brown and Deitzler, Lyman Allen and Columbus Hornsby, all of Lawrence, a young man who had come a year earlier to Kanzas Territory, had started the town of Mariposa, near the present site of Salina, which had been abandoned, and now was ready for further adventure—Preston B. Plumb, destined to become the town's most distinguished citizen in the Nineteenth Century, and to rise high in the councils of the Nation. These men were ten days in the saddle, selecting a site, so careful were they in their choice of a location for the new town. Brown at that time was editor of the Herald of Freedom, at Lawrence, and Plumb had worked for him there a short time.

The Town Company bought, from Joel Walker,[1] of Kansas City, executor of the estate of A. Hicks, the land on which Emporia was located. They divided equally among themselves the cost price of $1,800.00 into shares of $360.00 each, which they paid in cash.

The transfer is signed by Richard Hinton, land agent. The land originally was obtained from the

[1] The bill of sale given by Joel Walker hangs in the library of the State Teachers College, Emporia.

Federal Government as an Indian float,[1] covering 640 acres. An additional 320 acres on the south was included, and the entire one and one-half sections filed as a city site, in the surveyor general's office at Lecompton. The town site had been preempted and was ready to furnish deeds in December, 1858.

Young Plumb had insisted on no less than a section of land on which to start the town, that there might be no dividing line within a few years, such as might have developed had the town been located on a half section. At once the town began to grow and attract trade. A few settlements had been made in this section of the Territory as early as 1854-1855-1856, but the spring of 1857 the real tide of immigration began. Two thousand settlers came to Lyon County that year.[2]

Mr. Plumb was the only member of the Town Company whose home was in Emporia, and to him, more than to any other one man, the town owed its auspicious

[1] In the treaty concluded with Wyandot Indians at Upper Sandusky March 17, 1842, the Government, as an inducement to the Indians to accept the treaty, agreed to grant by patent in fee simple to Isaiah Walker and thirty-four other Wyandot Indians 640 acres of land, each, "out of any lands west of the Missouri River set apart for Indian use, not already claimed or occupied by any person or tribe." The Wyandots moved to Kansas in 1844, but none of the persons entitled to do so took up any of these tracts for several years. When Kanzas Territory was established it was impossible to secure absolute title to much of the land, as the surveys were incomplete. Then the Wyandots owning them began to sell these patents, for, as they could be located on any public land, they gave absolute title at once. As they could be laid on any portion of the public domain they were called "floating claims," or "floats."

[2] An attempt to start a free love colony on Taylor Creek, north of town, in 1857, got so good a start that two or three married couples swapped companions. They seem to have had as little regard for the marriage obligation as do some of the "advanced" thinkers of today. Other settlers complained of their actions, and they were summoned by the sheriff to appear at Agnes City, the county seat. And that was the last of the free love colony in Lyon County. The dissatisfied ones returned to their homes and the colony disbanded.

start in life. For Plumb brought a printing press[3] from Xenia, Ohio, where he had learned the printer's trade and been in the newspaper business. He started a newspaper here and advertised the town, also shouldered much of the work of the Town Company. The first issue of the Kanzas News[4] was printed at the corner which became Sixth and Commercial Streets, in an unfinished room of the new hotel building.[5] As many copies of the News as the editor had print paper were published, the Town Company buying 1,500 copies which were broadcast in the Eastern States. This was the only newspaper at that time between Lawrence and the Rocky Mountains, and for several weeks it was mailed at Lawrence.

[1]This first newspaper, in an editorial in its first edition, published the most important and forward-looking section of the town charter, which forbade the

[3] Noble Prentis, in his History of Kansas, says: "Napoleon said that every French soldier carried a marshal's baton in his knapsack; in Kansas, future governors, senators, chieftains and ambassadors, carried printers' rules in their pockets."

[4] The Kanzas News at once was recognized as a vigorous advocate of the Free State cause. It became the leading paper of that party in the Territory. "The News was surprisingly well edited," wrote Jacob Stotler, of Plumb's work in later years. "It took rank at once with the best in the Territory, and never occupied a doubtful position on any question."

[5] Two bronze tablets mark the spot where stood Emporia's first public building. In 1921 the Daughters of the American Revolution placed a small tablet on the northeast corner of the Citizens National Bank building, and in 1924 the Lyon County Old Settlers' Association put in place above it a much larger tablet, both commemorating the erection on this corner, in 1857, of the Emporia House, which was Emporia's first hotel and first public building.

[1] George Plumb, brother of P. B. Plumb, helped to run the press for this first edition of the News, and William Hammond got a job folding papers. Both were young boys in their early teens, both still are citizens of this community, and enjoy telling how they helped get out the town's first newspaper. These boys hauled water for the town with a horse and a barrel and a "lizard." Both are authorities on early-day history.

sale of liquor, and of gambling on the town site. Thus, Emporia's founders established the first prohibition town in the world, anticipating by twenty-three years the state prohibitory amendment, and by sixty-one years the Eighteenth Amendment to the Federal Constitution, which brought national prohibition.

[2]Volume 1, No. 1, the Kanzas News, published June 6, 1857, in an editorial on "Emporia," contains the two prohibitory paragraphs:

[3]"The parties bind themselves to each other that, in every sale or donation of any portion of the land which may be selected or located for a town site, they will sign no deed of sale, release, gift, grant or lease to the same, without a provision in such deed of sale, release, gift, grant or lease, that the lessee shall not make, store, sell or give away, to be used as beverage, any malt or spirituous liquor on such premises, or sold or conveyed away, and that any violations of such provisions shall be a forfeiture of all the rights, which such purchaser, donee, grantee, or tenant shall have acquired to such premises.

"And the parties further agree that they will also prohibit, in all deeds and conveyances, as above, and bind purchasers to extend the same provisions to their assignees, that no houses shall be allowed to be occupied for gambling purposes on any lot of said town; and any gambling for money, or otherwise, by which anything shall be lost or won, on said premises, with the knowledge and counsel of the purchaser, shall be a forfeiture of all the rights which said purchaser, donee,

---

[2] Volume I, No. I, the Kanzas News, carefully preserved and framed, hangs in the editorial office of the Emporia Gazette, and is one of the Gazette editor's valued possessions.

[3] The original agreement of the Town Company, framed, is in the library of the Kansas State Teachers College, Emporia.

grantee, or tenant shall have acquired to said premises."

In his salutatory, Plumb voiced the sentiment of the Free Soil settlers—largely in the majority in this section of the Territory—when he said:

"Standing on the broad principles of Humanity and Freedom, we shall not cease to strike at oppression in whatever form or wherever it may be found. We admit of no middle ground between right and wrong—no compromise with evil; and we shall act with no party that has not universal Freedom inscribed on its banners. The struggle now going on between freedom and slavery is a death one. One or the other must succumb. The agitation of this question will not and should not stop until every bondsman is made free, or until every poor man, black or white, is made a slave. This is the alternative presented. Believing this, we shall never cease our warfare with slavery."

[1]In 1858 Jacob Stotler bought a half interest in the News, and in January, 1859, Mr. Plumb sold his remaining half to Mr. Stotler.

Charles Vernon Eskridge, then and thereafter as long as he lived a citizen of Emporia, was appointed town clerk and general agent for the Town Company. The original boundaries of this county were fixed by

[1] Jacob Stotler came to Lawrence with Plumb from Ohio early in the spring of 1857, worked for a time on the Herald of Freedom, and came to Emporia in May of that year, as foreman for Plumb on the Kanzas News. He hauled the printing press, type and other equipment from Lawrence with a yoke of oxen. For more than a quarter of a century he was editor and publisher of the News—the name changed to the Emporia News—and the paper was one of power and influence, a credit to its editor and to the community it served. Stotler for four terms was a member of the lower house of the Kansas Legislature, two terms was speaker, and served one term as state senator. For two terms he was postmaster of Emporia, resigning at the beginning of the third term. Stotler died at his home in Emporia, January 26, 1901.

the "bogus legislature" of 1855. It was named Breckinridge in honor of the vice president of the United States, but this was changed by act of the State Legislature of 1862, honoring Gen. Nathaniel Lyon,[1] who fell in the Battle of Wilson's Creek.

The location of Emporia is ideal. On the south slope, almost to the top of the rise half-way between the Cottonwood and the Neosho Rivers, there is no probability of its ever being overflowed by either of these streams. The streets have excellent natural drainage, the heat of summer is much less oppressive than in those towns which hug the river banks, it is light and airy, open to sunshine and ozone, and almost free from mosquitoes. The trees planted throughout the nearly three-quarters of a century have grown within the town a forest which provides the shade so necessary to comfort in summer, and furnishes homes for thousands of native songbirds. Not a tree nor a shrub was nearer the town site than the rivers when the first settlers came, and the rolling plain was covered with bluestem grass, much of it as high as a man's head on horseback, say old settlers. The town long since went over the top of the hill to the north, and has overflowed its original boundaries on every side. Its beautiful elms, its lovely lawns bright with flowers from early spring until verdure is frozen in the autumn, its innumerable songbirds, make it a bower of peaceful beauty.

In 1858 the name of the Kanzas News was changed to the Emporia News, and the paper had enjoyed a steady growth. Mr. Stotler in 1860 had enlarged it to seven columns to the page, it having been a six-

[1] General Lyon was distinguished as the only abolitionist in the West Point contingent of the Union Army when the Civil War was declared.

column paper. In his first issue of the enlarged paper, he printed some reminiscences of the earlier days of the town, a part of which he quoted in his Annals of Lyon County, published in 1898. These quotations follow, in part:

"There were just three houses in Emporia at that time—the date of the first issue of the News—the hotel, the store of Hornsby & Fick and a small building used temporarily by N. S. Storrs for a store and dwelling, 14x16 feet. The type for the first number was set in one of the bedrooms of the hotel, while the press work was done in what afterward was the parlor, on loose boards laid down temporarily for that purpose. The printers were Jacob Stotler, Theodore W. French and C. C. Clawson. . . . . We do not exaggerate when we say that the regular appearance of the News during the first year of the history of Emporia, did more to save the town and establish it firm in the confidence of the people than all else put together. It betokened a purpose which put down the croakers who were prophesying that the town would fail. It inspired confidence in those already here, and induced others to come."

Evidently the News was *established* in the fourth building, when it was ready for occupancy, but Mr. Stotler's record does *not* say the first issue was printed on this corner. An Historical Sketch of Emporia and Lyon County, written by Mr. Stotler for the Lyon County Atlas, published in 1878, describes clearly the locations of these four earliest buildings. The sketch says:

[1]"The first building erected was on the site of Mr. Eskridge's building, (Emporia State Bank corner)

---

[1] John Hammond was the first contractor and builder in Emporia, and erected the three houses referred to.

northwest corner of Commercial Street and Sixth Avenue. The second was the Town Company's hotel, on the corner now occupied by the First National Bank. (Now the Citizens Bank.) The third was a storeroom, on the corner opposite the hotel. (Commercial National Bank.) The fourth was the old NEWS building, on the corner now occupied by the block of that name. In this the NEWS was established June 7, 1857, and printed there for fourteen years."

The News brought the first job and power presses south of Lawrence and Topeka, and had one of the largest and best printing plants in the state, outside of Leavenworth, Lawrence and Topeka.

In 1857 the town of Columbia, three miles southeast of Emporia on the Cottonwood, was supposed to receive mail once a week. Mail for this section at first was left at the post office on the Santa Fe Trail on One Hundred and Forty-two Creek at the home of Charles Withington, the county's first post office and first postmaster. For a time mail for this community was deposited in a hollow tree on the Neosho. Soon the post office was moved from Columbia[2] to Emporia,

[2] John Fowler, postmaster at Columbia, resigned that the change making Emporia a post office might be effected. John Fowler, with Mrs. Fowler and their fifteen sons and daughters, and several grandchildren, came to Lyon County in 1855, with "four wagons drawn by four yoke of oxen and one team of horses, and a buggy drawn by an extra horse," according to W. T. Dungan, in his Story of a White Slave. In 1832 the Fowlers had moved to Indiana from North Carolina, their mode of conveyance being "two cows and a rude frontier wagon." The Fowler school district, southeast of Emporia, long ago was overflowed by descendents of Mr. and Mrs. John Fowler, to the sixth generation. They have numbered among them the county's best citizens. Fred Fowler, commissioner from the First District, is a grandson of Mr. and Mrs. John Fowler. Eli Fowler, a son, was county commissioner twenty-five years earlier. Jefferson S. Pigman was the first postmaster at Columbia, having been appointed in 1855. Mr. Pigman later settled at Neosho Rapids, and died at his home there many years later. R. 'P. Snow had a blacksmith shop in

and for a time all mail matter for this post office was addressed to Box 500, Lawrence, the "Emporia Box," and brought here sometimes by immigrants or others who might be passing through the country. Sometimes a team was hired and Ira Hadley went to Lawrence on purpose to bring the mail. An occasional horseback mail was carried from Fort Scott to Council Grove, by way of Emporia. Late in 1857 a mail route was established, and a hack line started by the Walker Brothers, between Emporia and Lawrence. The hack made round trips weekly, the passenger fare for which was $15.00. The Walkers, along with their passenger business, secured the contract for carrying the mail once a week; time, two days; distance seventy-five miles. H. W. Fick was Emporia's first postmaster.

In August, 1859, Emporia and Emporia Township had 541 inhabitants, with registered voters numbering 180. Taxable property was valued at $150,000.00. New Year's day, 1859, there were four stores in Emporia—the Proctor general merchandise store, the hardware store of Edward Borton, the Fick & Eskridge and the P. G. Hallberg stores. The population of the entire county at this time was 3,500. The prairie sod had yielded well and the new settlements seemed on the way to prosperity. Then came what has come down in history as the Drouth of 'Sixty, although it began in the late summer of 1859. For sixteen months

---

Columbia in 1856. M. M. Snow, of Emporia, is his son. When the Snows came to Kansas from Lee County, Iowa, their two prairie schooners were drawn, one by a yoke of oxen, the other by a yoke of cows. The cows did double duty. They were milked night and morning, and the milk not immediately consumed was put into a churn, the churn firmly anchored in one of the wagons, and by noon, or night, at the furthest, there was a roll of fresh, sweet butter in the churn.

no rain fell in Emporia and Lyon County. This was the longest and severest of any drouth ever known in this section.

Settlers who had come well supplied for the first few years had reached the end of their resources, and were depending on the crops which so hopefully they had planted. Their clothing wore out, their extra food long since had been consumed, their money was gone, there was little work to be had and less money to pay for it. There was no surplus of food and grain from the past year as, the country only just getting a start agriculturally, the acreage was small. Committees to investigate the needs of the people were appointed, and their reports showed that many of the settlers, both in town and on the claims, must have help if they stayed in the state. Food and clothing and other supplies and, later, seeds for planting began to come from further east, and the immediate needs of the people were met. Comparatively few families left this section of the state—some of them stayed for the reason that they had no means of getting out of the state and "going back to my wife's folks," as many of the pioneers said with grim humor. Most of them hung on from sheer dogged determination to win in their fight to build their homes in Kansas. October 14, 1860, a soaking rain fell, and the relief and the rejoicing were unbounded. Hopefully, seeds were planted the next spring, and once more, to these Kansas pioneers, the promise of seed-time and harvest was fulfilled.

Breckinridge County was organized in 1855, under statutes enacted by the "bogus legislature," a body which had been elected in Kanzas Territory by votes cast largely by residents of Missouri. For a time Breckinridge was attached to Madison County for all "civil, criminal and military purposes," and Columbia designated the county seat, but no county business was transacted there. At a bona fide election, February 17, 1857, Arthur I. Baker was elected probate judge, and his residence, Waterloo, declared the county seat. About the same time, Breckinridge was detached from Madison County. Meantime, Americus had been established, and was a candidate for county seat honors. At an election held in the autumn of 1858, probably in September, Americus was made the county seat by a large majority of votes of the people. The first term of court in this county was held in Americus. Other officers elected at the time of Judge Baker's election were Christopher Columbia and Charles Withington, commissioners; Elisha Goddard, sheriff; Solomon Brown and George H. Reese, representatives to the Territorial Legislature.

Breckinridge County's south line originally was the Logan Avenue of today. Madison County, long since defunct, lay between Breckinridge and Greenwood. Emporia, with aspirations to become the county seat, pulled her wires successfully and secured three miles off the north end of Madison, which was added to Breckinridge. This placed Emporia nearer the center of the county geographically, adding to its eligibility for the county seat. At the November election of 1860 George H. Lillie, of Neosho Rapids, was elected representative to the Legislature over Perry B. Maxson, the issue being the location of the county seat. Emporia was chosen by 155 votes over Americus, at which place all county business theretofore had been transacted. Thus ended the county seat[1] war, which had been fought without bloodshed.

[1] The stone courthouse, which stood on the site of the Poehler Mercantile Company's plant until the new courthouse was oc-

December 21, 1857, Breckinridge County was divided into five townships—Agnes City, Americus, Cottonwood, Emporia and Kanzas Center. In 1859 Kanzas Center was changed to Waterloo, and Cahola, Fremont and Forest Hill townships were created. In 1860, Cottonwood was changed to Pike, and Forest Hill to Jackson. Cahola was abolished. When the twelve miles to the south off old Madison County were added, Elmendaro and Center were created from this new territory. Ivy Township was created in 1886, making eleven townships in Lyon County.

This community early realized the necessity for schools. Mary Jane Watson, daughter of Judge and Mrs. John H. Watson, opened the first school in Emporia, October 14, 1858, with fifteen pupils, in a small building on Commercial Street next door to the Emporia State Bank. This was a free subscription school, the young men of the town furnishing most of the money for its support, and securing the necessary building. Parents of school children who were able to subscribe, did so, but those who could not pay were urged to send their children, anyway. Within the next year, more than sixty children were attending school in Emporia.

There were few small children in town, and the pupils for this first school came mostly from outlying claims. Some of the children walked the two or three miles to town, some rode Indian ponies two or three to the pony, and some were brought each day by their parents, driving yokes of oxen, and carrying, perhaps,

---

cupied, was built in 1866 at a cost of $19,795.00. The contract for building the courthouse, from plans furnished by John Hammond, was let to Dr. Thomas Armor and Perry B. Maxson. Peter H. Hughes and Richard Howe did the stonework. George Plumb burned the lime for the mortar used in the stonework.

children from several families. The school bus is not a recent innovation in Lyon County.

T. M. Gruell taught a short term of school the summer of 1859, in the new Christian Church, before the building was plastered. Mrs. Margaret Gilmore, who attended this school, recalls as among other pupils, Fannie McCormick, afterward Mrs. W. T. Soden; Clara Weaver, who became Mrs. John A. Moore; her sister, Sarah, afterward Mrs. Ed Staley.

A school for older boys and girls was started the winter of 1858 in McElfresh's Hall, on the present Henning meat market site. This was called a "high school," because it was upstairs, says Mr. George Plumb, who was one of the pupils. Orlando Tripp was the teacher, and the other eight pupils were three of the Spencer girls, Elmira, Eliza and Amanda; two Hicks boys, George and Ellen Armor, and Will Plumb. All of these boys and girls lived on claims north of town, across the Neosho, and rode or walked to school.

Another early-day school was held in the Congregational Church, with about eighty pupils of all ages taught by a man named Foster, who lived in the Duck Creek neighborhood. He was well educated, and often gave free evening entertainments, with lectures and illustrations on chemistry. Miss Abraham and Miss Todd also taught in this school. The Rev. G. C. Morse, pastor of the Congregational Church, and also Lyon County's first superintendent of public instruction, had made a large and heavy wooden tray, in which he had fashioned of clay a plat of Jerusalem for use in his Sunday School work. During week-day school sessions this tray stood against the rear wall of the church— outside. Coke Watson hitched his Indian pony to this tray and gave himself and the other children what he called a "sleighride in Jerusalem."

School District No. 1, Emporia, was organized in December, 1859. W. F. Cloud was director; Edward Borton, clerk, and C. C. Dodge, treasurer. The first public school was opened January 14, 1861, with Miss Abraham as teacher.

Lack of water was one of the town's most serious handicaps in the beginning. Water was hauled in barrels on one-horse sleds made of forked pieces of timber—sometimes called lizards—from deep holes in the Cottonwood, and dragged the weary way over the dry grass and burning soil, or in freezing temperature in winter. In summer, the barrel was deposited on the shady side of a house, to keep the water cool as long as possible, in winter the sunny side was sought, to delay freezing.

John Hammond, contractor and builder, dug the first well[1] that brought a plentiful supply of water, on Mechanic Street between Fifth and Sixth, and great rejoicing followed his announcement that a strong flow of water had been struck. Hammond had saved the town, declared P. B. Plumb who, as member of the Town Company, had hired him to dig the well. Without water, the town could not have endured. After completing the well on Mechanic Street Mr. Hammond dug another well on the hotel lots—the Citizens Bank corner—and struck water at 180 feet. Also, he dug:

---

[1] "At one time," Mrs. Ella Pemberton relates, "the water in this well, from which most of the families got their supply, became curiously tainted. Fear was expressed that the water might have been poisoned, but no one thought of who would do a deed so despicable. The water smelled and tasted like camphor, and finally a man who lived in the east part of town confessed. He had bought a bottle of camphor, and on his way home stopped at the well to quench his thirst. The bottle dropped from an outside pocket into the well, the cork was jarred loose by the fall, and for many days the water was flavored with camphor. When it was found the taste and smell were harmless, the people laughed at the incident."

a well with a strong flow of water on the lots which were the first home of the Hammonds in Emporia, on what became the Major Calvin Hood home, Eighth and State. Major Hood built the residence now occupied by his son, Harry Hood and Mrs. Hood.

Ague—chills and fever—followed the breaking of the sod, a frequent occurrence in new settlements. Often entire families would be down with this scourge at the same time, and if their "chill days" and their "fever days" were the same, there was no one to wait on them. If the "days" alternated, members of the same families could care for one another. Probably no one ever died from ague, but many persons suffering from it wished they might die. Dr. Thomas Armor,[1] pioneer physician, made and dispensed "ague pills," for which settlers, hearing of their curative properties, came sixty to seventy-five miles to procure. Doctor Armor died many years ago, and the formula

---

[1] The late Mrs. F. E. Hawkins, of Americus, was a patient of Dr. Thomas Armor, coming to Emporia on horseback, without a saddle, to get his ague pills. Half a century later Mrs. Hawkins, coming to Emporia from Americus in an automobile to take treatments from Dr. Gladdis Armor, a granddaughter of "Old Doc" Armor, made laughing comparisons of her early trips to her later ones. The "Old Doc" was a born pioneer, and could not confine his activities to the practice of his profession. He built and operated a gristmill on the Neosho, selling the site to the city for its waterworks plant. He started a steam mill in Emporia, the beginning of the Teichgraeber mills. He settled and lived for years on the W. A. Gladfelter farm, north of the Neosho. He took contracts for several of Emporia's public buildings. He owned and operated a wholesale flour and feed business, across the street from the Poehler offices, and sent wagon trains of his products to Denver and other distant points. Doctor Armor brought the first kerosene lamp to Emporia, on his return from a visit to his native state, Delaware, in the sixties. It was a small lamp, with a No. 1 wick, and it was so great a curiosity that the house for several weeks was full of neighbors who had come to "see that new-fangled lamp." He was one of the founders of the defunct town of Fremont. He was public spirited and community minded. Dr. C. C. Slocum was one of the town's earliest physicians, and others of that day were Doctor Bailey, Dr. John

for making ague pills died with him, but the ague had been subdued in this county long before.

In 1860 William T. Soden, who had come to Emporia from New York State in 1857, began the building of the Soden grist mill, on the Cottonwood at the foot of Commercial Street. For years he was building—additions, alterations, repairs—and the mill did an enormous business. A furniture factory was operated in connection with the mill, by Arnold & Company, and it, also, was a thriving institution. After the death of W. T. Soden the mill was operated by his son, Justin R. Soden, until his death in recent years. Now the old mill stands idle, but for many years it was an important asset to the community. Mrs. Justin Soden and her son, Billie, live in the beautiful old Soden home near the mill. W. T. Soden earlier had been a part owner of the Haworth Mill, southwest of town on the Cottonwood, but this mill, which was a combined saw and grist mill, burned in 1862. Mr. Soden was a builder, owned much real estate in Emporia, and was one of the men who helped the town and community in many ways.

Hanford & Hirth ran a furniture factory and planing mill, on Sixth Avenue between Commercial and Mechanic, where they made much of the furniture for the community, of solid walnut, handsome and substantial. There are many pieces of furniture of their manufacture in use in Emporia today.

Mark Patty, another miller, came to Emporia in

A. Moore, L. D. Jacobs, J. W. Trueworthy, J. J. Wright, W. W. Hibben, Allen White, R. R. McCandliss, Doctor Newlon was Emporia's first dentist, and was also a physician. L. D. Bailey and Robert M. Ruggles were the first attorneys, and Preston B. Plumb the third. Later prominent attorneys were T. N. Sedgwick, E. S. Waterbury, Scott & Lynn, C. B. Bacheller, J. Jay Buck, W. T. McCarty, W. A. Randolph.

1859, and built a grist mill on the Cottonwood, eight miles southwest of town. This mill long did a flourishing business, but was burned and not rebuilt. The Patty's Mill site for years was a favorite picnicking place for Emporia people. The old Patty homestead, on a high hill a mile south of the mill, was a landmark for that section of the county. Early-day millers were necessary and valuable acquisitions to any community. Mrs. Anna Jaquith, house mother at Abigail Morse Hall, Teachers College, is a daughter of Mr. and Mrs. Mark Patty.

Numerous sawmills prepared the native lumber for use of settlers in the towns and on the claims. Without railroads, it was impossible to haul all the lumber needed from Kansas City or Lawrence. The first sawmills were operated by Doctor Armor, north of the Neosho, and Parham & Phelps, north of Teachers College, about where Lake Wooster is located. Other early-day sawmills were those of Gideon D. Humphrey, east of town; Joel Haworth, southwest of town; Daniel Rich, in the Rinker neighborhood; Fawcett & Britton, Rinker; Isaiah Jones, on the old Sowerby place and probably others.

There was no sparing of the walnut and oak, the ash and sycamore trees along the Cottonwood and the Neosho. Many old Emporia houses have much valuable timber in their framework which, if in usable form, would be worth many thousands of dollars. The Frederick Cowles homes, northeast of town, was built entirely of walnut, and the estimated value of the lumber even in that early day was $2,000.00. Kitchen floors of ash and hackberry, scrubbed with wood ashes lye to maintain their original whiteness, were the pride of many housekeepers. When cottonwood logs were sawed into lumber and used in buildings—

well, the owners wished they had used the harder woods. Cottonwood lumber warped and twisted and shrunk in wind and sun and rain, and cracks between the planks became unbelievably wide. But the despised cottonwood, a rapidly growing tree, provided the first shade from the glaring sun for the early settlers, and is now held in high esteem by those who appreciate its real value to the pioneers—or to families today on new places who wish to get shade quickly. But the cottonwood's strongest champions admit it doesn't make good lumber.

The Gilmores and the David Plumbs were neighbors on Plumb Creek. In 1859, one of the two horses belonging to each family had died, leaving them only a horse apiece. Young David Gilmore and young George Plumb put the two family horses together to make a team, and took Ellen Plumb, George's sister, to Leavenworth to take the train for Ohio, where she attended school. While in Leavenworth the boys met the president of the New England Emigrant Aid Society, who wished to send some spring wheat seed to settlers at the head of Walnut Creek. He hired the boys to haul the seed and, in trying to estimate the cost of moving it, asked the distance from Emporia to the Walnut. The boys didn't know, but at home it was decided that the Rev. Solomon Brown, who had walked all over this section of the country, preaching, might tell them the probable distance. The boys went to the Brown home at the foot of Exchange Street—way out in the country—met Miss Maggie Brown on the porch, and she called her father. He estimated the distance from Emporia to the Walnut by the length of time required to walk from one preaching place to another, and the boys made money enough from hauling the wheat to buy another horse for each family. But the most important part of this entire episode was that this was the first meeting between young Dave Gilmore and Maggie Brown, the beginning of the romance which culminated in their marriage. Dave Gilmore long has been dead, but Mrs. Margaret Gilmore lives at 423 Union Street, hale and hearty at 83, her mind filled with stories of early days in Emporia.

CHAPTER II—1860-1865

The beginning of 1860 was a discouraging period in the settlement of this section of Kansas. With no rain for many months, there seemed little use in planting, and those who risked their precious seed lost it, as it could not germinate in the dry, parched soil. The town was at a standstill, and the settlers could not encourage their friends in other states to come to Kansas. In Emporia Township, 340 acres of farm land yielded but seventy bushels of inferior wheat, and the best corn made one bushel to the acre. There were no potatoes or other vegetables.

But, in spite of all this, Christmas Day, 1859—no closing for holidays at that time—which came on a Saturday, was reported by the News to have been the biggest trading day in the history of the town. [1]Proctor & Company, who owned the largest store, sold goods to the amount of $350.00, and other stores did a rushing business. January 19, 1861, a snowstorm lasting thirty-six hours added to the moisture which had fallen the previous October, and put the soil in good condition for planting. Throughout 1860, the

[1] July 30, 1859, Addison G. Proctor, proprietor of this store, entertained with a party in the Emporia House in honor of his twenty-first birthday anniversary. Young Proctor in 1860 represented this section of Kansas at the first National Convention of the Republican party, which nominated Lincoln for President. It was said he was the youngest delegate ever sent to a National Convention from any state. Later, Proctor was a bodyguard on the Lincoln funeral train, on its way from Washington to Springfield, Illinois. He lived only a few years in Emporia, and most of his life was spent in St. Joseph, Michigan, where he died February 28, 1925, at the age of 87. Proctor opened his store in Emporia April 15, 1858.

condition of the people has been aptly described as "just hanging on." Too poor to provide properly for their families, the settlers also were too poor to leave their claims. They had no money for travel, no money for food and clothing and fuel, and without the aid sent from the East, many persons must have perished from hunger and exposure.

With the breaking of the drouth the people again took heart, and in the spring of 1861 fields were plowed and more sod broken, and crops planted with high anticipations. But the coming of the Civil War took the young and middle-aged men from the town and county, and little business or agricultural progress was made in the next four years. The first meeting for the organization of a military company in Emporia was held March 6, 1861. Some of the first Kansas soldiers to enter the service for the preservation of the Union were those enlisted from Emporia. April 27, 1861, three companies had been organized from Emporia and surrounding territory, as follows:

The Emporia Guards, 55 men, William F. Cloud,[1] captain.

The Emporia Artillery, 47 men, A. J. Mitchell, captain.

The Emporia Cavalry, 20 men.

May 13, thirty-three more men enlisted, and the next day the Guards offered their services to Governor Robinson. May 24 they left for Lawrence, and June 20 became Company H, Second Kansas Volunteer Infantry. A beautiful flag[2] was given this company by

[1] William F. Cloud had had experience in the Mexican War, and had been a drillmaster. He was a tailor by trade.

[2] In planning to make this flag the women could find no suitable material for the blue field. Mrs. Edward Borton gave for this purpose a "dress pattern" of lovely blue cashmere, which had been sent her from Cincinnati by her mother. Mr. and Mrs.

Emporia women the day it left, the presentation made by Miss Fannie Yeakley, of Americus, and it "was prayed over and blessed" by Father Fairchild, a pioneer Methodist minister. After the Battle of Wilson's Creek the flag again was given into Father Fairchild's hands by the remnants of the company, who brought it home, torn and blood-stained. The Battle of Wilson's Creek, for the number of men engaged, was one of the severest of the war. In the Emporia company four men were killed and eleven wounded.

Soon another company was organized in Emporia, and it reported at Leavenworth in September, 1861. Again Emporia women made a flag, which was presented by Miss Mary Jane Watson,[1] said the News, in an address "couched in beautiful language, appropriate and to the point." In the Battle of Springfield, August 10, 1861, five Emporia boys were killed.

September 20, 1861, Lemuel T. Heritage left Emporia with a company which was mustered in at Leavenworth as Company H, Eighth Kansas. In the spring of 1862 this company was transferred to the Ninth Kansas, becoming Company B of that regiment.

In July, 1862, when President Lincoln issued his call for 300,000 volunteers, to serve three years or for "the endurance of the war," the quota of Kansas was three regiments. Preston B. Plumb, elected to the Legislature in 1861, had been prevailed upon not to enlist until after the legislative session of 1862,

---

Borton came to Emporia from Cincinnati, Ohio, in 1857. Mr. Borton was proprietor of the town's first hardware store, which he opened August 10, that year. They were prominent citizens for many years.
[1] Daughter of Judge and Mrs. John H. Watson, a leading pioneer family. The Emporia battleflags have been carefully preserved, and are in possession of the Kansas State Teachers College, Emporia.

where he was expected to attend to important business for Emporia. This business related chiefly to the county boundary lines, whereby Madison County, on the south, would be abolished, and Emporia established, firmly and forever, as the county seat.

Lyon County originally was twenty-four miles square, its south line being the present Logan Avenue. Emporia wanted three miles off the north end of Madison County added to Breckinridge, and got it, by act of the Territorial Legislature of 1859. The north twelve miles of Madison County in 1861 was attached to Breckinridge, and the south half to Greenwood, eliminating Madison County. The Legislature of 1864 authorized the attachment to Morris County and Chase County of a two-mile strip off the west side of Lyon, thus leaving Lyon twenty-two miles wide, by thirty-nine in length. Lyon County contains 858 square miles, equaling 549,978 acres.

The summer of 1862 Plumb was authorized to recruit a company from six counties, including his own. In the News he advertised, August 16, "One Hundred Men Wanted," and announced war meetings for Neosho Rapids, Emporia, Americus and Council Grove on closely following dates. In a later issue the News announced that a bounty fund of $20.00 a year for each member of needy families of those enlisted in the Lyon County company would be paid until the close of the war. Plumb headed the bounty subscription with $100.00.

Plumb's speeches at the war meetings aroused the people as they had not before been aroused. He knew the people and their needs, their financial limitations, the hardships the families must endure when the men went to war. He put the matter up to them as a duty, and he secured the quota, but it required almost all of the men in the six counties.[1] Only the editor and the devil remained in the News office, and Jacob Stotler declared he would not be able to resist another call. "Our town is almost dried up," said the News, "since the boys left it is a rarity to see a man."[2]

Emporia was left largely to shift for itself, as were the other villages, as well as the prairie claims with their cottonwood shacks, a few acres of broken ground about them, and the stumpy clearings on the bottom lands, the log cabins with the women and children with two or three cows, perhaps, a team, a few chickens. Some of the stores were closed, some of them were opened[3] as an occasional customer might appear. Supplies were secured only under the greatest difficulties, and the courage and fortitude of the women at home gave encouragement to the men at the front, in camp, or on the march. It must be remembered that there were no railroads, few transportation lines of any kind, only occasional mail to most villages, that all of the settlements were new, almost all of the people having arrived during 1857 and the years following. War news was slow in coming, and often battles had been fought for days and weeks before the news of it reached the prairies. The suspense was hardest of all for the women to bear, but they bore it bravely and uncomplainingly, many of them doing men's work in the fields, trying to raise some corn that their children might be fed.

[1] Kansas furnished more than double her quota for the army, and more men, proportionally, than any other state in the Union. No draft was necessary.
[2] When all of the enlisted men had been enrolled, but two men eligible for military service were left on the town site—W. T. Soden, who stayed at home to keep his mill grinding that the people might have bread, and Jacob Stotler, editor of the News.
[3] The late Mrs. J. D. Gibson, of Americus, related how she kept their general store open on Saturdays, while Mr. Gibson was in the army, but said that not every Saturday were there customers.

Plumb reached Leavenworth with 144 enlisted men. Six were rejected because of their extreme youth, but Plumb insisted they be mustered in as musicians. September 10, 1862, 101 of these men were mustered in as Company C, Eleventh Kansas Cavalry, and the remaining thirty-three were mustered in as Company E, of that regiment. Plumb was captain of Company C, but at the completion of the regimental organization he was chosen major. Heritage, who had served as first lieutenant of Company B, Ninth Kansas Cavalry, was elected captain of Company C. Captain Heritage, in the Battle of Prairie Grove, received the wound from which he carried a limp all the rest of his life. He was helped from the battlefield by Eli Fowler, a member of his company. Charles Stotler, a young brother of Jacob Stotler, was killed in this engagement.

The Battle of Prairie Grove,[1] a decisive defeat to the Confederacy, was followed by the retreat of the Confederate army, and with it went the hope of the Confederacy in Missouri and Northwest Arkansas. In this battle, Plumb commanded a part of the Eleventh Kansas Cavalry, which never before had been under fire. The men fought like veterans, and had a large part in the victory of this engagement, giving assurance of the honorable record afterward made. In 1863 Plumb was appointed provost marshal of the District of the Border.

[1] The anniversary of the Battle of Prairie Grove has been observed in Emporia by its survivors and their friends each December 7 for many years. Thomas Barber, of Dunlap, had charge of the first celebration, at the Barber home in Dunlap, in 1889. He was one of the Prairie Grove veterans. The celebrations were continued under management of Capt. L. T. Heritage until his death in 1913, and since that time the Women's Relief Corps or the Ladies of the Grand Army have "put on" a Prairie Grove dinner and program in Grand Army Hall, in the courthouse, each year.

Colonel Plumb was the representative man of the Eleventh Kansas, says William E. Connelley in his Life of Plumb, and he declares no better regiment than this same Eleventh was in the Union Army. Early in 1865 Colonel Plumb was ordered to proceed with his regiment from Fort Riley to Fort Kearny, in a campaign against belligerent Indians. This campaign was carried out successfully, the Indians brought to peace terms, and most of the regiment was mustered out at Fort Leavenworth in September of that year. Their term of enlistment had expired with the surrender of the Confederacy, but Plumb declared that service in the Union Army was the only legitimate business for loyal men as long as a foe to the Government remained in the field.

Even during the terrible pinch of poverty and the sorrow and loss occasioned by the Civil War, Emporia progressed. C. V. Eskridge,[1] a representative in the Legislature of 1863, introduced a bill in the House providing for the establishment of a State Normal School in Emporia. The bill was presented in the Senate by Perry B. Maxson, and it became a law March 3, 1863. A commission to select a site was appointed by Governor Carney, and a 20-acre tract was secured.[2] The school opened with eighteen stu-

[1] C. V. Eskridge, the first town clerk, also was the first probate judge in the county, by appointment of the territorial governor. He was a member of the State Legislature in 1862-63, was state senator 1867-69, and was author of the law by which school districts were enabled to issue bonds for the purpose of erecting schoolhouses. He was lieutenant governor of Kansas under Governor Carney, 1869-71, and was again a member of the Legislature, 1871-73. He founded the Emporia Daily Republican in 1880. The town of Eskridge, in Wabaunsee County, was named in his honor.

[2] I. E. Perley, an Emporia merchant, secured the gift of this land from its owner, Giles E. Filley, of St. Louis, manufacturer

dents,[3] February 15, 1865, in the upper room of the newly erected Emporia public school building—the Old Stone. There was no furniture, and the equipment consisted of a Bible and a dictionary. Seats were borrowed from the Congregational Church. Lyman B. Kellogg,[4] a young graduate of the Normal University of Illinois, was the principal, and only teacher. From this small but significant beginning has grown

---

of the Charter Oak cookstoves. Mr. Perley was intimately acquainted with Mr. Filley, and went to St. Louis to offer the suggestion that he give the State the land on which to locate the Normal School. Mr. Filley complied with Mr. Perley's suggestion. The land, a tract of twenty acres, twenty rods wide fronting on Commercial Street and extending north for half a mile, was deeded to the State of Kansas. From time to time land has been added to the original tract, and the campus now covers forty acres. Mr. and Mrs. Perley came to Emporia in 1858, and Mr. Perley erected the first brick and stone building on Commercial Street. Public-spirited citizens, they served their community in many ways. Mrs. Justin Soden is their daughter. Mrs. Perley was a sister of Lyman Allen, a member of the Emporia Town Company.

[3] A list of the names of members of that first class—the Old Eighteen—follows: Zeruiah P. Allen, of Lawrence, a sister of Mrs. Perley; Mary Bay, Laura Burns, Ellen M. Cowles, Clarissa Fawcett, Frank E. Gillette, Heloise Hunt, Emma Hunt, Albert T. McIntire, John F. McLain, Sarah Manter, Mattie J. Nichols, Adaline Soule, of Eagle Creek; Josephine Slocum, Betty Maddock, Ella Spencer, Maggie Spencer, Martha P. Spencer. Betty Maddock was called the "sweet singer" of the class. She was a daughter of Mr. and Mrs. J. R. Maddock, and married M. H. Bates, an Emporia druggist. They moved to Missouri, where she died in 1875.

[4] Lyman B. Kellogg, first president of the State Normal School, opened that school of which he was principal and the only teacher by reading the Parable of the Sower and offering the Lord's Prayer. The Bible from which he read is one of the school's valued possessions. Mr. Kellogg later served his State in both branches of the Legislature, as probate judge of Lyon County, and elected attorney general of Kansas in 1888. Mrs. Kellogg, his law partner, was a daughter of the Rev. Daniel Mitchell, a pioneer Methodist minister of Kansas. She was appointed Judge Kellogg's assistant in the attorney general's office. Through Judge Kellogg's influence in the Legislature the salt lands endowment fund was secured to the resources of the Normal School, and the west wing added to the one building. Mrs. Kellogg was a sister of Mrs. J. E. Eckdall, of Emporia.

a magnificent institution, the Kansas State Teachers College of Emporia. The first class to complete the course, two in number, was graduated in 1867. These graduates[1] were Mary Jane Watson and Ellen Plumb.

In 1860, an attempt was made to hold a county fair, and a premium list was printed, but there is no record of a fair having been held that year of no rain and no crops. The first successful fair was held in September, 1864, on the Neosho near the present M. K. & T. bridge, north of town. The Fourth of July, 1860, was celebrated by an immense crowd of 2,500 people, and the town put on its first fireworks display. A tri-weekly service was started this year on the Emporia-Lawrence hack line, and the trip one way was made in a day.

The summer of 1860, Texas fever appeared among the livestock of Lyon County, following the trail of Texas cattle driven through this section. More than three hundred native cattle died within three weeks, occasioning serious loss to their owners. Many of these cattle were milk cows, and table rations were cut short.

During much of the war period, Emporia and Lyon County people were in constant fear of the Quantrill gang of raiders, or other like outlaws, but such depredations here were comparatively few. The burning of Lawrence, and the brutal murder of many of her citizens, by the Quantrill gang in 1863, filled the people here with terror. Emporia sent $500.00 to the relief of her Lawrence neighbors. In 1864, when the

[1] The Emporia News, speaking of the first graduation essays, said: "They well written and, what is unusual in female productions of this kind, both were well delivered." These women were valuable citizens of Emporia many years. In 1858, Miss Watson had opened the first school in Emporia. Miss Plumb also was a teacher, and later opened a book store in Emporia, of which she was proprietor for many years.

Confederate General Price and his army came north and threatened to overrun the state, 300 soldiers of the Eleventh Kansas under Colonel Plumb went to the eastern border and helped to drive back the enemy. A company of soldiers, many of them Emporia men, camped most of one winter at Humboldt, guarding the state from the inroads of the Confederates. Though Emporia experienced many Indian scares in the early days, none but friendly Indians ever visited the town. They came principally from the Kaw Reservation, and were a thieving, lazy lot, but further than small purloinings they made little trouble.

The first railroad meeting in Emporia was held July 21, 1857. Col. C. K. Holliday, of Topeka, spoke for a road from Topeka, and John O. Wattles for one starting near Jefferson City. The Emporia & Topeka Railroad was incorporated in 1859. "Railroad talk" was revived in 1864, when a location for what became the Santa Fe station and yards, south of the M. K. & T. holdings, was secured. September 12, 1865, the first vote for railroad bonds was taken—the Lawrence & Emporia road, one of whose sponsors was James H. Lane. The road did not materialize, and the town did not pay out on the $125,000.00 bonds it had voted. In May, 1866, a meeting was held in Emporia to discuss the prospects of the Topeka & Emporia Railroad, afterward the Santa Fe. This road, and the "Katy," came only a few years later.

CHAPTER III—1865-1875

With the return of the men from the army, in the months following the surrender of the Confederacy, Emporia and Lyon County again took up business and farm life and home-building. It was a difficult task. The men had contracted wandering habits during their army life, and it was hard for them to settle down. There was little money in the community. Scanty crops had been raised by the few old men and the women and boys, but there was no surplus. The private soldiers, paid $13.00 a month by the Government, had saved little, or nothing. Men with families had sent home their savings to their wives and children. It was a discouraging period.

In the latter part of 1865, however, began a steady stream of settlers to Kansas from states further east, many of them ex-soldiers whose time of service was deducted from the regular requirement of five years' residence before a homesteader could prove up on his land. This was in accordance with the Homestead Act of 1862. The new settlers brought some money, some provisions and other supplies, livestock, field and garden seeds, but more important, even, than all these, they brought an enthusiasm for the new country which served to kindle anew the smouldering fires of enthusiasm of those older settlers who had come in the fifties.

The Indian troubles on the frontier lasted from 1864 until 1868, and, although Emporia never experienced an Indian raid, always the people were fearful, not knowing at what moment the savages might swoop down upon them.

The livestock business was becoming an important industry, and it is recorded that $80,000.00 worth of cattle changed hands in Lyon County in 1866. In the autumn of 1871 the first Texas cattle were driven into Lyon County, south of the Cottonwood. Major Calvin Hood had come to Emporia from Sturgis, Michigan, in 1871, and he and P. B. Plumb formed a partnership in the cattle business. They were successful from the start, and many thousands of longhorns were brought to Kansas for pasture. Other men with a little money, or with no money if their credit were good at the banks, went into the Texas cattle business, with great profit, once they had learned how to handle these cattle. Cattle were driven from Texas and delivered to Kansas buyers for a dollar a head, it is authoritively stated. The late Jacob Holderman, who lived in Northern Greenwood County and operated a large farm and cattle ranch, riding through waving bluestem as high as his horse, remarked that "Bluestem is what puts the 'taller' on a steer." Fenced pastures were unnecessary, and the cost of keeping a steer was negligible. As a rule steers were taken off grass and marketed, without other feed than the bluestem.

There was constant war between the "big cattlemen" and the settlers. Fences were inadequate—this was before the days of barbed wire, the long hauls and high prices and their scarcity made rail fences a luxury—and when a herd of cattle roaming the prairie at night, as was a frequent occurrence, sniffed the delectable odor of growing corn, it didn't stop for a weak rail fence. Cattle in a cornfield in one night often destroyed all of the work of the spring and summer for a farmer, and there was little in the way of redress.

Early settlers on the divide between Eagle Creek and the Verdigris were discouraged by the cattlemen, who told them they would starve to death trying to farm the prairie land. To the reply from one homesteader that "God made the land and made man to till it. I think this quarter section is the land He expects me to till, and I'll be damned if anyone is going to run me off it," the cattleman said: "Well, but us cattlemen just can't have you there. We want the prairie left unfenced and unimproved so we always will have free pasture for our cattle." Another cattleman, in reply to a farmer's complaint that his field of corn had been ruined the night before, replied: "I do wish you farmers had money enough to fence your land properly." And that was all the farmer got for his complaint.

It wasn't so difficult to guard the fields during the day, though that was hard enough, but night after night farmers and their families would be roused out of bed by the noise of cattle in the corn, and men and women and dogs would chase them out of the fields. The story is told—and it is a true tale—of a prairie woman who, probably because she couldn't afford a nightgown, slept in her old-fashioned long muslin chemise—only she called it "shimmy." One bright moonlight night she heard cattle in the corn, roused her husband, and together they hurried to drive them out. Her shimmy was wide as well as long. She raised it over her head, and with one mighty whoop she rushed into the face of that herd, and the herd turned tail and fled. The story got out, and the cattleman complained that he never did get all of those stampeded steers rounded up.

The Osage orange hedge was the salvation of the prairie farmers. The tiny slips were planted carefully in the hedgerows outlining the farms, and in a few years grew into a fence that would turn the biggest, longest-horned steer. Now, and for many years, the hedge fence has been condemned, and with cause. Its roots sap the soil of nourishment which belongs by rights to the crops, keeping it properly trimmed is an everlasting job, if allowed to grow it shades the roads and encourages mudholes, cuts off the vision at crossroads, leading to accidents, is objectionable in many ways. Yet it served an important purpose for the early day prairie farmer. Hundreds of miles of hedge fences have been removed from Lyon County farms.

Sometimes the longhorned Texas steers were savage, and frequently showed fight with disastrous results unless the men they attacked could outrun a Texas steer. Often steers on short rations, in winter, weak from lack of feed, mired in the waterholes where they drank, and sometimes had to be pried out of the mud with rails. Rails were kept near many waterholes for this very purpose, and were handy unless some settler, out "jayhawking" for fuel, hauled the rails home and used them for firewood. The men who went to a steer's rescue mounted their horses hurriedly as soon as a steer was on his feet, to escape goring by the long, sharp horns of the ungrateful animal. The story is told of a kind-hearted man on foot who discovered a steer mired in a waterhole. With a rail he helped the steer to his feet, then used the rail to beat off the ferocious beast until he could climb the one nearby tree. He stayed in that tree for hours, the steer bellowing and pawing beneath him, until a man on horseback chanced that way, drove off the steer, and the man slid down the tree to safety. It was his last good-hearted effort to help a mired steer out of the mud.

Many fortunes were made—and lost, some of them —in Emporia and Lyon County in the Texas cattle business, through the seventies and eighties and extending into the nineties. The longhorns for many years have been superseded by the Herefords in Texas, as well as in Kansas, and the native longhorn Texas steer is almost extinct.

The first bank in Lyon County[1] was started in March, 1867—the Emporia Banking & Savings Association—by J. R. Swallow & Company, L. T. Heritage and W. T. Soden being associated with Mr. Swallow. This institution became the Emporia National Bank in 1872, through the efforts of P. B. Plumb, who was its first president. Captain Heritage for many years was its cashier. The financial panic of 1873 taxed heavily the new bank's resources, but its officers managed to keep its doors open and its credit good. The first bank was located in a corner room of the old News building, northeast corner Sixth and Commercial. The Emporia National's home was the present Fidelity Bank corner.

September 1, 1869, the second bank, the Emporia Savings Bank, was organized by Riggs, Dunlap & Company. Its directors were S. B. Riggs, P. B. Maxson, Howard Dunlap, J. Jay Buck, J. J. Wright and T. N. Sedgwick.

[1] George Plumb enjoys telling his experience with the first bank check he ever saw. It was given him in the sixties in payment for a flock of sheep he had sold to a man who was buying for a newly established firm in Kansas City. The buyer assured him the check was as good as money, but young Mr. Plumb had his doubts. He accepted the check, telling the buyer he would investigate, and if the check were no good he would follow him and take back the sheep. Mr. Plumb brought the check to the new bank and showed it to Captain Heritage, the cashier, who said he believed he had heard the name of the firm. Among his letters he found the name and assured Mr. Plumb the check was all right. The check bore the signature of P. D. Armour!

Kansas in 1873 experienced another season of dry weather and hot winds, which ruined the growing crops, and left the settlers in bad financial condition. Following this, in 1874 came the great plague of grasshoppers which devoured every green thing, and left the farms and orchards which had given abundant promise, stripped and bare. The hoppers came in great clouds, obscuring the sun, and for a time the people did not understand what was darkening the sky. Again were the settlers deprived of the sustenance for which they had labored, and again did the people of more fortunate states come to their rescue. The grasshoppers covered the entire state, and every settlement was more or less destitute. Peach trees, full of fruit almost ripe, were left with bare seeds hanging to the denuded limbs. Cabbages were eaten down to the stalks, then the hoppers burrowed into the stalks and hollowed them out to the furthest roots. Some families built smudges of dry grass and leaves and saved a part of their cabbage. Corn was eaten, stalks and all in many cases, and nothing was left.

There had been previous visitations of grasshoppers, but never, before nor since, anything like this in numbers and destructiveness. In the spring of 1875 eggs deposited by the hoppers began to hatch, but the hoppers did not appear in great numbers, and not sufficient of them came to life to alarm the people greatly. The baby hoppers took flight, starved out, no doubt, by the depredations of their parents the year before, whose greed left the young ones nothing to live on.

This year—1875—the farmers, the most optimistic people in the world, again took heart and planted a larger acreage than ever before had been planted. Many new farms were started, and thousands of acres of sod was turned. Faith and labor were rewarded by an abundant harvest of field crops, vegetables and fruits. For many years there was no crop failure, and the state reached a high degree of prosperity.

In June, 1867, county bonds were voted in the sum of $200,000.00 to aid in the construction of the M. K. & T. Railway through Lyon County, this road then being called the Southern Branch of the Union Pacific. The first train on this branch—long known as the Neosho Valley Branch of the M. K. & T.—reached Emporia from Junction City December 22, 1869, amid great rejoicing. And ever since the "Katy" has been a means of transportation up and down the Neosho, from Junction City to Parsons, and has had an important part in the development of the country.

In June, 1869, bonds in the same amount were voted to bring through Lyon County the Atchison, Topeka & Santa Fe Railway. An instance of the grit and determination of the people who built Lyon County is the fact that, with a population of but 5,000 to 6,000, within two years the county voted upon itself a railroad debt of $400,000.00. But the railroads brought settlers by thousands and added, more than any other one factor, to the material prosperity and the growth of the town and county. They gave work to farmers and laborers in building the roads, putting into circulation money that was greatly needed and highly appreciated.

The Santa Fe, since the first track was laid into Emporia in 1870, the first train arriving here September 14 of that year, has built the Southern Kansas Branch running south out of Emporia, connecting many thriving communities with this town; has built the Ottawa Branch, a short line to Kansas City; the Belen cut-off, whose trains travel on the main line to

Newton, but giving Emporia all the benefit of the shorter distance to the Southwest. It has improved the roadbeds of all its lines with substantial rock ballast, has laid thousands of miles of double track and treble track, and its record throughout Kansas and other states has been one of continuous improvement for the betterment of its service to the people. Since 1923, the Santa Fe has been engaged in a 5-million dollar building and other improvement project in Emporia, which will be completed in 1929 or 1930, probably.

Kansas, in 1869, made her first public effort looking toward universal suffrage.[1] Many Emporia people were interested in the movement, and did all in their power to aid the speakers who came here in the interest of votes for women. Susan B. Anthony, Lucy Stone Blackwell, Elizabeth Cady Stanton, Antoinette Brown and George Francis Train were among the national suffrage workers who came to Emporia, which was suffrage headquarters for this section of the state. Speakers were taken from here to smaller towns to speak, and not always were they cordially received. Mrs. J. V. Randolph used to tell how, when she and Mr. Randolph, in their buckboard, had taken Susan B. Anthony to another town to speak, all three at the beginning of the meeting were rotten-egged. But

---

[1] Dr. Allen White, a Democrat, father of William Allen White, voted for the equal suffrage amendment in 1869. He believed women at this time were ready for the franchise and that the Negro was not ready, and the injustice of investing the Negro with the franchise before he had learned even the elements of citizenship aroused Doctor White's indignation. Susan B. Anthony was entertained at the home of Dr. and Mrs. White on one of her visits to Emporia. Mrs. White also was an ardent suffragist. In 1867, during the campaign for suffrage, seventy-five Emporia women published a card, declaring they wanted to vote.

Susan B. wiped off the egg smears and made her speech, and the crowd listened respectfully.

The proposed equal suffrage amendment to the State Constitution was defeated that year, and again in 1894, and was passed by a majority of only 10,000 in 1912. Today, few men in Kansas will admit that they voted against the amendment.[1]

When Dr. Anna Shaw spoke in Emporia in the interests of suffrage in 1912, Grady's Band called the people together to hear Doctor Shaw speak early in the evening, from an open car at the corner of Fifth and Commercial. Most of the big crowd that had assembled followed her to the Whitley Opera House, to join another big crowd, where the speaker was accorded the utmost respect and attention.

The first school building erected in Kansas under the bond system, and the largest district schoolhouse in the state, was the Old Stone, Emporia's first school building, which stood many years on the Senior High School grounds, at the northeast corner. The building was completed in 1864, and had been undertaken after much discussion and many doubts as to the advisability of risking so much money in a school building. Bonds in the sum of $5,000.00 were voted June 25, 1863, for its erection. The school board at this time consisted of J. R. Swallow, director; Jacob Stotler, clerk, and John Hammond, treasurer. John Hammond did the carpenter work on the building, Thomas Murdock the stonework, and J. V. Randolph the plastering. T. M. Gruell[2] was the first principal in the

---

[1] In 1861 Kansas women were given the right to vote in school elections, and in 1887 in municipal elections. Only six states, Colorado, Wyoming, Idaho, Utah, Washington and California preceded Kansas in granting to women the right of suffrage.

[2] The first kindergarten teacher in Emporia was Miss Copley. One evening in 1865 a group of children was hanging around the

new building, and Miss Mary Jane Watson was his assistant.

Twenty-nine schools were in session in Lyon County in 1868.[1] In 1872 there were sixty-two schools with 3191 pupils. County teachers' salaries mounted up to $81,816.00, district school tax was $33,813.00, and the sixty schoolhouses were valued at $68,000.00. Schoolhouses were built in every settlement of Lyon County as early as there was a sufficient number of children to warrant the organization of a new district. Three- and four-year-old children sometimes were counted as of school age in order to make up the number necessary for the organization of a new district.

The next big job for Lyon County's representatives in the Legislature was to secure an appropriation for a building for the State Normal School in Emporia. Jacob Stotler went after it, following his election to the session of 1865, and he got it. In 1866 the contract for a building to cost $15,000.00 was let to Howe

---

News office, says Mrs. Ella Pemberton, watching for the arrival of the stage, on which was expected the new teacher, Miss Copley. She came, and with her two huge trunks, and the town was set to wondering how in the world any woman could have clothes enough to fill them. With the opening of school it transpired that one trunk contained school supplies, among them being colored beads and wools and other kindergarten paraphernalia. Miss Copley was a graduate of the New York State Normal School, and came here soon after the opening of the Normal School in Emporia. But she was a teacher in the town school, and was not connected with the Normal.

[1] The meeting of the Kansas State Teachers' Association, held in Atchison in 1865, was attended by a considerable number of Lyon County people. President Kellogg, of the Normal School; County Superintendent and Mrs. J. M. Miller and their 2-year-old baby, who lived in Fremont; Miss Mary Jane Watson, Clarissa Fawcett, Ellen Plumb, Ellen Cowles and Frank Gillette, all traveled together. Their conveyances consisted of a covered wagon, a two-seated carriage and a one-horse buggy. The trip required three days each way. One night each way the party slept in a hotel in Burlingame, the other night in a farmhouse.

MRS. G. W. NEWMAN
1857

MRS. MARGARET GILMORE
1856

& Hughes,[2] for the stonework, and John Hammond for the carpenter work. The building, of stone construction, was dedicated January 3, 1867. In 1873 a brick building, larger than the first, was built in front of the stone building, and both were destroyed by fire in 1878. The loss was about $85,000.00, besides the loss of time to students and faculty. Emporia joined with the State in the erection of a new and larger building, which was dedicated in 1880. Justice David J. Brewer, of the United States Supreme Court, made the dedicatory address.

Emporia was organized as a village February 6, 1865, with a board of trustees as its governing body. Robert M. Ruggles was chairman of this board; other members were J. C. Fraker, John L. Catterson, William Clapp and John Hammond.

Emporia was incorporated as a city of the second class in 1870. The first election under the new charter was held April 4 of that year. The following men

[2] Richard Howe and Peter H. Hughes, who had the contract for the stonework on the first Normal School building, built many of the stone houses of the early years in Emporia. Mr. Hughes was elected register of deeds of Lyon County in 1869, and re-elected in 1871. He lived for many years, until his death in 1928, in the stone house he built at 718 Merchant—now covered by stucco. Mrs. Robert Howe and her family live in the stone house erected by Richard Howe, at the foot of Exchange Street. Evan Davis, who lived for years at Eighth and Congress, also was stone mason and worked with Mr. Hughes and Mr. Howe. Davis was an aide to P. B. Plumb during the Civil War, and was one of the builders of the old Eldridge House, at Lawrence, before coming to Emporia in 1857. With Peter Hughes in 1857 came to Emporia Ellis Owens, Tom Jones, John Roberts and John Bennett, a group of singing young Welshmen. The last night before they reached Emporia they camped near the home of Oliver Phillips, on Duck Creek. The Phillipses insisted on the young men coming into the cabin to sleep, and they sang Welsh hymns and folks songs until long past midnight. The coming of travelers was to the Phillipses, as to all early settlers on lonely claims, an eagerly welcomed event. John Hammond, at the time the Normal School was built and for twenty-one years thereafter, was state-house commissioner, and was on the job looking after the erection

were elected to city offices: Mayor, H. C .Cross;[1] police judge, E. W. Cunningham; marshal, H. B. Lowe; councilmen, First Ward, C. V. Eskridge, R. D. Thomas; Second Ward, G. W. Frederick, M. G. Mains; Third Ward, L. N. Robinson, Charles Wheelock. The town was growing, and the Emporia post office became a money order office in 1867.

---

of the Normal building almost day and night. Col. W. F. Cloud, writing from Kansas City in 1901 in response to an invitation to attend an Old Settlers' meeting said, in part: "Any mention of early times in Lyon County would be incomplete if no recognition were made of the persistent and successful efforts of John Hammond in helping to secure the location of the Normal School for Emporia. His was a labor of love and a work performed without the promptings of avarice; and when Emporia deifies her saints and heroes and enrolls their names among the gods, John Hammond's name should be placed on high as a friend of schools and education and a benefactor of Emporia."

[1] H. C. Cross, first mayor of Emporia, served Lyon County as chairman of the Board of County Commissioners, became president of the First National Bank and of the M. K. & T. Railway. The old Cross home at Sixth and Union, then one of the choicest residence districts of the town, built in the early nineties, was, according to Stotler's Annals, "one of the largest, most complete and elegant in the city." The house has been remodeled, and now is an apartment house.

CHAPTER IV—1875-1880.

The half decade from 1875 to 1880 was one of prosperity[1] to town and county alike. The soil responded to the efforts of the farmers, each year more and more sod was broken, with corresponding increase in crops. The virgin soil yielded wonderfully, and as many as eighteen to twenty successive corn crops were grown without fertilizer. Rotation of crops in those days was not considered necessary. In Emporia, business houses were enlarged to make room for larger stocks, due to increasing trade, and many new places of business were established. Settlers continued to come in large numbers, new neighborhoods were formed and new school districts organized. Some district schools held their early sessions in private houses, so insistent was the demand for schools, before there had been time to vote bonds and build schoolhouses. In 1879, 184 buildings were erected in Emporia. The population of the town in 1878 was 3,400.

Col. P. B. Plumb,[2] who had served his community and State in the Civil War and in the State Legislature, and in many other capacities, January 31, 1877, was

[1] The people were freeing themselves from the biting poverty which the majority of them had experienced and in 1876, Centennial year, probably there was more travel from this county for anything else than the most urgent business than had been done in the two preceding decades. Everyone who possibly could, made the journey to Philadelphia. The tallest stalk of corn on the exhibition grounds was raised by James O'Toole, of Neosho Rapids.

[2] Colonel Plumb was independent in his views and actions, says William E. Connelley in his Life of Plumb. He had helped to form the Republican party in Kansas, yet he was not bound by partisan alignment. He supported Horace Greeley for the pres-

elected to the United States Senate by the Kansas Legislature.[3] He began his senatorial career March 5, 1877, and it ended only with his death, December 20, 1891. As a member of the Senate committee on public lands he had been enabled greatly to aid his State, as well as other States, in which much of the land still was in the hands of the Government. Few men in the Senate worked so tirelessly as Plumb, and always he accomplished the ends he sought.

In 1878-1880, thousands of Negroes arrived in Kansas from the South—the largest numbers from Tennessee and Texas, but Mississippi, Alabama, Arkansas and Georgia, and other former slave States, were represented. The railway companies, eager to advertise their transportation facilities, put on many colonist excursions during this decade, and brought to the Middle West from the Atlantic seaboard French and Swedish, German and Swiss, Mennonite and Dane, and other foreign groups, at a purely nominal cost. Also, large groups of Negroes were brought to Kansas in what was known as the Exodus, and the Negroes were called Exodusters. Representatives of the railways had been sent to the South, offering free, or almost free transportation, telling of the opportunities afforded by Kansas soil and climate, the free land which might be secured from the Government; above all, the attitude of Kansas people toward the Negro. Kansas had fought for free soil, and had won over

---

idency in 1872, for the reason that Greeley, with his New York Tribune, and by word of mouth, had been a most powerful friend of Kansas during the anti-slavery struggle. Plumb boldly worked and spoke for Greeley during the campaign, and Greeley lost the State by but two votes.

[3] At that time, and until 1909, when the ruling that United States senators be elected by popular vote went into effect, senators were elected by vote of the members of the Legislature.

great odds from those who wished it to come into the Union a slave state. Hence, emissaries of the railroads declared, the Negroes would be warmly welcomed to Kansas, a "land flowing with milk and honey, where, in addition to the forty acres of land which would be given to each man by Uncle Sam, he also would be fitted out with mule and wagon and farming implements, helped to build his cabin, with a free title to the land at the end of five years."

The Negroes, ignorant and credulous, believing implicitly in the Government which had given them their freedom, only a few years from slavery, eager to better their condition, which had been an anomalous one since the Emancipation Proclamation, were disappointed. The Government, as to all citizens, offered land for homesteading, but other allurements held forth to the Negroes were false or misleading. The Negroes came here, penniless, most of them, and would have suffered for food and clothing had not kind-hearted citizens and towns come to their rescue. In some communities, the State built barracks to house the Negroes. In Emporia, the town cared for them. Several families lived for weeks in the old Friends Meeting House, at Sixth and Sylvan, and other buildings were donated for their use.[1] Private citizens and the town fed them.

---

[1] The late John Gunkel provided for two of these Negro families. He built small houses for them on his farm, seven miles southeast of Emporia, and helped them to get on their feet. He furnished teams, farming implements and seed, and provisions as well—everything—and rented them farm land. In winter they chopped wood on shares in Mr. Gunkel's timber. One of these families stayed on the Gunkel farm six or seven years, the other not so long, both families moving to Emporia. Mrs. John Gunkel, upward of eighty, lives on the farm, which Mr. Gunkel settled in 1856. Their son, Jesse Gunkel, lives in Emporia at 1405 Highland. Mrs. J. C. Ames, 1006 Union, is their daughter.

The Negroes were unused to the colder climate of Kansas. Some of them died from exposure, some returned as soon as possible to their native States, but a large proportion of them remained. Today, many of the best Negro citizens of Emporia are those who came in the Exodus, or their descendants. At Dunlap, just over the line in Morris County, an academy for Negroes was built and maintained for several years by a body of Presbyterians. A few miles southwest of that town, Negroes were colonized on five- and ten-acre tracts on long-term payments, and this colony throve for several years. Now, but one or two Negro families live on the colonist land, a few families are on farms east of Dunlap, and the Negro population of Dunlap—once half Negro—does not exceed fifty. The Negro population of Emporia is between 700 and 800. A large majority of these own their homes, most of them are industrious, honest and ambitious, and are a credit to their race and to this community. They educate their children and maintain churches. Many of the Negroes of the third and fourth generations since the Exodus are High School graduates, some of them having received high honors. Previous to the Exodus there had been few Negroes in Emporia.

They were brought here, largely, under false pretensions, and were bitterly disappointed. Yet in none of the states from which they came, say the old men and women, could they have had the opportunities or lived in the comfort they have enjoyed in Kansas. After the first shock, they braced up and made the best of the situation, which they found was not so bad, after all.

In 1879, President Rutherford B. Hayes and Gen. William Tecumseh Sherman passed through Emporia, on a tour of the West. Two thousand citizens turned out to greet them. The President made a short speech, and General Sherman appeared on the rear platform of their special train.

July 5, 1880—the Fourth came on Sunday that year —Gen. U. S. Grant, on a tour of the West a few years after his two terms as President, visited Emporia, and made an address at Soden's Grove. Thousands of people drove many miles through rain and mud—many of them in lumber wagons—to see and greet the Civil War hero and former President. There was a monster parade, and the street decorations surpassed any previous attempts in that line. The General was accompanied by Mrs. Grant.

Waterworks bonds to the amount of $50,000.00 were issued following the city election of 1879. The waterworks was formally opened in June, 1880[1]—the first in the State. Water at that time was obtained from the Cottonwood River, the plant being located south of town at the foot of Congress Sreet. The waterworks plant was moved to the Neosho in 1886.

A destructive cyclone visited Emporia and vicinity in 1880, with much property damage. In 1881, four persons were killed in a cyclone which struck immediately north and west of Emporia. Many persons were injured and many buildings demolished.

An important part of the cultural and educational life of Emporia is, and long has been, its City Library, founded when the town was a struggling village. A group of citizens met December 14, 1869, and formed a library association. They had no money for library purposes, and dues of $3.00 a year for men and $2.00 for women were determined on as a means of revenue.

[1] The Emporia News for January 9, 1880, carried a first-page, five-column cut of "the mammoth engines and force pumps to be used by the Emporia waterworks."

Money with which to buy books was raised by lectures and strawberry festivals. In 1870, the front room of the Bates & Perley drug store was rented for library use, and the library and reading room was open Tuesday, Thursday, Friday and Saturday afternoons. Reading room privileges were extended visitors not members of the association. The Emporia City Directory for 1870 contains the list of library officers, as follows: President, J. M. Steele; vice president, R. M. Overstreet; secretary, C. H. Riggs; treasurer, H. C. Cross. In 1873 it was recorded by Miss Blake, librarian, that a festival had netted sufficient money for the purchase of forty-nine books.

A new library association was formed in 1884, with Mrs. L. B. Kellogg, president; Mrs. L. A. Platt, secretary; Mrs. O. D. Swan, treasurer. In 1891 Mrs. Amanda J. Carpenter was elected librarian. She served until 1893, when Mrs. Amanda Wicks was elected to succeed her. In 1902 Mrs. Martha Whildin became librarian, and Mrs. Mary Gridley, assistant, served as librarian during the spring of 1907. Then Miss Mildred Berrier was elected librarian, and served until her health failed, compelling her resignation. Miss Nora Daniel, the present librarian, has served in that capacity since 1920.

A branch library was established in the Grace Methodist Church, in the southwest section of the town, in 1917. When the new church was built, following the destruction by fire of the old building, rooms were set aside for library use. Mrs. J. K. Maddern is in charge of the branch library, where the books are in constant use. The main library hours are, week-days, 9 A. M. to 9 P. M., Sundays, 2 to 6 P. M.; branch library hours, week-days, 3 to 6 and 7 to 9 P. M.

The directors for the first year following the reorganization of the library association were Jacob Stotler, L. B. Kellogg, S. B. Riggs, J. M. Steele, Harvey Bancroft, L. N. Robinson, H. C. Cross, Mary Jane Watson and Mary M. Bancroft.

An interesting entry in the library record follows: "In December, 1894, the librarian was authorized to give the city attorney a list of delinquent patrons from whom she had failed to recover books kept over time, and also to remit fines when, in her judgment, the parties were unable to pay."

The Emporia City Library is housed in a handsome building, the gift of Andrew Carnegie, at Sixth and Market, the lots a gift of Mrs. P. B. Plumb. This building was opened to the public February 23, 1906, with a reception to the townspeople. Capt. L. T. Heritage, in his will, left $10,000.00 in trust for the library, the interest of which is used for buying books additional to those supplied by the city tax levy for library purposes. The annual report for December 1, 1927, shows a circulation of books during the year of 88,157, and at the branch library, 10,112 books were taken out during the year. Besides the librarian, there are two assistants in the main library. Present officials are: Mrs. Howard Dunlap, president; E. E. Anderson, vice president; George Bordenkircher, secretary; Mrs. G. W. Newman, Miss Mabel Edwards, L. A. Lowther, Davillo Spade, W. L. White; C. A. Bishop, mayor.

CHAPTER V—1880-1890.

The first three-quarters of this decade was a period of building. Many of the public and business buildings theretofore had been of wood, and these, as time and more prosperous conditions called for larger and more substantial structures, were replaced by brick and stone buildings. The public school buildings came in for many important improvements.

The Union Street School, built of wood in 1869, was replaced by brick in this decade, and has been rebuilt a second time. In the Third Ward, in 1881, a brick building was erected, which later was replaced by the Maynard[1] building. The Fourth Ward brick building, at Eighth and Sylvan, now the Century, Tenth and Commercial, and the Central Avenue, a frame building, now Riverside, were built in 1882 and 1883, respectively. The Walnut, a frame building, erected in 1885, was replaced in 1910 by a brick building. The Kansas Avenue School, a frame building of 1885, in 1927 was replaced by the handsomest public school

[1] The Maynard building in the Third Ward was erected after the death of Miss Mary Maynard, a teacher in the city schools for many years. Her savings, amounting to more than $12,000.00, she left to the schools she had loved and toiled for. The Third Ward, in need of a new school building, was selected as the beneficiary of Miss Maynard's bequest, and sufficient money was added to it to build the large and substantial structure which for years has housed most of the school children of the Third Ward.

[1] Governor Eskridge, in his Emporia Republican, alarmed for the morals of the town, printed the following editorial, about this time: "Every afternoon, about the time the eastern mail is distributed, the post office lobby is invaded by a lot of young girls, going home from school, who are very rude in their manner, both as to their actions and their conversation, and who ought to know better and act like ladies."

building in Emporia. The Lincoln School, then at the extreme west edge of town, was purchased from District 57, an addition built, and a two-room school was maintained in that building for many years. Bonds were voted at the city election of 1929 for the erection of a new building in the First Ward, to care for the rapidly increasing population in that section of Emporia. This building, whose pupils will include those who attended the Lincoln School, has been named the Mary Herbert School, honoring the woman who was principal of Lincoln School for many years, who gave a longer term of service to Emporia schools than any other person, and who, it was made known after her death in 1928, left a bequest for use of Emporia school children.

The Garfield, the first High School building, replaced a one-story frame on the site of the Senior High School. The present building, with grounds and equipment, is valued at $250,000.00, having been erected 1912-1914. The beautiful new Junior High School, across Sixth Avenue south from the Senior High, was built in 1925, its total value being $450,000.00. The total cost of Emporia's public school buildings from 1881 to 1885 was $52,000.00—at a time when building materials and labor were less than one-fourth their present cost. Each High School sits in a block of bluegrass lawn, graced with fine old trees and brilliant flowerbeds. They form a most fitting gateway on the west to the business section of Emporia. Strangers in town are impressed by the beauty and dignity of these buildings as well as by the fact that they stand for the training of Emporia's boys and girls. The total value of all of Emporia's public school buildings is $975,000.00. L. A. Lowther is superintendent of the Emporia public schools, Rice

Brown is principal of the Senior High, and Humphrey Jones, the two latter born and brought up in Emporia, is principal of the Junior High.

In October, 1882, the Presbyterians of Kansas, at their annual meeting of Synod, in Ottawa, appointed a committee to confer with citizens of Emporia regarding the location of a synodical college in this town. July 16, 1885, the cornerstone of the first building of the College of Emporia was laid. The ceremonies were conducted by Dr. F. S. McCabe, of Topeka, a pioneer Presbyterian minister of Kansas, and Dr. J. D. Hewitt, afterward for several years president of the College. Citizens of Emporia gave thirty-eight acres of land, the beautiful campus on which the College buildings stand, and $40,000.00 toward the erection of a building. The incorporation was completed in 1883, and classes were held in downtown buildings, beginning November 1 of that year, and continuing to be held there until the College building was ready for occupancy in 1886. A. H. Horton, of Atchison, chief justice of the Supreme Court of Kansas, was president of the first College Board of Trustees, and Emporia members of the board were S. B. Riggs, secretary; Dr. J. F. Hendy, Rev. Robert M. Overstreet, P. B. Plumb, H. C. Cross and J. M. Griffith. Doctor Hendy was the first president of the College.

The first building, Stuart Hall, built of stone, burned in 1916. The beautiful new administration building, completed in 1929, was begun in 1917, but construction was delayed by lack of money, first occasioned by World War conditions, and by the continued financial stringency of the College. Now, the College is free from debt and is on its feet, financially. The administration building is valued at $275,000.00. A $35,-000.00 organ is in War Memorial Chapel of this building. Other College buildings are Lewis Hall of Science, Mason Gymnasium, Anderson Memorial Library, the gift of Andrew Carnegie; Emporia and Dunlap Halls, dormitories for women; Thomas Hall, a dormitory for men; heating plant. Gemmel Hall, the residence of the president of the College, is located at 617 Union Street, and is valued at $13,000.00.

There are thirty-three faculty members of the College of Emporia, and the enrollment is 375 to 400. Graduates number 983. Of these, 367 are educators; ministers, missionaries and other religious workers, 153; wives of these workers, 23; others, 440. In all parts of the world alumnae of this institution are upholding the banner of righteousness and strengthening educational and cultural life—the College's chief reasons for existence—in all kinds of religious and business and professional work, to the honor of the institution they represent. To the original thirty-eight-acre campus has been added a small strip of land to the west; nine acres immediately east of Newman Memorial County Hospital, and nine acres on the north side of Fifteenth Avenue—Thomas Hall and farm—have been purchased and may be classed as a part of the campus, about fifty acres in all.

In this decade, Emporia began to take on city airs. December 16, 1880, the first gas for lighting was used. In 1881 a franchise for a street railway was granted by the City Council, a telephone company was organized, the waterworks plant was ready for use, a Board of Trade was organized. The Hotel Coolidge, on the site of the Broadview, was opened, and its fame spread beyond the bounds of the state. It was owned by a stock company for a short time, then was purchased by the late Col. H. C. Whitley, and as the

Whitley Hotel it served the public until the building burned in 1913. Later, the name was transferred to the hostelry which had been called the Fifth Avenue Hotel, built about the same time as the Whitley. Other public buildings of the eighties were Jay's Opera House, Fifth and Commercial, used for other purposes for many years, and remodeled and enlarged in 1929 by the Palace Clothing Company; the Masonic Temple, greatly enlarged and improved in recent years.

Many substantial residences, some of them highly ornate, were built during this period. Among them were the homes of the elder William Jay, Twelfth and West, the site now of the Gufler home; the P. B. Plumb residence, superseded in 1895 by the present building, the latter a gift in 1919 of the sons and daughters of Senator and Mrs. Plumb to the Emporia Young Women's Christian Association; the Major Calvin Hood residence, altered not at all in the passing years and still comfortable and dignified; the H. C. Cross home, one of the show places of the town for many years, built about the time the Plumb house was rebuilt, in the early nineties. It became the home of the I. E. Lambert family in 1907, and now is an apartment house. Red Rocks, built by Judge Almerin Gillette in the eighties, was rebuilt by Mr. and Mrs. W. A. White in 1920-1921. They bought the property in 1900.

On Twelfth Avenue, the most desirable and exclusive residence section of the town at that time, lived the Eskridges—their lovely home, the discarded music hall of Teachers College; the Isaiah Joneses, the Cunninghams, the Richard Thomases, east of the Normal, and to the west the homes of the J. M. Griffiths, the R. J. Edwards family, the DeCamps, and, a little later, the beautiful home of Mr. and Mrs. G. W. Newman. That part of East Twelfth mentioned has largely been taken over by Teachers College, to make room for its rapidly expanding needs. Other handsome homes of the earlier days were those of W. T. Soden, which retains its old-time dignity and beauty; the Dr. John A. Moore home, now a sorority house; the old Slocum place, at First and East, remarkable for the beauty of its lawn and hedges, its flowers and trees, when these were much less frequent than now; the Sterry home immediately south, Mrs. Sterry a daughter of Mrs. Slocum; the L. W. Lewis home, Fifth and Market; the William Martindale home, on Constitution, home of the Chester Martindales; the Gilchrist home on West South Avenue, a suburban home, vacated in 1928 by the Roy Kramms, because of the encroachments of the Santa Fe; the big three-story dwelling at Sixth and Garfield, far out in the suburbs, home of the Col. David Taylor family, vacant for years. "Too big," says Frank Dale, who has it in charge. "Tastes have changed and people want smaller houses." Those were the days when, the bigger the house, the greater the indication of the hospitality and prosperity of the owner.

The dry summer of 1887 cut short the crops in this State, and Lyon County felt again the depression of hard times. But with continuous good crops since 1875, there was a surplus of the necessities of life, no more was felt the bitter poverty of the Drouth of Sixty, or of the Grasshopper Year, in 1874, and soon the town and county rallied. Followed five years of excellent crops, of more diversified planting, of deeper and better and more scientific cultivation of the soil, and Kansas and Emporia and Lyon County indeed were prosperous.

In 1882 H. Parkman—father of Harrison Parkman, postmaster of Emporia during the Wilson administrations—who, with his family, had come from Philadelphia and settled on and named Sunny Slope farm, three miles northwest of Emporia, raised the first alfalfa grown in Kansas, at a time when the introduction of this drouth-resisting crop was most welcome. Mr. Parkman, who recently had been in Chile, South America, observed alfalfa growing there, investigated its nutritive as well as its drouth-resisting qualities, and after he came to Kansas, sent to Chile for seed. He sowed this seed on a part of the quarter section of land across the road south from the Sunny Slope residence, and the first year raised a seed crop. Blackshire Brothers, Chase County ranchmen, bought some of this seed, and sowed ten acres to alfalfa as an experiment. Now alfalfa is one of the State's most important crops. It is grown successfully in dry seasons without irrigation, its long, penetrating roots being able always to find water at no matter what depth. It is equally valuable as hay and as pasture, and from three to five crops are cut for hay in a single season. Mr. Parkman represented an English cutlery house in South America, Mexico, Japan, the Islands of the Pacific, and Russia. The Czar of Russia once gave him a letter recommending the horseshoe nails which Mr. Parkman had sold to the royal shoeing shop.

In 1884 the Ottawa Branch of the Santa Fe was built, thereby shortening the distance from Emporia to Kansas City, this being of particular advantage to the railway company on its freight hauls. In 1886 a branch of the Missouri Pacific Railway was built across Northern Lyon County from east to west, greatly benefiting that section of the county. Three new towns—Allen, Admire and Bushong—were an immediate result of the railroad's coming, and later Miller was added to the Missouri Pacific towns.

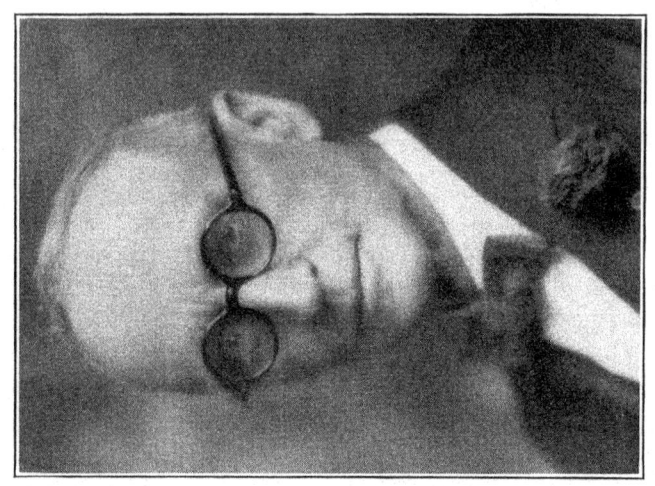

MR. AND MRS. WILL WAYMAN, 1855-1864

The Ladies' Benevolent Society—the forerunner of Emporia's efficient Welfare Association—during these years cared for the needy of the town, and in the files of the newspapers of that time frequent mention is made of this society's activities. In March, 1885, the town was stirred when Dwight L. Moody, world-famous evangelist, held a two-day meeting in the skating rink, Eighth and Commercial. That year Belva Lockwood, candidate for president of the United States, visited Emporia and spoke to large audiences. Always the town was looking forward to more railroads, and frequent meetings were held to discuss the probability of attracting different railway companies to Emporia. Also, the town began to consider a sewer system and electric lights. In December, 1885, the first electric lights were installed, at a price which would make the electricity user of today gasp—$12.50 a month for private consumption.

The waterworks location on the Cottonwood had proved unsatisfactory, and the city and the owner of the water rights, W. T. Soden, could not come to terms. After much deliberation, it was decided to move the plant from the Cottonwood to the Neosho, and in 1886 Emporia voted bonds to the amount of $162,000.00 for the removal to and the establishment of the waterworks plant in its present location. The change was beneficial in many ways, and particularly so in that the water of the Neosho, rising in the sandstone of Morris County, is comparatively soft, while that of the Cottonwood, which has its source in the lime rock of McPherson County, is extremely hard.

In 1885 occurred the famous Walkup murder trial, which held the interest of almost every person in Kansas. J. R. Walkup, a resident of Emporia for many years, a widower of 49 with grown children, married

Minnie Wallace, of New Orleans, a girl of 17, and brought her to his home in Emporia. Shortly afterward, Mr. Walkup died of what was pronounced arsenical poisoning, and Mrs. Walkup was charged with having administered the drug. In the trial, she was acquitted and soon afterward left Emporia. The town and community almost were rent asunder by the violence of the discussion between those who were positive of the guilt of the accused woman, and those who were equally certain of her innocence. Early in the case, Mrs. Walkup had attracted the attention of the elder William Jay, one of the town's capitalists, who adopted the young woman as his daughter and used his money and influence in fighting for her release. This was, and ever since has been the town's most sensational murder case.

The population of Emporia in 1886 was 9,107, and of the county 22,819. In 1887 the first Santa Fe stockyards was built in Emporia. It was confidently asserted by town boosters that four new railroads would built their tracks through Emporia this year—but the railroads did not materialize. Emporia was well on the way to become a railroad, educational and financial center, these men declared. And their prophecy is largely true. The town, with the ever-widening facilities of the Santa Fe, has become one of the most important railroad towns in the state, without the addition of a single new road. As an educational center, Emporia is second to no Kansas town, and its financial condition is firmly established. January 30, 1887, real estate sales of more than $100,000.00 were reported for the day before, and sales of $500,000.00 the previous week. The three daily newspapers—the Republican,[1] the News and the Globe —were filled with stories of big deals and of the town's brilliant future. Real estate transfer records filled much space on the first pages of these papers.

Street cars, drawn by mules, transported citizens and strangers back and forth, east and west, from the Katy to the Santa Fe stations, and back and forth, north and south, from the Normal to Soden's Grove. The town's banks overflowed with cattle money, and the population of the county had jumped to 25,000.

An important step in the emancipation from long hours of labor was the agreement, among Emporia grocers, to close their stores at 8 o'clock sharp each evening, April 1 to November 1, except Saturdays. Of the ten stores entering into this agreement only two, Brooks & Son, then Brooks & Lyon, and the Ireland grocery, now are in business in Emporia. Since that time, gradually all of the stores have come to a 6 o'clock closing hour all the year round except Saturday nights and a few nights at the Christmas holiday season.

Free mail delivery was established in Emporia July 1, 1887. In February, 1888, a bill was introduced in Congress by Senator Plumb, providing for an appropriation of $100,000.00 for a federal post office building in Emporia, but it was many years before the building materialized. A new wing at the Normal School, three stories and basement, was opened February 7, 1888. Dan Hammond and Frank McCain, contractors, built this wing. Lyon County again responded liberally to the call sent out for help from Western Kansas counties, the result of crop failures in that part of the State. William Grafenstein, of Center Township, in 1889 raised 13,000 bushels of apples on eighty acres of land, and other orchards made proportionally heavy yields.

Madison, never satisfied with the change in county

boundaries which left her high and dry near the northern line of Greenwood County, this year agitated the matter of the reinstatement of old Madison County, with Madison as the county seat. The defunct town of Elmendaro had been the county seat, but the county's namesake always had had aspirations for that honor. Governor Eskridge, in his Daily Republican, proposed that a few miles off Northern Greenwood, including the town of Madison, be taken into Lyon County. Neither proposition got anywhere. Allen, in the north part of Lyon, also was working for the establishment of a new county, to be formed of parts of Lyon and Wabaunsee Counties, but this plan "died a-borning."

The annual encampment of the Grand Army of the Republic, department of Kansas, in April, 1890, brought 5,000 Civil War Veterans to Emporia. J. M. Griffith, an honored citizen of Emporia, was elected department commander. In Olpe this year occurred the golden wedding celebration of Mr. and Mrs. Michael Sterbenz, the date being also the silver wedding anniversary of their son, Michael Sterbenz, jr., and Mrs. Sterbenz, and at this double celebration two of the elder couple's grandchildren were married—Michael Sterbenz III to Therese Kelling, and Katie Sterbenz to Frank Hagerman.

In 1889 the first annual commencement exercises of the Lyon County Schools were held in the Whitley Opera House, and this custom ever since has been observed. A. A. Stephens was county superintendent at that time.

The Farmers Alliance, which later went into politics and became the Populist party, and a force in local as well as State and National politics, was organized in Lyon County in 1889, with a large and influential membership. Soon an Alliance Exchange was incorporated and a general merchandise store opened in Emporia. The directors of the Alliance Exchange were William Ernst, J. B. Moon, R. J. Rudisill, Perry Edwards, O. B. Wharton, W. H. Wyckoff and W. L. Spencer. Alliance stores were established in other Lyon County towns, and flourished for several years.

In the eighties William Austin, of Lyon County, received a considerable inheritance from relatives who had lived in Scotland. A community-minded man, Mr. Austin generously contributed money for the completion of the auditorium at the College of Emporia which, until the destruction by fire of the first building, was called Austin Chapel. A more enduring monument he established was the long rows of elm trees which he planted bordering the half-circular drive on the College campus. Mr. Austin invested also in thoroughbred horses, and carried on a breeding stable for several years, housed in a large barn which he erected immediately north of the Santa Fe station property. He built for himself and his family the beautiful home on the Neosho, a mile north of town, now owned and occupied by the Ptacek family. But Mr. Austin was an inexperienced business man, and heavy financial losses brought him to poverty in his old age.

CHAPTER VI—1890-1900.

During the two or three decades following the passage of the prohibitory amendment to the Constitution of the State of Kansas, in every Kansas town occurred more or less litigation with law-breakers, who sought in various ways to evade the provisions of the law which, they argued, was a curtailment of the liberties guaranteed them by the Constitution of the United States. A movement to resubmit the liquor question to the people of the State at the general election of 1890 was overcome, and no resubmission vote ever has been taken in Kansas. A few Emporia citizens for years frequently were haled into court, charged with liquor law violations, and frequently they paid heavy fines or served jail sentences. They persisted, and as persistently the law enforcement element of the town—always in the majority—fought them.

Some of the drug stores, under pretense of keeping within the law by selling liquor on prescription from physicians for alleged medicinal purposes, did a thriving business. When the Legislature "cracked down" on the drug stores, several of these places in Emporia quit business. Without a liquor revenue, they could not exist. "Original packages," another method of law evasion, were sent often to Emporia from outside the State, and many were the "original package" cases tried in court. For years, of the dozen or more drug stores in Emporia, it was authoritively stated that only one did not sell liquor or carry a stock of it—these drug stores holding state permits to sell liquor under certain restrictions, keeping generally within the letter of the law. The one drug store which did not sell liquor or permit it on its premises was established in 1892 by A. E. Kraum, and has been in business all these years, conforming not only to the letter, but to the spirit of the law. The Kraum drug store was located in the five hundred block on the east side of Commercial, but moved a good many years ago to 203 Commercial. A. E. Kraum died in 1928, and the business is carried on by his son, Clarence R. Kraum.

This year—1890—Lyon County sent money and food and clothing to Stanton and Hamilton Counties, where the people were suffering from the effects of a drouth the year before. "Nelly Bly"—Lillie Corcoran, the first woman to go around the world unaccompanied by a man, and who, under auspices of the New York World, made the circuit in seventy-two days, passed through Emporia, and was interviewed at the Santa Fe station. The Postal Telegraph and Cable Company this year opened an office in the Whitley Hotel.

At the city election the spring of 1890, the town voted that a sewer system be installed. The matter was put in the hands of the City Council, and since the completion of the first sewers, the system has been enlarged and improved as the needs of the town required. Census frauds this year were charged against the city, the assertion being made that the population figures had been raised from 7,851 to 10,309, ten thousand being the required population to secure free mail delivery. In July, it was authoritively stated that the population was 8,241. But, fraud or no fraud, Emporia has enjoyed free mail delivery since its installation in 1887.

Col. H. C. Cross this year was made president and general manager of the Missouri, Kansas and Texas

Railway, following his services as receiver for that road. The death of John Fowler, who had settled in Lyon County with his family in 1855, was recorded this year—1890. The death of Senator Preston B. Plumb occurred in Washington, December 20, 1891. The entire State, and particularly Emporia and Lyon County, was saddened thereby. All of the nine-column first page of the Emporia Republican was devoted to the story of Plumb's death and burial, and to his achievements. At the opening of the January term of the Lyon County District Court, memorial exercises were held for Senator Plumb. The Grand Army, the Masonic orders, and other organizations of which he had been a member, honored the memory of the town's foremost citizen in like manner.

In 1892, when preparations were made by teachers and pupils in the city schools for the celebration of Kansas Day, it was found that no Emporia school owned a United States flag. Emporia homes lent flags for this occasion, and the Kansas Day celebration was graced by Old Glory. Now, no school in Emporia and Lyon County is without a flag. All of the city schools, and a part of those in the country, have been presented flags by the women's patriotic organizations of Emporia. The churches, also, have been supplied with flags by these women.

Emporia in 1890 experienced her first epidemic of La Grippe—the disease was indicated thus—in severe form. An editorial on "La Grippe" in the Emporia Republican, said: "No malady can hold out long against the profound medical wisdom of the present enlightened age." And still the grip gets in its deadly work.

The Young Men's Republican Club was making a stir in local politics. W. N. Smelser, now a judge in the Department of Labor and the Bureau of Immigration, Washington, D. C., was its president; C. G. Harvey, vice president; W. L. Huggins, secretary; Ed Eskridge, treasurer. John L. Sullivan, passing through town on the Santa Fe, was greeted by a large crowd during a few minutes' stop at the station. He was referred to by the Republican as "the once festive pugilist and notorious individual."

The telephone was coming into general use, and instructions on "How To Use the Telephone" were printed in the daily papers. The Santa Fe made extensive improvements in its Emporia stockyards, and R. H. Burr, of Emporia, was appointed to superintend the work in the city and in the yards. The experience of an Emporia man who had been graduated from the Keeley Institute, at Dwight, Illinois, was published in an interview printed in a daily paper, and the patient advised all persons afflicted by the drink habit to take the Keeley cure.

April 7, 1892, an 80-mile-an-hour gale was recorded as the swiftest windstorm ever experienced in this section of Kansas. Considerable damage to property resulted. The wind was accompanied by rain. The sixth annual department convention of the Ladies of the G. A. R. was held in Emporia this month, and Mrs. Matie Huffman, of Emporia, was elected department president. At the Fourth District Republican Congressional convention, I. E. Lambert was elected a member of the Congressional committee. John Carter, the oldest resident of Plymouth, died, and the death of Edward Borton, of Emporia, one of the town's early citizens, occurred this month. D. D. Williams bought the jewery store of I. D. Fox & Company, and continued in this business until his death in 1928. Hughes & Todd now own and operate this store.

Emporia school children, by donations of their pennies and nickels, were happy to be able to send $50.50 to storm sufferers at Wellington and Harper. The Ruggles farm, near Americus, settled in the fifties by Judge and Mrs. Robert M. Ruggles, was sold to J. O. Patterson, of Chicago. The 1,500 acres, much of it Neosho Valley land, sold for $40,000.00. Mrs. Almerin Gillette, wife of Judge Almerin Gillette, a magazine writer of considerable prominence, died in June, 1892, and in July occurred the death of H. E. Norton, who came to Emporia in 1856.

The Santa Fe this summer completed its double tracks to Kansas City, and the Populists opened their campaign with a monster picnic in Soden's Grove. Old Settlers' Associations representing Ohio, Illinois, Iowa, Indiana, Pennsylvania and other states, as well as the Welsh contingent, held their annual picnics and reunions. The Emporia Republican was running five and one-half columns of delinquent tax list, chinchbugs were destroying the corn, cattle were dying with Texas fever in Lyon, Chase and Greenwood Counties. Later, it was announced that the Texas fever had been placed under control, that the chinchbugs were routed by infected bugs, put in the fields by E. C. Hickey, field agent for Chancellor Snow, of the State University. That autumn, taxes were paid with reasonable promptness, and again "Bleeding Kansas" redeemed herself.

"Nora," correspondent for the Republican from Fremont Township, predicted free rural mail delivery for the United States within the next ten years, possibly within five years. The Normal School, at its opening in September, announced the largest enrollment in the history of the school—811. The cornerstone of the new Baptist Church, Fourth and Merchant, was laid October 4—and in 1929 another new Baptist Church, built by the same congregation, at Eighth and Constitution, was completed and dedicated.

Invitations were received in Emporia for the marriage, December 1, 1892, of Arthur Capper and Miss Florence Crawford, of Topeka. Mr. Capper was referred to as a "rising young newspaper man." The bride was a daughter of former Gov. and Mrs. Samuel J. Crawford, and formerly lived in Emporia. The "rising young newspaper man" has been governor of Kansas and was elected to the United States Senate in 1919. Mrs. Capper died in 1926.

The new Chicago Mound Methodist Church was dedicated in November, 1892, the Rev. Bernard Kelly, presiding elder, preaching the dedicatory sermon. Rev. R. T. Harkness was pastor of this church, and the cost of the new building was $2,248.00.

In the early nineties there was general complaint of the large number of bicycles on Emporia streets. They frightened horses, causing disastrous runaways, and were a menace to pedestrians, many persons having been struck by careless riders when crossing the streets. There was serious consideration of ruling these dangerous transportation devices off the streets, but no such action was taken.

Rural education took another step forward when it was announced, in 1893, that henceforth the rights and duties of citizenship would be taught in the district schools. The study of civics ever since has been a part of the regular course of study in the county schools. Emporia was honored this year when one of her citizens, Mrs. Belle C. Harris, was invited to sing at the World's Fair, on Women's Relief Corps Day. This invitation was extended to no other Kansas woman. Hundreds of Lyon County people made the trip to Chicago to attend the World's Fair, where but very few were able to go to Philadelphia for the Centennial celebration.

Many Emporia and Lyon County people this year made the race for the opening to settlement of the Cherokee Strip, in Oklahoma. Many of them secured land and made that territory—a state since 1916— their permanent homes. Charles S. Cross, president of the First National Bank and owner and breeder of the world's largest and best herd of Hereford cattle, was awarded the prize for the finest Hereford calf in the United States, at the Interstate Fair, in Kansas City. Mr. Cross at this time was the owner of Sunny Slope, and was internationally known as a breeder of Herefords.

Emporia's most destructive fire up to this date occurred September 15, 1893, when the north half of the six hundred block, from Mechanic to Commercial, was burned. The loss was estimated at $75,000.00, and twenty-five horses, in the Barwick livery stable, were burned to death.

The town, which was building sidewalks as rapidly as possible, complained because the state provided no sidewalks in front of the Normal School building. Walks at that time were almost entirely of stone, replacing the first ones of boards. Some of the stone walks remain, rough and uneven, but most of these have given way to cement. The first cement walks in Emporia were built at the Normal School, in 1900.

The city school children this year provided Thanksgiving dinners for the needy people of the town, and these were distributed under direction of Marshal Tom Fleming. In the following January the Emporia Relief Association was organized, with Mrs. D. S. Kelley as president; Mrs. I. E. Perley, vice president; Mrs.

Belle C. Harris, secretary; Mrs. Kate Smeed Cross, treasurer.

With the declaration by the United States Congress of war with Spain, in May, 1898, came to Emporia her second opportunity to offer her boys to the service of the country.[1] Company E, John C. McGinley, foreman of the Gazette's composing room, captain,[2] was made up of Emporia young men and those from surrounding communities. This company was assigned to the Twenty-second Regiment, Kansas Volunteer Infantry. It left Emporia in May, after being presented a flag in the name of the Women's Relief Corps by Mrs. Marian G. Stratton. Most of the townspeople were at the Santa Fe station to wish them God-speed, the Second Regiment Band playing "There'll Be a Hot Time In the Old Town Tonight," and "The Girl I Left Behind Me." This company, with others, was in camp at Topeka several weeks, then was sent to Camp Alger, Virginia, near Washington, where the men sweated and sweltered and swore through a long, hot summer, with no opportunity for service. The Twenty-second Regiment was discharged and mustered out November 3, 1898.[1]

Company H, the College company, made up from students of the State Normal School, the University of

[1] In his History of Kansas, Noble L. Prentis said: "When the call for volunteers came to Emporia, the quota assigned to her was filled within four hours."
[2] Carl Jilson, another Emporia printer, was first lieutenant of Company E.
[1] The late Judge Joseph F. Culver, an honored citizen of Emporia, as well as being an active church and temperance and political worker, was an A. P. A.—a member of the American Protective Association, which was unfriendly to persons of foreign birth. He was a Civil War veteran, prominent in the Grand Army. Between Captain McGinley, Irish and Catholic, and Judge Culver, Methodist and A. P. A., commander of Grand

Kansas and the Agricultural College, at Manhattan, of which W. C. Stephenson, a member of the Normal School faculty, was captain, had much the same experience.

November 16, 1898, came Emporia's greatest tragedy—the closing of the First National Bank, long the financial bulwark of the town, and the suicide of its president, Charles S. Cross. The reports of the bank examiner had indicated that the bank was in a failing condition, yet such was the confidence of the people in an old and honored institution, and in the personal integrity of its officials, that they did not realize the danger. Charles Cross, son of one of the founders of the First National, knew, no doubt, that this was the end for him, financially, and had not the courage to face the future. The cashier, D. M. Davis, left the United States never to return, and William Martindale, the vice president, turned over all he possessed, with the exception of his home in Emporia, to the creditors of the bank. He died, many years later, a heart-broken and disappointed man. He had known nothing, he declared, of the precarious condition of the bank.

The failure of the First National also was the beginning of the end for the Emporia Republican and for its founder and editor, Charles Vernon Eskridge.

Army Post No. 55, existed a bitter and long-standing feud. When the "boys came marching home" in November, a delegation of Grand Army men, most of the membership of Post 55—they were younger then—marched to the Santa Fe station to welcome the returning soldiers. A formal reception in Albert Taylor Hall at the Normal was tendered the soldiers of the two wars, and Captain John McGinley and Post Commander Culver marched side by side at the heads of their commands from the Santa Fe station to the Normal. Their feud was ended.

Governor Eskridge, unable to recoup his losses occasioned by the bank failure, November 10, 1900, shot and killed himself.

In addition to all this was the loss to hundreds of men and women of their savings, often of a life-time, and the consequent wreck of their hopes for an old age free from financial worries. The bank, at the hands of a receiver, paid small sums from time to time to the ever-hopeful depositors, until about 60 per cent of the shortage was returned to them. But this money came to them in "dribs," and many of them never again attained what could in any sense be termed financial security for themselves in their declining years. The town for many years felt the effects of this tragedy, not only financially, but it suffered in the loss of its misplaced confidence.

In 1899 Emporia, recovering somewhat from the shock of the First National failure, planned a monster street fair, September 27, 28 and 29, the climax of which was a parade in which the first horseless carriage, the automobile, ever driven in Kansas, was a part. The news spread that an automobile would be driven down Commercial Street, and a crowd, the like of which never before had filled the town, came on the big day to see with their own eyes this wonderful vehicle. It was owned and driven by Edgar Browne, of Chicago, and an Emporia friend, W. A. White, had induced him to ship the machine to Emporia for this occasion. No sensible person at that time would have remotely considered driving an automobile from Chicago to Emporia. With Mr. Browne and Mr. White, as the car rolled slowly and proudly down Commercial Street, were the guests of honor—the chief executive of Kansas, Gov. E. W. Stanley, and a Pottawatomie chief from the Indian reservation near Topeka. The horseless carriage was followed closely by another horseless vehicle—a Roman chariot, with a yoke of oxen hitched thereto, driven by Miss Maude Hainer, an Emporia young woman, now Mrs. Harry Baker, who has lived for years in New York and Paris.

This had been an exceptionally good crop year, and the exhibits, displayed in booths lining Commercial Street, of field and garden products, livestock and poultry, sewing and cooking and canning, and other arts and industries, all contributed to make this fair a most successful event. But the big drawing card was the horseless carriage—a small, awkward, graceless affair which today would hardly be classed as an automobile.

EMPORIA PUBLIC LIBRARY, 1906
Free for use of every Lyon County Citizen

CHAPTER VII—1900-1910

Rural free delivery of mail was established in Lyon County with the beginning of the new century, and in 1900 five routes were being carried out of Emporia. C. E. Fowler in 1913 carried the first mail by automobile over a Lyon County rural route. Now, all of the ten rural carriers use cars.

The scarcity of houses engaged the attention of the newspapers and real estate men during August—they were concerned as to how the numerous new families expected in Emporia for the beginning of the school year were to be housed. But the shortage was met by families doubling up and living in more crowded conditions than formerly. In this decade the first apartment houses were built in Emporia, and they were looked up as a distinct innovation. A monster street fair, on a much more elaborate scale than the previous year was planned, but was only a partial success because of rain. The Benevolent and Protective Order of Elks was organized in Emporia December 6, 1900, and ever since has been one of the town's strong and useful organizations.

The contract for the erection of the new courthouse, located at the corner of Fourth and Commercial, was let early in 1901 to D. L. Thomas, of Emporia, the contract price being $47,639.00. At that time, and ever since, much dissatisfaction has been expressed concerning this location, as being slight improvement, so far as freedom from disturbance by trains and street traffic is concerned, over the old location at

Third and Commercial. There was long and bitter discussion before the location was decided by vote, causing considerable delay in the erection of the building. The cornerstone was laid July 4, 1901, under direction of Emporia Masonic orders, Judge J. Jay Buck delivering an address. The new courthouse was completed in 1903 at a total cost, including furniture and fixtures, of $55,000.00. It was accepted for the county by Major W. H. Mapes, First District, chairman of the Board of County Commissioners; Elias Moorhead, Second District; and John Langley, Third District.

E. W. Cunningham, one of Emporia's pioneer attorneys and a leader in all moral, religious and civic enterprises, in 1901 was honored by the appointment as associate justice of the Supreme Court of Kansas, by Gov. E. W. Stanley, to fill an additional place in that body created by the Legislature. Mrs. Carrie Nation about this time began her saloon wrecking campaign in Kansas. Although she found no saloons to wreck in Emporia, her work was indorsed by the W. C. T. U. and the Ministerial Association, and by a majority of Emporia citizens, which was but another indorsement of that section of the town's charter which made this from the start a prohibition community.

The City Federation of Women's Clubs was organized in 1901, with Mrs. L. B. Kellogg as its president; Mrs. J. E. Evans, vice president; Mrs. Charles Harris, recording secretary. Through all the years of its work in Emporia it was an intellectual, civic and moral force in the town, and from it has succeeded the Women's City Club. The Parliament Club this year sponsored the first rest room for women, in a second-floor room between Fourth and

Fifth on Commercial. In 1904 the City Federation took up the work of the rest room, secured the use of the large basement room in the courthouse now occupied as several rooms by the County Health Unit, and fitted it up with a large reading table, easy chairs and rockers, cribs for babies, curtains at the windows, and provided for its care. This was one of the outstanding activities of the City Federation for many years, until the establishment of rest rooms in the department stores made it no longer necessary.

The Emporia State Bank opened for business in March, 1901, with its founder, Will Wayman, as president, an office he ever since has held. This institution has grown to be one of the leading state banks in Kansas. Albert R. Taylor, for nineteen years president of the State Normal School, resigned, to become the head of a college at Decatur, Illinois. Jasper N. Wilkinson, who for several years had been vice president of the school, succeeded Mr. Taylor.

The Orient Railway Company, capitalized at two and one-half millions, announced that its road would be completed from the Gulf of California through Emporia to Kansas City by June, 1901. The first dirt for the establishment of the Orient's grade through Emporia was thrown in May, by Miss May Madden, daughter of Judge and Mrs. John Madden. The first spike—a gold one—was driven July 4, at Second and Cottonwood, by W. W. Sylvester, an Orient official, as a part of a celebration in honor of the occasion. The grade was completed through Emporia, but the road did not materialize, and at frequent intervals since talk of its completion has been revived. The purchase of the Orient right of way by the Santa Fe, in 1928, as a part of the Santa Fe's expansion plan, ended whatever hope the Orient promoters might have held for a road through Emporia. The people of this town had great faith in the plans and promises of the Orient. In an account of the celebration, the Gazette for July 5, 1901, said in part:

"Thus was driven the first spike in what seems destined to be one of the great commercial arteries of the Nation, and probably one of the great factors in opening up commerce with our new Island possessions —the Philippines—and with oriental nations."

Later, the Santa Fe asked an injunction to stop the work of the Orient, and action was withheld when W. W. Stilwell, the Orient's president, declared the road would be ready for operation in a couple of years.

The summer of 1901 was hot and dry, and to the general discomfort was added an ice famine, and an order from the city prohibiting the use of water on lawns and gardens. Crops were threatened, but August 14 came heavy rains, and again the corn was "saved." The First Methodist Church was burned September 5, also the Randolph coal yard and the Sprague planing mill, all by the same fire. High wind blew sparks from the planing mill to the church, and many neighboring buildings were endangered. The church officials met immediately and started plans for rebuilding, following which the present main building was erected. Other destructive fires about this time were those of the Newton livery barn and the Jones & Stone grocery stock, the latter the result of a gasoline explosion. This month the town paused in its activities to hold memorial services for President William McKinley, following his assassination.

Emporia banks in October announced deposits of two million dollars, evidence of the increasing prosperity of the town and county. Intellectual progress was marked by the organization of a Chautauqua Association, with Major Calvin Hood as president, and J. G. Hutchison, secretary. This association flourished many years, bringing to the town the country's best speakers, musicians and entertainers, and was greatly appreciated and largely patronized. Another evidence of the town's progress was that 6 o'clock closing of all stores, from April to October, was instituted. The installation of rural telephone lines was being discussed.

In August, 1901, 11.63 inches of rain fell, a record rainfall for this month, and equal to the rainfall for the five preceding Augusts, according to the State Weather Bureau report. This was the wettest and the coolest August in the history of Lyon County. Much wheat in the shock was lost, and there was considerable damage to other crops.

William Meffert, an Emporia physician, was deprived of his license to practice medicine by the State Board of Medical Examination, following charges of malpractice brought against him by Emporia citizens. Later, Meffert petitioned that his license be restored, and after much opposition, in 1907 it was restored, and he practiced in Emporia until his death in 1921. Much bitter feeling was engendered in this matter, and half the town and county were lined up either for or against Meffert. The case was dragged through all of the State Courts, and through the United States Supreme Court.

Nineteen-two opened cold and dry, stock water was scarce over the county, and the ice crop threatened to be two thousand tons short. The water situation was not materially relieved until May, when heavy rains fell. The need of street paving was being discussed, a special bond election was held April 1, when $30,-000.00 bonds were voted for the erection of a municipal electric light plant. The cornerstone of the new Methodist Church was laid April 8, 1902, and the dedication was June 7, 1903, with Dr. Charles Bayard Mitchell, son of a pioneer Methodist minister, preaching the dedicatory sermon.

Andrew Carnegie announced the gift to Emporia of $20,000.00 for the erection of a building in which to house the city library. Mrs. P. B. Plumb presented the library site to the city, and work was started on the building May 3, 1904. The building was opened to the public with an all-town reception, May, 1906, at which Joseph H. Hill, of the Normal School, formally turned over the building and its equipment to the city.

In 1902 the Federal Government began work on a post office building in Emporia. Lots, at the northwest corner of Fifth and Merchant, had been bought several years earlier from E. W. Cunningham, Mrs. A. Harley, William Martindale and Mrs. E. J. Bancroft, the price paid for all having been $10,100.00. The building, 40x80 feet, was completed in May, 1903, at a cost of $40,000.00. The stars and stripes were raised over it by the Grand Army of the Republic, February 20, 1904. An addition, 20x80 feet, in 1911 cost $30,-000.00. The present valuation of the building and grounds is $145,000.00. The building is inadequate to the rapidly increasing needs of the office, and plans for another addition are being formulated. Receipts of the Emporia post office when the present postmaster, Harry Osborn, took charge in August, 1923, were about $92,000.00 a year. Receipts for 1928 were $108,000.00.

The county superintendent in 1903 announced the largest county teachers' institute in the history of the county schools, with an attendance of 170. County teachers' wages this year averaged $43.00 a month, denoting a steady increase. Lyon County teachers were in demand by other counties, the demand being greater than the supply. A state meeting of school boards in Emporia discussed the new truancy law, and C. C. Rhodes was appointed the first truancy officer in Emporia. The regents of the Normal School began plans for what has developed into the splendid athletic field at that institution. The Upper Room Bible Class, a group of Normal students organized in 1898 by T. M. Iden, an instructor in the school, was a strong factor for righteousness in the town, and this autumn moved to commodious quarters above the Gazette office, fitted up by Mr. Iden especially for his class. Several years later Mr. Iden was called to the University of Wisconsin, and left Emporia, but the influence of his work remains.

The Rock Valley Gazette correspondent in June made the laconic announcement that "Our telephone line starts today." A Lena Valley item under date of July 13 announced that "Many of the neighbors have purchased steroscopes, and are well qualified to entertain and amuse." A day electric current was turned on in Emporia in July, and in the autumn manual training classes were started in the High School. The first manufactured ice was used in Emporia this year. The Whitley Opera House's published list of attractions for the winter included "Way Down East," and such actors as Hanford, Mantell, Beresford and Isabelle Irving in Shakespearian roles.

Many Russian settlers, alarmed at the prospect of war between Russia and Japan, took out their final naturalization papers.

Eighty-three valuable Hereford cattle, owned by C. A. Stannard, were burned to death in a barn fire at Sunny Slope. Howard Dunlap, president of the Emporia Savings Bank, in 1903 became president of the Emporia National Bank, on the merging of these two financial institutions. Mr. Dunlap this year offered prizes for the best and most attractive flower gardens in Emporia, thus stimulating many residents to greater efforts in beautifying their homes and the town. This custom was continued for several years by Mr. Dunlap, with gratifying results.

Oil and gas talk resulted in the formation of the Wyckoff Oil & Gas Company, and wells were drilled near Neosho Rapids and in Humboldt Park in Emporia, without result other than the loss of considerable sums of money for many individuals, and for the city, which had put down the well in Humboldt Park. An eel, forty-nine inches long, stopped the Soden Mill when it was caught by a big wheel in the waterway. Assessors' reports for the year showed farm improvements totalling three million dollars. This autumn W. E. Biederwolf, a nationally known evangelist, held a series of revival meetings, in which almost all of the Protestant Churches participated, and at which 650 conversions were reported.

Early in 1904 the Santa Fe appropriated $84,000.00 for stockyards improvements at Emporia, and there was "talk" that a Harvey eating house might be established here. The talk materialized, and the site was staked out early in the autumn. The Second Presbyterian congregation dedicated a new church building at Fourth and Market, and the State Federation of Women's Clubs held its annual meeting here, May 3 to 5. The Department of Kansas, Grand Army of the Republic, came to Emporia for its annual convention which was held May 19 and 20. Charles Harris, of Emporia, was elected department commander. Gen. Nelson A. Miles was the principal speaker at this convention. Fifty High School pupils were graduated this year, and the county graduates numbered 150.

The Poehler Mercantile Company bought the old courthouse site from the county for $5,000.00, and Charles Grimmet, of Americus, paid the county $650.00 for the old stone building. The Poehler Company started on the erection of its warehouse and office building as soon as the old building had been razed and the ground cleared. The Rev. Frank Ward, pastor of the First Congregational Church, alarmed for the morals of the town, after considerable investigation, made the statement from his pulpit that the moral condition of the town was worse than at any time during his five years' residence. The Law and Order League, he said, had $800.00 at its command with which to push the prosecution of law-breakers, and needed $700.00 more for that purpose. Pearl Tipton, of Emporia, son of Mr. and Mrs. David Tipton, at the general election was chosen a presidential elector, by the Republicans, the first colored man so honored by Lyon County.

Miss Ida Tarbell, of New York City, nationally known writer and publicist, in 1905 visited friends in Emporia, a reception was given in her honor to which the town was invited, and she made a stirring address at the Normal. An early spring favored the farmers, corn planting was well under way by April 25, and some farmers had finished planting by that date. The Santa Fe announced its intention to build the Belen Cut-off, a branch line running from Emporia through Southern Kansas, Oklahoma and Texas, to Belen, New Mexico, making connections at that place with the main line. The object of this was to eliminate mountain hauling for heavy freight trains, and to shorten the distance between the eastern and western terminals. The Belen Cut-off has grown in importance and in convenience until now several passenger trains a day, as well as many freight trains are run over its rails. This summer four thousand sheep were sheared in the Santa Fe stockyards, and the ten men necessary to do the work were hard to find. This was before the days of shearing by electricity.

The Gazette printed a list of paid-up liquor sales at Emporia drug stores, thereby calling down wrath upon the head of its editor. Colonel Whitley's Old Fiddlers' organization took all the prizes in a state contest in Topeka, before an audience of 1500. The contestants were Jehu Trueman, Dudley Smith and Nathan Main. The judges were T. A. McNeal, Eugene Ware and W. H. Davis.

W. W. Finney, of Neosho Falls, bought a controlling interest in the Independent Telephone Company, in Emporia, which moved the Bell Telephone Company to make rates to farmers of 25 cents a month. Later, the companies were consolidated, and there has been but the one company since that year, under control of Mr. Finney. The city advertised for its first paving bids, for State and Union Streets, and the first paving was laid on Union, the work starting June 26, 1905.

The Emporia Republican, which had been in business since 1880, suspended publication June 3, 1905, and in 1908 the building was sold to J. W. Burkett and C. D. Huested. Dr. Frederick J. Sauber, seventeen years pastor of the First Presbyterian Church, resigned his pastorate, and Dr. John C. Miller, president of the College of Emporia, also announced his resignation. The Rev. John H. J. Rice, of Oberlin, Ohio, in 1906 accepted a call to the pastorate of the First Congregational Church, Emporia, succeeding the Rev. Frank Ward. For twenty years Mr. Rice filled this pastorate, and in 1913 was elected police judge of Emporia. He resigned from the work of the church in 1926, but retained the job as police judge on the theory, apparently, that it is easier to find a pastor than a police judge. He still administers that office, to the great satisfaction of the town.

The closing habit was growing on Emporia. In 1905 the stores were closed for half a day on Decoration Day, and all day the Fourth of July. The county's population in 1905 was 25,230, and a new city directory gave the city's population as 12,850, exclusive of students. The post office at Lang was discontinued, as being unnecessary since the establishment of rural routes. The bank of Hartford, formerly the I. A. Taylor bank, in 1906 became a national bank, with W. M. Willcox president and C. A. Johnson, cashier. Gas was found at Elmdale, and Americus, Hartford and Madison all drilled for gas and oil, without results. The town began to feel the need of a Y. M. C. A. building, and the City Federation advised the organization of a Humane Society.[1]

Sunday trains were put on the Howard Branch of the Santa Fe for the first time in 1906, and ever since a seven-day-a-week service has been maintained. The

[1] Dr. W. C. Templeton, who in 1912 became pastor of the First Presbyterian Church, was interested in the enforcement of humane laws, and was elected president of the Humane Society. He worked on the job, warned parents who were mistreating or neglecting their children, and teamsters who were abusing their horses, that continuance of such practices would result in their arrest. He put the fear of the law into the hearts of these persons, and few arrests were necessary. Doctor Templeton left Emporia in 1918, and the Humane Society has ceased to function. The late Mrs. Cora Borton Ryder was one of the interested members of this organization.

M. K. & T. Railway Company filed in the office of the Lyon County register of deeds a mortgage for $4,000,-000.00, covering its entire system—the largest such entry ever made in this county, the fee for which was $40.00. Building permits from April to July, totalled $112,300.00. The issuing of building permits by the city was a new departure, and the amount in this short period was surprising to Emporia citizens.

Among other forward steps of the county schools was a reading course, a corn growing contest for boys, and a sewing, cake and bread-making contest for girls. Ninety-two boys and fifty-nine girls entered the contest the first year. The opera house was filled to hear Eugene Debs on "Social Problems," the Poehler Mercantile Company moved into its new $200,000.00 building, and the Gazette devoted two stickfuls of type to the Teddy Bear, the fuzzy-wuzzy toy which became popular with all children and some grown persons this year. Also, the Gazette issued a Blue Book, setting forth the advantages of town and county, which was an effective piece of advertising. Juvenile court records for 1906 showed that no boys had been sent by this court to the Boys' Industrial School for more than two years, and that but two girls during that period had been sent to the Girls' Industrial School at Beloit.

For the inauguration of Joseph H. Hill as president of the Normal School, following the resignation of J. N. Wilkinson, A. R. Taylor, former president of the Normal, came from Decatur, Illinois, to make the inaugural address. President Hill served the school until 1913, when he resigned, and Thomas W. Butcher has since been the president.

Emporia had more speakers—eight of them—at the

meeting of the State Teachers' Association, than any other Kansas town. Complaints of crowded conditions in the Garfield building, which housed the High School, was the beginning of the agitation which resulted in the erection of the Senior High School, in 1912. The Maynard library of 3,000 volumes was turned over to the High School in accordance with the will of Miss Mary Maynard, a former High School teacher.

Nineteen-seven was marked by the town's largest and most imposing celebration—the fiftieth anniversary of the founding of Emporia. Two days, one of them the Fourth of July, were devoted to this celebration, which was held in Soden's Grove. The most important speaker was George W. Brown, president of the Emporia Town Company, who came, a venerable figure in frock coat and high silk hat, from his home in Rockford, Illinois, to talk to the people and to rejoice with them in the prosperity and happiness of the town to which he had devoted much time and energy. This was one of the town's happiest celebrations.

Early in 1907 the contract was let by the Santa Fe to S. N. Parker, of Emporia, for the erection of a Harvey eating house. When the Harvey House was opened in the autumn with a formal reception, it was pronounced by Inspector D. Benjamin "as near perfection as possible." County Treasurer J. D. Eastin reported the past year the biggest, in point of money paid in, in the history of the county, the amount of tax money having been $162,819.00. The Henry Pratt farm, seven miles southeast of Emporia, was sold for $40.00 an acre, and a herd of 325 Herefords, sold at the Santa Fe stockyards, brought the high price of $45.00 a head. At Sunny Slope this year was the largest herd of Herefords in the world, numbering 425 head. A post office substation was established near the Santa Fe station for the convenience, chiefly, of the residents of the Third Ward. For the first time, this year an entire new set of officers was sworn in at the courthouse, this having been made possible by the change in the state laws from annual to biennial county elections. Marriage licenses were granted this year to 594 persons, and 146 divorces were granted. The Mutual Building & Loan Association was incorporated and opened for business, and a second edition of the Blue Book was published. The County Fair Association awarded $50,000.00 worth of premiums, and its gate receipts were $65,000.00.

A road drag which had been recommended to the State by the Legislature was put into use on Lyon County roads, much to their benefit. Mrs. Marian S. Nation was elected state president of the Woman's Relief Corps, and Henry Coe Culbertson, of Iola, became president of the College of Emporia. J. E. Evans installed the first machine for dictating letters on a phonograph, and again the Gazette had kept tab on drug store liquor sales, and was happy to announce that there were 4,467 less in 1906 than in 1905.

The hottest March on record for more than forty years was followed by three-eighths of an inch of ice in April, which killed the budding fruit, the temperature dropping to 24 degrees above zero.

In May, unusually heavy rains fell, and it was said there was not a dry spot in Lyon County. The annual report of the chief engineer at the waterworks showed the plant to be on a paying basis, the total amount of water pumped for the year having been 391,058,264 gallons, an average per day of 1,074,132 gallons.

Dr. John Northington was the first Emporia man to own and drive an automobile, and Captain Heritage probably was the second. "Buzz-wagons," as the Gazette termed them, were becoming common in 1907, twenty-four up-to-date motor cars being in daily use on the streets, and at least eighty Emporia people enjoying a spin every day. The amount of Emporia money invested in automobiles was estimated at not less than $15,000.00, and a list of cars and the names of the owners was printed in the Gazette. But automobiles were considered unsafe for long trips, and Emporia people spent $7,000.00 during June, July and August for railroad fare to Colorado. "This is a sign of prosperity," commented the Gazette, "Colorado is a luxury, not a necessity."

Five thousand persons heard William Jennings Bryan in his "Cross of Gold" address at the Chautauqua, and this was followed by a big reception to the Great Commoner at the home of Mr. and Mrs. J. M. McCown. Mr. Bryan spoke many times in Emporia, and always large audiences heard him. The new Christian Church, at Seventh and Market, built at a cost of $27,000.00, was dedicated this year. The Rev. W. A. Parker was its pastor, with a congregation of between 350 and 400.

Normal School boarding clubs, in line with other mounting expenses, announced an increase in the rate of board from $2.25 to $2.50 a week. It was carefully pointed out that this was an increase of but $10.00 in a forty-week term. Mr. and Mrs. Andrew Hinshaw, the first couple married in Lyon County, in 1907 celebrated their golden wedding anniversary. David Tipton, for many years one of Emporia's outstanding Negro citizens, spoke on "Twenty Years as a House-mover," at a meeting of the Negro National Business League, in Topeka. Mr. Tipton at that time had in his employ fifteen men, with $4,000.00 invested in house-moving equipment. He died in 1910.

An evidence of Emporia's stand for morality is the following: "Black Crook, Jr.," as it was advertised in Emporia, drew a large crowd of men to the Whitley Opera House. When the curtain was raised for the first act, according to a newspaper account, every seat was occupied and not a woman in the house. The Rev. W. A. Parker, of the Christian Church, heard that the manager of the opera house was not selling tickets to women, but on inquiry was told he had been misinformed. However, Parker learned there was not a woman in the house, and told the manager if an indecent show were being given he would be arrested. The manager declared he was not responsible for the show, and advised Parker to see the manager of the troupe. Parker replied: "I will hold you responsible if an indecent show is put on, and not the manager of the troupe." This action produced the desired effect, and the company, according to the statements of several of its members, did not put on the show it had advertised.

"The Call of Kansas," the most popular and outstanding Kansas poem ever written, by Esther M. Clark—now Mrs. Hill, of Chanute—was printed in the Gazette May 16, 1907, its second newspaper appearance. It was printed first in the Lawrence Journal. The Gazette said of it: "A Kansas girl is spending her vacation out in California and she is homesick." The poem follows:

EMPORIA POST OFFICE, 1903

THE CALL OF KANSAS

Surfeited here with beauty, and the sensuous-sweet perfume
Borne in from a thousand gardens and orchards of orange-bloom;
Awed by the silent mountains, stunned by the breakers' roar—
The restless ocean pounding and tugging away at the shore,—
I lie on the warm sand beach and hear, above the cry of the sea,
The voice of the prairie calling,
       Calling me.

Sweeter to me than the salt sea spray, the fragrance of summer rains;
Nearer my heart than these mighty hills are the wind-swept Kansas plains.
Dearer the sight of a shy, wild rose by the roadside's dusty way,
Than all the splendor of poppy fields, ablaze in the sun of May.
Gay as the bold poinsettia is, and the burden of pepper trees,
The sunflower, tawny and gold and brown, is richer, to me, than these.
And rising ever above the song of the hoarse, insistent sea,
The voice of the prairie calling,
       Calling me.

Kansas, Beloved Mother, today in an alien land,
Yours is the name I have idly traced with a bit of wood in the sand.
The name that, flung from a scornful lip, will make the hot blood start;
The name that is graven, hard and deep, on the core of my loyal heart.
O higher, clearer, and stronger yet, than the boom of the savage sea,
The voice of the prairie calling me,
       Calling me.

A new law, passed by the State Legislature at the 1908 session, provided for the office of county assessor. In compliance with it, the Board of County Commissioners elected W. L. Spencer as the first man to fill this office. Also, this Legislature made a ruling that all estates remaining unsettled in the probate court be settled at once. Probate Judge W. T. McCarty found there were 670 unsettled estates in Lyon County, which he closed as rapidly as possible. The City Federation of Women's Clubs about this time gave a book shower to start a library for use of prisoners in the county jail, and more than seven hundred books and magazines were donated.

Cattle were turned on pastures of native grass the middle of April. Never had the farmers been so well along with their plowing for corn; wheat and alfalfa were in excellent condition, timely rains were welcomed. By April 16 all the pastures were filled with cattle, the price being $4.00 to $4.50 a head for the season. A freeze, later, endangered fruit and vegetation, but little harm resulted.

The Emporia post office this year became a weather observation bureau. Ed Howe, celebrated Atchison editor and author, lectured to a large audience in the Christian Church. O. H. P. VanSickle, superintendent at the county farm, reported that the farm had sold hogs, chickens and eggs, in April, to the amount of $80.00, whereas, usually, there was little or no income from such sources.

In 1908 the first carload of automobiles was received in Emporia, by the Bishop Auto Company, three Buicks representing an outlay of $15,200.00. John S. Watson purchased the best Buick built, with speed of forty to fifty miles an hour. J. R. Soden and Floyd Hagins bought the remaining two Buicks in the carload. The assessed valuation of Lyon County this spring was $40,000,000.00. Three private libraries were listed at $5,000.00 each—those of Major Calvin Hood, Mrs. P. B. Plumb and W. L. Huggins. Major Hood owned the most valuable cow in the county, listed at $50.00, and the highest priced gold watch, worth $75.00. The number of gold watches listed was 565.

Emporia people, wishing to secure a franchise for natural gas, made up a delegation of five hundred citizens to assist in the celebration of the bringing of natural gas to Cottonwood Falls and Strong City. Shortly afterward, a natural gas franchise for fuel and light was granted to G. W. Shaw, of Strong City, for furnishing gas to Emporia. The Elmdale field, from which gas was piped to Emporia, was not strong enough for so great a drain, and after wrestling with an insufficient gas supply for two winters, Emporia, disgusted and disappointed, went back to coal and wood for heating purposes, and electricity was installed for lighting in almost every home.

Hundreds of citizens who had installed gas as fuel in their homes, shivered in their heaviest clothing as they set up discarded coal and wood heaters, or tore the gasburners out of the furnaces. From that time until 1928 natural gas was considered a sorry joke in Emporia. Thousands of dollars had been invested in gas equipment which was of no use and for which there was no sale after the gas supply failed.

However, in 1920 Carl Wyckoff, of Grand Rapids, Mich., took active management of the old plant for manufacturing gas, rebuilt the plant and the mains all over town, and several years before natural gas again was brought to Emporia, had been supplying an excellent quality of gas at a reasonable rate. With the second advent of natural gas, the plant discontinued the manufacture of gas, and the company was consolidated with the Kansas Electric Power Company.

In May, 1908, 3.60 inches of rain fell, accompanied by heavy hail. In the Summit items in the Gazette appeared this: "The Jay Ames family had ice cream for dinner May 14, frozen from hail which fell May 5. Drifts of hail lined the creek banks five to six feet deep, and did not entirely disappear for ten days." Wheat fields in the Neosho and Cottonwood Valleys suffered, and at least two thousand acres of wheat was destroyed. Ninety-day corn was planted following the flood and hail, and made a fair crop.

Hartford in 1908 observed her fiftieth anniversary with a two-day celebration. The High School announced a new course for the beginning of the fall term, when bookkeeping, typing, commercial law, penmanship and business methods were offered. The town was declared "paving mad" by non-progressives, five petitions for street paving having been brought before the City Council in as many weeks.

The Emporia Gazette, January 9, 1909, printed an editorial under the head, "A Dying Fad," rejoicing "that newspapers which claim to be respectable are dropping the 'comic supplements' which have made them ridiculous for several years. . . . . In a year or two they will be as rare as the shinplasters of half a century ago."

January 14, 1909, I. E. Lambert, of Emporia, was burned to death in a fire which destroyed the Copeland Hotel in Topeka. Many Emporia people were in the hotel at the time, which was legislative headquarters for Kansas Republicans. Lambert had enjoyed the largest private practice of any Kansas attorney.

The Kansas Medical Society, meeting in Emporia for its forty-third annual convention, urged the necessity for keeping up a fight on tuberculosis. The city health authorities thereafter declared war on dirty alleys, stagnant pools, pigpens, cowlots and manure piles in an effort to eradicate the mosquitoes which followed every heavy rain. Threats of prosecution to follow failure to observe this order brought results, and the town was cleaned up as never before. A fine of $5.00 and $5.00 costs was imposed on citizens who failed to do so. A time limit for the removal of manure piles was fixed for June 21. Improved fire protection facilities were ordered for Emporia business houses, for hotels and the Normal School and the College of Emporia, with a special order that all doors on public buildings be made to open outward.

In September, 1909, the town turned out to welcome home Mr. and Mrs. W. A. White, their children and Mr. White's mother, Mrs. Mary A. White, from a five-month tour of Europe. Many out-of-town friends participated in this happy event. . . . . Emporia citizens were urged to unite in a project for road improvement, and twenty Emporia men offered to contribute $100.00 apiece for twenty years for permanent road improvements. The Business Men's Association was urged to get behind this proposition, and also to take a stand in favor of the commission form of government for the city.

CHAPTER VIII—1910-1920

February 18, 1910, at a special election called to vote on whether or not the City of Emporia should adopt the commission form of government, the proposition carried. At the city election the following April, Frank McCain, of the Third Ward, was re-elected mayor; William Corbett, also of the Third Ward, was elected commissioner of streets and public utilities, and William Lawler, of the Second Ward, commissioner of finance. During their administration, Mayor McCain and Commissioner Corbett advanced the idea of busses as a means of public transportation, but they received no encouragement from the people of the town, who considered the scheme a visionary one, and jeered at mention of the subject. Neither of these men lived to see the bus plan put into execution in Emporia, many years later, after street cars a second time had failed to solve the town's transportation problems. The old mule-drawn street cars had been junked a quarter century earlier. A street car proposition was brought before the commission by Albert Emmanuel and Dennis Dwyer, of Dayton, Ohio, which included the lease of the city's electric plant to them. They secured a franchise, and later the municipal light plant was sold to them, street cars were put in operation October 26, 1911, and the town was supplied with electricity by the street car company. The street cars never were satisfactory, as so small a portion of the town was reached by the tracks, and so few persons, comparatively, were served advantageously. The cars were replaced by busses in 1926.

The coldest weather on record since 1872 occurred early in 1910, when snow and ice lay on the ground from December until February. The Merchants Delivery System, installed this spring by Ed Mitchell, and adopted by a majority of the grocers, has been functioning successfully ever since. The city brought suit against the Orient Railway Company, after protests by property owners in the Second Ward, demanding that that thoroughfare be vacated, and that the grade built for its proposed railroad tracks by the Orient company become again a part of the street. This demand was granted March 1.

To Miss Hannah Edwards, daughter of Mr. and Mrs. R. J. Edwards, and her class of twenty-five boys of the First Presbyterian Sunday School, credit is due for the first active work looking toward a city Y. M. C. A. building for Emporia. This group had been raising money in various ways, and setting it aside as a definite Y. M. C. A. building fund. One of these money making plans was the giving of a play, and another was bringing to Emporia Judge Ben B. Lindsey, of the juvenile court, of Denver, Colo., to give a Y. M. C. A. benefit lecture. Thus was aroused the first public interest in this project, and led the way, a few years later, to the erection of the substantial building for Emporia's boys and young men. Among the twenty-five boys of this class were Fred Bowers, jr., of the Bowers Plumbing & Heating Company; Lieut. Loy Hege, who fell in France; Arnett Grigsby, son of the Rev. S. L. Grigsby, pastor at that time of the First Presbyterian Church; Adrien Foncannon, a cousin of Dr. Frank Foncannon; Dr. Harry Everett, of Emporia; Lee Cochran, a student of the College of Emporia.

Miss Edwards for many years has been Mrs. Fred Honhart, of Detroit, and has a son and daughter of her own.

A tornado, May 5, swept a path one hundred fifty to two hundred feet wide and a mile in length over the south part of Emporia. More than one hundred buildings were wrecked and the Randolph orchard, at Riverside, one of the best in Lyon County, was a complete loss. There was no loss of life. The Eskridge family, one of the oldest in the county, this spring gathered at the old home on Twelfth Avenue for the last time, before going to California to live. Their home was sold to the State for use of the Normal School, and before the erection of Beach Music Hall, was used by the music classes of the school. This year the Normal established a model rural school in the old Red Brick, the predecessor of the Whittier school, in which students might gain real experience in teaching in a rural school. The total population of children of school age in Lyon County this year was 7863.

The new Santa Fe stockyards was completed at a cost of $90,000.00, enlarging the capacity several times over for the benefit of shippers. George H. Randolph built the first cement silo in Lyon County, at his dairy farm at Riverside. Mrs. Belle C. Harris, of Emporia, was elected national president of the Women's Relief Corps, at its annual meeting this year. The Good Fellows was organized early in December by George Jones, for the purpose of providing Christmas cheer for every child in the community who might otherwise have none. This organization functions regularly and happily each year, and long has been considered one of the town's permanent institutions. The first year, ninety persons subscribed $123.50 to its fund. At the end of 1910 Emporia boasted of eight and one-half miles of paved streets.

The post office was closed on Sundays by an order of the Federal Department to all offices having an annual business of more than $40,000.00, and a postal savings bank was established. Mrs. Roy Fees—now Mrs. Walter Madison—this summer was awarded a Carnegie hero medal because of the heroic action of her husband, Roy Fees, who lost his life in the Cottonwood while endeavoring to save a friend from drowning. The award was a silver medal, $600.00, and a pension of $30.00 a month.

The King's Daughters, an organization of business and professional young women of the First Presbyterian Church, removed much of the prejudice against moving pictures—which theretofore had been looked at askance by conservative Emporia people—when they defied the elders of their church and sponsored a "movie" at the Electric Theater as a King's Daughters' benefit. The manager, P. J. Concannon, gave the King's Daughters all of the profits, as their sponsoring the show was worth much to him as advertising. The King's Daughters cleared $105.00, and when a portion of this money was turned over to the trustees of their church as part payment on the Commercial Street paving in front of the church building, no member objected to accepting the money. Thereafter, there was no opposition to church organizations sponsoring moving pictures. The theaters then charged an admission of ten cents, having advanced from the nickelodeon stage of five cents admission.

There was ample employment for all laborers in 1911—a new pipe line was installed for the waterworks, street paving was in progress, the street car line was being built, a new gymnasium at the College of Emporia was in course of construction, a new freight depot at the Santa Fe, improvements at the county farm, and a great deal of building by private citizens was under way. The contract for the new Catholic Church had been let. There was talk of the formation of a country club, to include golf links, and a list of names of eighty-one prospective members had been secured.

Alfalfa had come to be considered the leading crop in Lyon County, and five thousand bushels of seed had been sold in the county, bringing $40,000.00. An alfalfa mill was started by Grant Wolfe, and almost every farmer had at least a small field of alfalfa. E. W. Barker this year paid Morris Pyle $60,000.00 for Sunny Slope farm, the original home of alfalfa in Kansas. C. A. Stannard, years earlier, had bought Sunny Slope for $28,000.00. F. C. Newman sold his farm, a mile north of town on the Neosho, to W. A. Gladfelter, two hundred twelve acres at $125.00 an acre, a total of $28,000.00. Mr. Newman had paid $55.00 an acre for this farm.

County teachers' salaries, slowly mounting, this year averaged $45.00. The Normal School had gained almost one thousand students in the five years last past, half that number in the past two years. Twelve hundred students attended summer school at this institution. An action to enjoin the City Board of Education, which had forbidden the organization of fraternities in the High School, resulted in victory for the board, and was the end of fraternities in this school.

The Lyon County Equal Suffrage Association was organized November 1, 1911, with Mrs. I. E. Perley as president; Mrs. J. M. McCown and Miss Mary Whitney, vice presidents; Miss Mabel Edwards and Mrs. W. A. Randolph, secretaries; Mrs. Fremont Miller, treasurer. After the year's campaign, which resulted in the passage of the suffrage amendment in Kansas, Mrs. W. A. Johnston, of Topeka, president of the State Suffrage Association, declared that the work of the Lyon County Association was the greatest in volume and the most effective of any county in the State, and that there had been sent out from Emporia a larger amount of effective publicity than from any other Kansas town. Suffrage Associations functioned in every Lyon County town, seventy women of the Normal School organized to aid in the fight for votes for women, and ministers preached from their pulpits on the equal suffrage question. The Lyon County vote for suffrage at the general election was 2999, and the opposing vote was 2362.

William Lawler, city commissioner of finance, who had been urging for some time the need for a city market, in 1912 was authorized by other members of the commission to establish a market, on the east side of Commercial between Third and Fourth, which was opened about the first of May. 'This market was the beginning of the present efficient city market, and it has been running ever since. In January, the High School was closed a few days because of cold classrooms, and this probably helped the vote for the issue of bonds for the erection of the new high school building, which went over by a big majority at the city election in April. The Santa Fe freight depot was opened for business, the Good Roads Association held its tenth annual meeting in Emporia early in the year, and later Lyon County sent twenty delegates to the meeting of the National Old Trails Association in Kansas City. A contract for the erection of a Country Club building was let for $11,250.00, with additional expense reaching $15,000.00. The building, on a beautiful knoll overlooking the Neosho Valley, was formally opened January 1, 1913.

A chapter of the Daughters of the American Revolution was organized in Emporia this year, by Mrs. George Guernsey, of Independence, and Mrs. J. P. Ramseyer was elected regent. The Women's Relief Corps erected a soldiers' monument in Fremont Park, dedicated to the memory of Civil War veterans, the ceremony of dedication taking place September 13. W. A. White was made national committeeman for the Progressive party in Kansas, and Theodore Roosevelt[1] was a drawing card at a political meeting in Emporia. Jackson Township farmers demanded road improvement from the county commissioners, and the commissioners pledged themselves to improve and maintain one hundred seventy miles of county road within the year.

Boarding prices for Normal School students again were increased, this time to $2.75, $3.00 and $3.50. An Emporia homecoming, held in Soden's Grove the week of October 13, was a five-day festival in which thousands of citizens and former citizens participated.

[1] Theodore Roosevelt visited over Sunday, September 22, 1912, in Emporia, during his last campaign for the presidency. Being a member of the Dutch Reformed Church, he attended the services of that denomination—St. Paul's—while here. The Rev. T. F. Stauffer was pastor of the congregation of thirty-one members Mr. Roosevelt was accompanied to church by W. A. White, at whose home he was a guest. He took part in all of the services, sang the hymns and contributed to the offering. The minister made but one slight reference to the great man by whose presence his church was honored. After the benediction everyone in the building shook hands with the former President, and he walked home with his host, with the same lack of ostentation as would any other private citizen. Mr. Stauffer had been informed that Mr. Roosevelt would attend his church that morning. It was a great day for the little congregation. This organization, never large, since has disbanded, and the Calvary Evangelical Church owns the building and holds it services at Ninth and Constitution, where once Roosevelt worshiped!

Weather conditions were ideal, and every plan of the promoters was successfully carried out. A Gospel Team training conference held in Emporia this autumn resulted in the formation of many such teams, men and woman, who went to surrounding communities preaching the gospel of righteousness.

Capt. Lemuel T. Heritage, who died in January, 1913, left a bequest of $40,000.00, the accumulations of which are used for the purchase of clothing and books and other school supplies for children whose parents are unable to provide for them. Since that time, many Emporia children have profited by Captain Heritage's generosity, and have been kept in school when otherwise they could not have gone. Capt. Heritage left substantial bequests to the City Library and to the First Congregational Church.

The first person in Emporia to mail a package by parcel post was Mrs. F. M. Davis, in January, 1913, who sent a six-pound parcel to Seiling, Oklahoma, for 36 cents. The parcel post business increased rapidly. Real estate men declared that this year there were five prospective tenants to every farm for rent, and that farm sales for the December just past exceeded those for many years. Numerous farms were changing hands, and there was an excellent opportunity for persons owning farms to secure desirable tenants. The Gazette noted the coming to Lyon County of three Bohemian families—the Anton Ptaceks, the Mareshes and the Joseph Prchls, all of whom are highly desirable citizens. Farmers plowed in their fields every month during the winter, and the first alfalfa was cut May 15. Two new banks were established in Emporia this year—the Lyon County State Bank, William M. Price, president, and the Commercial State Bank, which in a few years became a national bank, F. M.

Arnold, president. The cattle business was good. The demand for houses in Emporia was greater than the supply.

Mrs. Nellie Ashley was appointed the first matron in the Santa Fe station, and a year earlier Mrs. Maggie Wood had been the first city matron, appointed by the City Commission. Mrs. Nina V. Riggs for years following was city matron, and has been the juvenile court officer since the necessity for such an officer became apparent. The stores in 1913 agreed to a 9 o'clock closing hour for Saturday nights, with 5 o'clock closing for five days in the week during July and August. These closing hours ever since have been adhered to. The Whitley Opera House, built in 1880, burned June 18, with a loss of $40,000.00. In the business rooms on the first floor were a meat market, a barber shop and grocery store, all of which were destroyed. The opera house stood on the northeast corner of Sixth and Merchant.

This was a hot, dry summer, but fear of a water famine was allayed when the city "hooked up" with the Cottonwood, to augment its water supply. Drinking water was boiled and filtered as precautionary measures, the ice plant was compelled to split orders, householders were limited as to watering lawns, and finally, forbidden to water them at all. The Gazette printed a story of an early-day drouth, from the Americus Sentinel of October 27, 1860, which proved that the drouth of that year and its attendant hardships were much more serious than those of 1913. In September, light rains brought relief, and three inches of water fell in October.

Mayor Fessenden this summer entertained fourteen hundred Emporia children with a picnic at Soden's Grove, and two thousand persons paraded on Commercial Street, Labor Day. Average salaries paid to teachers in the county schools were, men, $51.00, and women, $48.50.

With the summing up of the fire losses for 1913, the City Commission decided that a paid fire department had become a necessity for the safeguarding of Emporia property. The fire loss for the year, $60,000.00, never had been so large. Salaries for a paid department were fixed at $75.00 a month for the chief, $60.00 a month for three regular firemen, and $15.00 a month for three substitutes, seven men being employed instead of the eleven who had made up the volunteer department. Building permits during the year past had been issued to the amount of $200,000.00, and the first half of the 1914 taxes was $298,859.35. Births registered numbered 211, and deaths 179.

Three hundred Lyon County women met at luncheon to discuss the duties of their newly acquired citizenship. The Lyon County Federation of Women's Clubs took up the need of a mothers' pension law, to be presented to the Legislature; the censorship of amusements, especially for moving pictures, and a committee to investigate conditions at the county farm was appointed. At the city election in the spring, pool halls had been voted out of existence in Emporia, by a vote of 1923 to 1312. The women of the Rinker neighborhood organized a cooperative egg-selling association, which functioned with profit for several years. When the money-raising campaign for a $75,000.00 city Y. M. C. A. began this year, Miss Hannah Edwards's Sunday School class made the first contribution—$500.00. Miss Catherine Jones, daughter of Mr. and Mrs. D. O. Jones, of Emporia, was honored by being requested to sing before Queen Alexandra, in Queen's Hall, London.

The county commissioners ordered twenty steel road

drags of special construction for use on the county roads, and announced that fifty Lyon County men would be regularly employed to keep the roads in good condition. H. L. Popenoe became Lyon County's first farm adviser, when the Farm Bureau was organized this year. School opened in the new High School building April 20, with an attendance of four hundred fifty-nine. The building program for the year amounted to $550,000.00.

Soon after the declaration of war in Europe the women of the County Federation took up Red Cross work. W. Harrison Roberts gave the first sack of flour of the one thousand barrels sent by Lyon County to the starving Belgians. Wheat was $1.07 a bushel, and increasing in price almost daily.

An evidence of Emporia's ethical progress during 1914 was found in the fact that charitable, religious and public gifts this year totalled $108,089.00, and in addition to this were thousands of dollars in private charities and in gifts other than money—time and energy and the neighborliness for which the town was becoming more and more known. A censorship had been placed on the operation of pool halls under a prevailing city ordinance, and a vote at the city election on their reinstatement without censorship was defeated, 1767 to 153. When this matter again was voted on, later in the year, again it was defeated. Mrs. Robert King was appointed the first policewoman in Emporia, with the idea of "strengthening her authority as a member of the Board of Censorship."

Margaret Templeton and Valetta Gates, College of Emporia students, operated the first jitney—transportation at five cents a haul—in Emporia when, using the car belonging to Miss Templeton's father, Dr. W. C. Templeton, they met trains and transported pas-

SENIOR HIGH SCHOOL
Erected 1912

sengers. They gave the money thus earned to the College endowment fund. Soon other jitneys were on the streets, and the business flourished for a time.

The winter of 1914-1915 was a hard one, much of the distress being occasioned by war conditions. Fifty tramps slept in the city jail during January, according to Officer Sam Marsh. The price of wheat reached $1.50 in January, and millers and bakers were experimenting with substitutes by which to conserve the wheat for use in Europe, and at the same time provide proper nourishment for the people. The 5-cent bakery loaf was discontinued in Emporia, and has not been reinstated. Cattle feeders were hard hit by the continued mud and cold weather, and their profits fell off. Five inches of rain in May delayed the planting of crops. In spite of these drawbacks, Earl Armstrong and Vernon Johnson, Lyon County farmers, received silver medals for their corn exhibits at the Panama-Pacific Exposition in San Francisco, and Edward Palmer was awarded a gold medal for his corn from Lyon County. R. V. Dyer, who lived eleven miles northeast of Emporia, harvested a 20,000-bushel crop of apples, the largest crop to this date ever raised in a Lyon County orchard.

A disastrous epidemic of hog cholera, the worst in many years, was checked by vaccination, under direction of the county farm agent, H. L. Popenoe, thus proving to the skeptical that the work of the farm agent is an important aid to farmers. The Lyon County Teachers' Institute, held for a month each summer, was abandoned, a five-day session of intensive work given instead, and this method still prevails.

Frank A. Beach, head of the music department at the Normal School, provided by parcel post instruction in rural school music for the schools of the state, with great success. This year, 40 per cent of the Normal students were sons and daughters of farmers. Work was started razing the old Normal administration building, to give place to Plumb Memorial Hall, and this year moving pictures became a part of the educational work of this school.

Stuart Hall, the main building at the College of Emporia, built in 1884, was burned with a loss of $100,000.00. Immediately work was started to secure money for the erection of a new building, but this was delayed because of war conditions. The beautiful new administration building, called the War Memorial, completed in 1929, takes the place of Stuart Hall. City library privileges this year were extended to all residents of Lyon County, without cost to the persons taking out books.

Lyon County spent $60,000.00 in road improvements in 1915, and plans were made for the construction of the present permanent road to Maplewood Cemetery. One thousand automobiles were listed by the assessors as belonging to Lyon County citizens. Emporia banks gained a half million in deposits this year, the total being $3,610,420.00, and building costs reached $400,000.00. The Welfare Association bought the five lots at the corner of Fourth and Merchant, paying for them $4,000.00, plus paving tax of $740.00.

Company L, Kansas National Guard, composed largely of Emporia and Lyon County boys, was in training under command of Capt. Clayton Patterson throughout July, in preparation for possible service in Mexico. This company was mustered into the service of the United States Government in 1917, and went into training at Camp Heritage, adjoining the town on the northwest. After a couple of months this company left Emporia, and later was ordered to Deming,

New Mexico, to assist in guarding the border. Red Cross classes were at work in the towns and schools, and soon almost all of the women of the county were organized for service, and the town and county were ready for whatever action might be required of them. Camp and Field, a daily column in the Gazette, grew into many columns of news devoted to the men in the service, and to the letters they sent to their families and friends. This was the most popular department ever instituted by the Gazette. Sixty-one Lyon County men lost their lives in the World War.

A Draft Board, with Sheriff Tom Owens as president and the late G. A. Hege as secretary, was organized for the purpose of registering the 2250 men announced by the War Department as the military quota for Lyon County. June 5 was registration day. The town formally indorsed universal military service, girls and women took the places in the fields and stores and shops of the absent men, united efforts were made in the conservation of food, and the community market and garden clubs supplied quantities of vegetables. Wheatless days, meatless days, lightless nights, union church services to save heat and light, all became a part of the regular program of events made necessary by the World War. The 1917 wheat crop yielded as high as 48 3-10 bushels per acre in a few fields, and was unusually abundant all over the county. Bakers' loaves went up in price to 15 cents, and were made largely of wheat substitutes. Prairie hay sold for $16.00 a ton. Many Emporia persons adopted French war orphans. Mr. and Mrs. John Wilkie, now living in California, were the first to take charge of an orphan.

Miss Linna Bresette, representing the Kansas Industrial Welfare Commission, this year and for several years, spent considerable time in Emporia, looking after the enforcement of the rulings of the Commission regarding women in industry. The result was greatly improved conditions, without hardship to the employers. The City Federation pledged its help in the enforcement of these laws, and was a valuable aid to the Commission.

The first action looking toward hard-surfaced roads was taken this year, the Rotary Club was organized in Emporia, and the Women's Relief Corps, the Rinker Community Club, and almost all of the women's organizations in town and county became Red Cross auxiliaries, for the carrying on of the work of organization.

Paul Culbertson earned the first Cross of Honor bestowed upon an Emporia boy. Three times was he cited by the French Government for bravery under fire—November 26 and 27, 1917, and March 26, 1918. Young Culbertson was an ambulance driver and in each case went back into the lines under heavy fire to carry out wounded men. He is the son of the late Dr. and Mrs. George Culbertson, and grew up in this town.

School districts all over the county gave Red Cross benefits. At a pie social at the Summit schoolhouse, the receipts were $87.00. At a "last day of school" in District 60, Gladys Bruce, teacher, a goose given by Mrs. John Gilligan sold at auction for $13.31. There were many other such instances, all for the Red Cross. The Young Men's Commercial Club, under direction of Frank Lostutter, a merchant, worked after business hours in the fields for farmers who were short of help, and helped to save many acres of wheat. Lyon County this year had a wheat acreage of 17,657 acres, 5,000 acres more than any previous year. Cattle pasture brought $17.00 a head.

All registered nurses were required to register for service on call, and the names of many Emporia women were enrolled. Mrs. J. H. Starbeck and Mrs. A. S. Young were awarded each a Red Cross, for one hundred or more hours of service in the hospital garment sewing department, having worked one hundred fifteen hours each during April and May, 1918. The Normal gymnasium became a barracks for the S. A. T. C., as did the College of Emporia gymnasium. The Beligian Relief Committee in one day collected 8,500 garments for the needy Belgians. The lowest county teachers' salaries this year—and there were but two so low—were $50.00 a month, and the average was $60.00 to $65.00. The new administration building at the Normal was dedicated in May, 1918, and the Normal cafeteria was opened for use of the students and faculty.

The first epidemic of influenza took a heavy toll. Almost all Emporia physicians were out of town on war duty, medical attention was difficult to secure, hospital accommodations inadequate, nurses were scarce. The Chamber of Commerce rooms and rooms in the Masonic Temple and the Elks Club, and in private homes, became temporary hospitals. Many Emporia citizens volunteered their services as nurses, doing all they could for their fellow townspeople. Schools and churches were closed, and there were few public meetings. The Country Club building was turned into a smallpox hospital. January registered the coldest weather in thirty-one years, eleven days being below zero. Trains on the Howard Branch were snowbound for twenty-four hours in drifts between Eureka and Madison the day before Christmas, 1918, with no food and the prospect of relief postponed from hour to hour. Snow plows moved slowly because of the five feet of snow on the level, and the heavy drifts. Rural mail deliveries were held up several days.

Dr. W. C. Templeton about the first of the year resigned his pastorate of the First Presbyterian Church, and Dr. R. A. B. McBride, who had been in war work in France for the Y. M. C. A., was called to the church.

Emporia and Lyon County's response to the need for war work was spontaneous and sincere. The Red Cross paid no rent for workrooms, no advertising bills, no gas or light or water bills, the different business houses esteeming it a privilege to help in this way. Red Cross headquarters was in the new Y. M. C. A. building, where the general offices were located. Here the Rev. Carl Nau, county chairman, then rector of the Episcopal Church, did his work. A stenographer, his assistant, drew the only Red Cross salary in Emporia. Mrs. J. P. Ramseyer, chairman of the women's work for town and county, gave nearly all her time to it. The Gazette some days carried a dozen Red Cross stories, and always its columns were open to the slightest need of the Red Cross, as were those of the Emporia Times. The knitting department was located in the basement diningroom of the Y. M. C. A., with Mrs. George Plumb as supervisor, and Mrs. J. W. Lostutter as knitting instructor. Here all of the yarn for the thousands of knitted garments was given out, and dozens of women bought their own yarn, that those who could not afford to buy, but could knit, might keep busy. Here, also, was headquarters for the twenty-three auxiliary Red Cross chapters of Lyon County. Mrs. Charles Harris was supervisor of the auxiliary supplies.

The big diningroom of the Masonic Temple was the

workroom for the surgical dressings department, where one hundred fifty workers could be accommodated, and where Mrs. J. E. Eckdall was supervisor. The Masons furnished not only the room, but heat, light, water, gas and janitor service. The diningroom of the Elks Club, with its adjoining kitchen, was turned over to the hospital garments sewing department, with the same generous donation of supplies as was the Masonic Temple. Sixty women worked here, and the use of five sewing machines was donated by the Singer Sewing Machine Company. The light company provided electricity, and installed fans during the hot weather. The gas company provided gas. These women met every day to sew, held many all-day meetings, and lunched together at noon. Coffee was furnished by an Emporia merchant, cream by an Emporia woman who had little time to sew, and the Elks provided many of the luncheons. Mrs. R. L. Hershberger was supervisor of the sewing room.

Two big rooms at the Normal School were devoted to the making of surgical dressings, where sixty persons could work at one time. Every person in any way connected with this school, man or woman, boy or girl, faculty member or student, was required to work at least an hour a week on surgical dressings. This time was greatly exceeded. Forty-four Emporia women held Red Cross instructors' cards.

Twenty workers were accommodated in the room at the College of Emporia set aside for Red Cross activities, and it was occupied with busy workers many hours each week. Pupils at the High School, the city schools and the parochial school were making gun wipes, snipping for comfort pillows, sewing refugee garments, and the boys in manual training made packing boxes for the shipment of supplies. In the domestic arts department at the Normal School refugee garments were made under supervision of the head of that department, Miss Elizabeth Bye.

The town civilian relief committee looked after the welfare of soldiers' families, urged all soldiers to take out insurance, and in one collection of garments for Belgian relief, in half a day three and one-half tons of clothing was secured. In the county schools more than 80 per cent of the pupils held paid memberships in the Red Cross at 25 cents a member.

Six first aid classes were taught by physicians who took no pay for their services. A class in home nursing and care of the sick was taught by the Normal School nurse, Mrs. Kirtland. As each army contingent was called the Red Cross gave a dinner for the boys at which men of the town were hosts. At one of these dinners, besides the army contingent, one hundred fifty men and women were present. Each Lyon County soldier was given a sewing kit, with his initials embroidered on it by women of the Red Cross. A salvage committee of boys and girls gathered all waste materials, sold them, and turned over the money to the Red Cross. The Chamber of Commerce kept an up-to-date list of the names and addresses of the Lyon County boys in the service of the Government. Every change of address was recorded as soon as received. The total registration for Lyon County was 2121, and the total number of men mustered into the service was 1042.

Lyon County was represented in the branches of military service, as follows:

Artillery: Light, Field, Heavy, Coast Defense.

Infantry: Machine Gun Companies, Marines, Tank Corps, Labor Batallions, Engineers.

Signal Corps: Airplanes, Observation Balloons, Radio.

Navy: Submarines, Submarine Destroyers, Light Cruisers, Heavy Cruisers, Gunboats, Battleships, Shipbuilding.

Service of Supply: All departments.

Early in 1919 the soldiers who had been discharged began arriving in Emporia, and many of them went to work at once on the jobs they had held before the war. They were joyously welcomed. When Company L came a big town demonstration was held, with a monster parade. Memorial Day observance was the most universal in the history of the town. On the return of portions of the Eighty-ninth Division, Emporia fed five hundred soldiers at the Santa Fe station.

Memorial services were held for Theodore Roosevelt soon after the death of the former President. The death of George W. Newman, founder of the Newman Dry Goods Company in 1868, occurred February 21, 1919, and was a town and community loss. Mr. Newman in his will gave $50,000.00 as a start for the founding of a hospital in Emporia, and this sum was augmented by a 2-mill tax levy voted at the next general election. This was the beginning of the Newman Memorial County Hospital, a plant worth now $244,839.18, according to the 1929 inventory, and of inestimable value not only to Emporia and Lyon County, but to many of the surrounding counties.

The first airplane landed in Emporia February 4, 1919, seeking an air mail landing place.

Lieut. Harry Martin, son of Mr. and Mrs. John E. Martin, of Emporia, was awarded a distinguished service medal by the Federal Government, and A. G. Marsh, of Emporia, was given a croix de guerre by the French government. Red Cross activities were moved from the Masonic Temple to the Whitley Hotel, and the canteen at the Santa Fe station was closed, after a year's activity. The American Legion and the Women's Auxiliary effected organizations, which have functioned regularly since. Legion membership is 350. The Red Cross T. N. T. Club, composed of women who worked in the sewing department during the war, is another permanent organization.

The Preston B. Plumb home, following the death of Mrs. Plumb, was presented to the City Y. W. C. A. by the owners, Miss Mary Plumb, Mrs. Caroline Plumb Griffith and Mrs. Ruth Plumb Brewster, as a memorial to their father and mother, the late Senator and Mrs. Plumb. This gift was augmented by another of $10,000.00 each from A. H. Plumb and Preston Plumb, the sons, bringing the total value of the Plumb gift, at a conservative estimate, to $50,000.00. J. S. Kenyon and other citizens gave an additional $3,000.00 when it was needed in construction work on the large annex to the original building.

The handsome Y. W. C. A. building on East Sixth Avenue is the home of many Emporia business and professional women, and a meeting place for scores of town and county organizations all the year round. The building was formally opened for use of the Y. W. C. A., December 17, 1919. A successful joint drive for a $5,000.00 maintenance fund for the Y. M. C. A. and the Y. W. C. A. was put on soon afterward. Miss Lina Tulloss is secretary of the Y. W. C. A., and DeWitt Lee of the Y. M. C. A.

President Woodrow Wilson passed through Emporia October 2, 1919, and was given an enthusiastic welcome by thousands of Emporia people. King Alfred, Queen Elizabeth and Prince Leopold, of Belgium, were greeted at the station by a great crowd of Emporians, to whom the King expressed his appreciation of their welcome and of their assistance in Belgium's great need. Miss Lillian Davis, the county's first school nurse, went on duty this year.

CHAPTER IX—1920-1929

January 13, 1920, the doors of the Southwestern Farm Mortgage Company were closed, because of serious shortages, and its president, Edward J. Conklin, was missing. The losses were said to exceed $50,000.00. Conklin organized this mortgage company and the Farmers State Bank in 1917, and was granted a charter by the State Charter Board against the protest of the presidents of all other Emporia banks. R. M. Hamer was appointed receiver for the defunct mortgage company, and found assets of but $400.00. The bank earlier had severed its relations with Conklin, it was reorganized and a new president elected. It remained in business only a few years.

A warrant was issued for Conklin's arrest, but for more than three years he evaded the officers. Early in April, 1925, he was arrested in New York City and brought to Emporia for trial. He pleaded guilty to five embezzlement charges and received a sentence of from five to twenty-five years in the penitentiary. He was paroled after a year or two, and is said to be living in Wichita. Many persons lost all of their savings by the failure of this company, in whose stock they had invested. Thirty-five per cent of their investments were returned to the stockholders in 1921.

The Citizens National Bank, with which the Emporia National Bank—following the death of its president, Howard Dunlap, in 1920—was consolidated in 1921, was organized in 1886, with William Jay as president; T. J. Acheson, vice president; D. W. Eastman, cashier. The bank was reorganized in 1892, and F. C. Newman elected president; L. L. Halleck, vice president; H. W. Fisher, cashier.

The Citizens Bank was located first on the northeast corner of Sixth and Commercial—Emporia's original bank corner—but moved to its present location following the failure of the First National, 1898. In 1924 was erected the handsome, five-story building which houses this bank. The Citizens National is the most important financial institution in the Fourth Congressional District, and much of its success is due to the efficient management of the man who, for many years, has been its president—Frederick C. Newman.

The Emporia National, which long was the oldest banking business in Emporia, having been the town's first bank, organized in 1867, was reorganized in 1872 as a national bank. Preston B. Plumb was its first president, Major Calvin Hood its second, and Howard Dunlap its third.

Dan Dryer, city commissioner of public utilities, authorized by the other members of the commission, issued an order to the effect that Emporia people should limit the quantity of water in their bathtubs to four inches, in an effort to conserve the shrinking water supply. This order called down the scorn of newspapers all over the country, but saved the town from a serious water famine.

The Rev. J. C. Brogan, pastor of the Grace Methodist Church, elected mayor in 1920, took his oath of office wearing overalls, and led an overall parade of one thousand citizens through the streets of Emporia, as a protest against profiteering, which was taking the cost of living out of reach of ordinary persons. All domestic commodities were higher than ever before, sugar reaching 27 cents a pound. Building in

Emporia this year exceeded all that of 1916, 1917 and 1918, though materials were higher in price than ever before. But the slump in building during the war period made it necessary now, even at advanced prices.

April 2, 1920, a two-inch snow fell, accompanying a hard freeze, and the advanced vegetation was frozen to the ground. The new Strand Theater was opened the first of April. Three thousand persons attended the Labor Day celebration, and Hartford and other Lyon County towns held their usual pre-war fairs, which had been temporarily discontinued. A successful county fair was held in Emporia, and a new celebration—Armistice Day—was observed for the first time.

In 1921 the Whitley Hotel burned, with a loss of $150,000.00, and the death of one guest, James Daniels, of Topeka.

Wheat had sold at $1.60 the first of January, but at harvest time had fallen to a dollar, and sugar prices had dropped to 14 cents a pound. The yield of wheat was large, and farmers held most of it for higher prices. Six months of dry weather occasioned a serious water shortage in midwinter, and many farmers hauled water several miles for their livestock. Wells and cisterns were dry, and until rain fell, February 22, the situation was alarming. The scarcity of water had prepared the way for the voting of waterworks bonds in the sum of $75,000.00. This included the raising of the Ruggles dam on the Neosho, and other details of a plan offered by the City Commission.

A hearing before state officials in Emporia, concerning the wages of women employed in Emporia stores, impelled some working women of the town to experiment on living on 60 cents a day, as it had been asserted at this hearing they could do. The experiment, which lasted a week, proved most conclusively that no person could be well nourished on the food this sum of money would purchase.

Early in 1923 the Santa Fe announced an improvement program for Emporia, amounting to five million dollars. The Orient, however, blocked this program for several years, its officials announcing that the company was getting on its feet and that the line through Emporia to Kansas City from the Pacific yet would be completed. The Orient owned land, required by the Santa Fe for its improvements, which it finally secured. The Santa Fe bought, after condemnation proceedings, the residence properties west of West Street between Third Avenue and South Avenue, running west to include several farms. The houses were moved to lots in other parts of town, some of them by their former owners, and that section of the town for a time, before improvements were started by the Santa Fe, was indeed a deserted village. This year the Santa Fe completed a branch line from Elinor to ElDorado. Thirty blocks of street paving had been laid in Emporia, and the Sixth Avenue paving extended to the Chase County line on the west and to Coffey County on the east. The Madison oil fields, only a short distance from Emporia, promised to lead the state in production.

For the city election of 1923, which included the voting of bonds for a Junior High School building, 5546 voters registered, the largest registration the town had experienced, and the bonds for $40,000.00 carried. Two million dollars had been spent in the erection of new homes in Emporia the past year, and the Soden Bridge, built in 1869, and in continuous use since that date, was razed to give place to a new structure. The population of the town, 12,030, showed a gain for the year of 699. Twenty-five hundred students attended the Normal summer school, and Kellogg library records showed that 2,700 students, in one day during the winter, availed themselves of library privileges. The name of the Normal School this year was changed to that of Kansas State Teachers College.

The new Broadview Hotel, costing $400,000.00, was opened September 20, 1923, filling a town and community need. The County Health Unit had been established and was at work. D. C. Schaffner, treasurer of the College of Emporia, announced that the College at this time spent fifteen times as much for maintenance as in 1898. The Normal School put on the first money-raising campaign in which it asked the aid of the town, for the erection of a student union building, and the $50,000.00 project was successfully carried out.

In August, the Gazette issued a morning edition announcing the death of President Harding, and town memorial services were held honoring the dead President. The Women's City Club this year provided milk lunches for under-nourished children in the city schools, with satisfactory results, and the practice has been continued each year. Two hundred old settlers were the guests of the Newman Dry Goods Company an afternoon in December, and this "party" has become an annual event. Also, in this month the county treasurer received $89,492.38 in one day, the largest tax-paying day on record. Emporia led the State in the scope of its telephone service, having 4281 telephones with a population of less than sixteen thousand. The A. M. E. Church, which had been badly damaged by fire, was rebuilt, and citizens of the town joined with the congregation in the financing of the handsome building at Sixth and Congress.

LOWTHER JUNIOR HIGH SCHOOL, 1925

E. J. Alexander, a Negro who lived a few miles northeast of Emporia, left his estate of thirty acres of Neosho Valley farm land and $1190.00 for the use of orphans and needy children of the community. Also, his will provided that an acre of land be set aside as a cemetery for the use of persons unable to buy lots for the burial of their dead. The disposition of this property was similar in intent to that of the Heritage estate. Mrs. Emeline Johnson, the town's oldest citizen, died at the age of 102. James H. Rayburn, evangelist, announced 1422 converts as a result of revival meetings held by him in Emporia this winter.

Thirteen fire alarms in four days were turned in during the early part of January, 1924, many of the fires resulting from overheated furnaces during the extremely cold weather at that time. A blizzard, with intense cold, piled high with snow the streets and highways, February 3, and five inches of snow on March 16 was welcomed by the farmers. Lyon County the past year had invested $127,620.00 in road improvements, including eleven bridges, twenty culverts and 223 miles of dirt road dragged. The town paid $7,000.00 for a street flusher.

Memorial services for Woodrow Wilson were held in Albert Taylor Hall February 3. The Fidelity State & Savings Bank, W. W. Finney, president, was opened for business March 3. Monthly tuberculosis clinics were established by the County Health Unit, from which much benefit has been derived. Abigail Morse Hall, a dormitory for women, named in honor of an early-day Emporia educator, was opened at Teachers College. At the celebration of the sixtieth anniversary of the founding of this school, 1925, members of the first class were guests at the annual commencement exercises. Three sisters, of these former students, were members of the pioneer Spencer family, and were among the guests. They were Mrs. Ella Brown, Los Angeles, Calif.; Mrs. Margaret Hollingsworth, Emporia, and Miss Martha P. Spencer, Washington, D. C. Other members of the class present were Mrs. George Plumb and Timothy McIntire, Emporia.

The Grace Methodist Church, South Avenue and Neosho Street, was destroyed by fire in May, 1924. A new church, of brick construction, was erected on the site of the old building, and dedicated in December, 1926. The new church embodies many modern features of social and community work, and is a real community center for the southwest section of the town. In it is housed Branch No. 1, of the City Library, and this is greatly appreciated by the residents of this neighborhood. The Rev. J. C. Brogan is pastor of this church.

Robert M. Hamer, who had served his community in the Legislature, as postmaster, as mayor, and as a commissioner to the State Supreme Court, died May 20. The death of Mrs. Mary A. White, an Emporia pioneer, occurred May 6, and that of Eli Fowler May 13.

Emporia citizens at a special election voted as in favor of busses for public transportation to supersede street cars. Four bus lines began operation November 1, extending their service into each ward considerably further than had been reached by the street cars.

The new Junior High School, completed in 1925 was, on petition of the Grade Teachers' Club, and indorsed by almost every Emporia citizen, named in honor of L. A. Lowther, superintendent of the city schools. At that date Mr. Lowther had served the schools twenty-seven years, still holds the job, and the town feels that this honor could have been no more fittingly bestowed. The State Teachers meeting in November brought a large gathering of educators to Emporia, the county schools were serving hot lunches to the pupils, and the cause of education, as always in this town and county, steadily moved forward.

From June 15 to July 30, 1925, the temperature ranged from 94 to 103, and sixty-one days in June, July and August, was above 90. A two-inch rain in August alleviated the heat somewhat, but there was no continued cool weather until late September. Health conditions in town and county were improving steadily, and the fight of the Health Unit was bringing results.

In 1926 the Santa Fe moved into its $100,000.00 new passenger station which, in addition to passenger service, houses one hundred officers and employees.

A new county home was erected in 1926, and opened May 6, to the gratification of the many organizations and individuals interested in securing better conditions for the county's dependents. To the County Association of Rural Clubs credit is given for having accomplished most toward this desired end. Town and county women provided for the furnishing of the Nurses' Home at the Newman Memorial County Hospital.

The G. W. Newman Dry Goods Company, in business in Emporia since 1868, late in 1926 was sold to the Rorabaugh-Paxton Dry Goods Company, which had been in business here thirty years. This firm took possession of the Newman building and stock early in 1927. The City Y. W. C. A. in January announced a membership of 600, with many working organizations meeting regularly in its building, and with its financial affairs in good condition.

The town observed its seventieth birthday, February 20, and the observance of Founders' Day has been continued as an annual event.

A "pioneer room" in the New Student union building at Teachers College was provided with old-time furniture, and dedicated to the pioneers of the school and community. Beach Music Hall at Teachers College was opened, and city building permits for March totalled $72,000.00.

The State Federation of Women's Clubs, at its annual meeting here in May, 1927, elected Mrs. J. H. Wiggam, of Emporia, its state president. The Business and Professional Women's Club also held its state meeting in Emporia this year. Sixty Kansas editors were entertained at a garden party in Emporia this summer, honoring W. M. Jardine, then secretary of agriculture, and the first Kansas man to become a member of the President's cabinet.

In 1928 a contract was let for $75,000.00 worth of all-weather road improvements, and the city started work in improving Soden's Grove, which had been purchased from Mrs. J. R. Soden for $12,000.00. The death of J. S. Kenyon, Emporia's oldest merchant, who left a bequest of $100,000.00 to the College of Emporia, enabled that institution to announce, for the first time in its forty-seven years, that it was free from debt. The new $375,000.00 administration building was named Kenyon Hall in honor of the man who had made possible its immediate completion, and opened the way for greater accomplishment.

The College this year graduated sixty-five students —its largest graduating class. The budget for the College was announced as $160,000.00 for the next year. The new president, Dr. John Bailey Kelly, of New York City, took up his work, his installation and the dedication of the new building having been held November 1, 1929.

Land valuations were announced in August, for improved lands, in Lyon County, $36,121,464; unimproved land, $24,355,738.00. An Emporia official flag was adopted, with the understanding that the national flag is to be displayed on all patriotic occasions. The new flag carries the colors of three big schools—yellow—Old Gold—for Teachers College; red for the College of Emporia, and black for the Senior High School.

The new St. Mary's Hospital, at the head of State Street, was opened in November, 1928, its furnishing and building cost having been $250,000.00. At the beginning of 1929, checking up the building activities of the previous year, it was found that building permits totalled $300,000.00, aside from the Santa Fe's building program. The Santa Fe this summer began work on a subway beneath its tracks at Mechanic Street, this being the third Santa Fe subway within the city limits, safeguarding human life, and property as well, by making unnecessary the frequent use of grade crossings in town. A storm sewer to cost $108,-000.00 is under way, and a new grade school building, for which bonds of $100,000.00 were voted in April, was built this year. This school is located on a two-block tract between Seventh and Ninth Avenues, between Sherman and Wilson Streets. The seven classrooms will serve six grades and a kindergarten department. In the building also will be located the second branch of the City Library, a clinic room, auditorium-gymnasium, office and wide, light corridors. This handsome building has been named the Mary Herbert school, in memory of a veteran grade teacher who died in 1928, many of whose pupils will attend this school. Miss Herbert had taught forty-five years in Emporia, and died in the fiftieth year of her life as a teacher. She was principal for many years of the Lincoln school. After her death it was found she had left a bequest of $1,000.00 to the Emporia schools, the interest of which each year is to be divided into three scholarship prizes of $25.00, $15.00 and $10.00 for the Junior High School.

January 6, 1929, began a storm of rain and sleet turning to ice, followed by snow which covered it, putting streets and highways in the worst condition ever known in this county. Going was unsafe for man, beast and motor car alike. All traffic-ways were ice-bound for weeks, and after thawing began, the bottom seemed to have dropped out of the dirt roads. At many mudholes, on high ground impassable to ordinary traffic, county trucks and caterpillars were stationed to pull cars through the deepest mud. March 14, the Gazette announced that all roads in Lyon County were open to travel and in fairly good condition. No stronger argument for all-weather roads could have been advanced than that put up by Nature the first two months of 1929.

As evidence of prohibitory law enforcement, it was announced that 221 liquor law violators of the town and county had been convicted and sentenced during 1928.

The Grand Army of the Republic, Department of Kansas, with one hundred forty Civil War veterans in attendance, in May assembled in Emporia for its annual convention. Coincident with this gathering were held the annual meetings of all the auxiliary bodies of the Grand Army, which brought to Emporia more than five hundred delegates and visitors.

Newspapers all over the State expressed their surprise—in fact, were stunned—when their editors read in the Gazette that a group of property owners had appeared before the Emporia City Commission, July 25, asking that the city tax levy be increased from 11 mills to 11.4 mills, as they were convinced that more money should be available for fire and police protection. Their request was refused.

Dr. Albert R. Taylor, president of the State Normal School in Emporia from 1882 until 1901, died at his home in Decatur, Illinois, August 11. His body was brought "home" to Emporia for interment in Maplewood. President Taylor, as his Kansas friends never ceased to call him, was one of the strongest men ever at the head of this school, and the value of his influence—spiritual, moral, educational—cannot be estimated. With all of his high qualities in so many directions it is the universal opinion of the students who learned to be useful men and women under his direction, and the citizens of the town and the State in general, that the greatest of all his really great qualities was love, and that he exemplified Paul's letter to the Corinthians in which he tells them that the greatest of all good gifts is love.

The Granada Theater, the largest and most pretentious building of its kind in Emporia, costing $350,000.00, was opened October 3.

The will of Mrs. Charles Ryder—Cora Borton Ryder, daughter of the late Mr. and Mrs. Edward Borton, Emporia pioneers—designated a fund approximating $200,000.00 to be known as the Borton-Ryder memorial hospital fund, the interest and accumulations of which are to be used, according to the wording of the will, "for rendering medical care and assistance to the children of Emporia, Kansas, who are unable to provide for such medical attendance for themselves, ... to alleviate the sufferings of the children of poverty." Mrs. Ryder died at her home in Emporia, in October, 1929. She left several substantial bequests, and many smaller ones, mostly to friends in Emporia, where she had lived all of her life. Mrs. Ryder was the last of her family.

Late in 1929 plans were formulated and work started for a cheese factory in Emporia.

LYON COUNTY TOWNS

AMERICUS

Americus, established in the autumn of 1857, has had for its proudest boast during the years that never has a saloon been located on the town site. The town's paramount interests have been its churches and its schools, and the quality of its citizenry attests to their influence. The Americus Town Company consisted of T. C. Hill, G. H. Rees, E. Yeakley, John Moser, E. Columbia, William Grimsley, E. M. Sewell, B. Wright, N. B. Switser, A. I. Baker, J. W. Voak, J. Voak, W. Thompson, David Swim, F. Barrett and Elisha Goddard. Officers of the Town Company were A. I. Baker, president; T. C. Hill, treasurer, and David Swim, secretary.

A post office was established in 1858, and E. Yeakley was the first postmaster. School District No. 2 was organized in 1858, and G. W. Torrance was its second teacher. A log schoolhouse was replaced the next year by a frame building, and a handsome brick building now houses the Americus schools. The first jail in the county—then Breckinridge—was at Americus, when that town was the county seat. Its walls later were weatherboarded and the building still stands as a landmark in Americus. A sawmill was established in 1859 by J. Kuhns. Americus for many years was noted for the manufacture of cheese, and Thomas Anderson was the proprietor of the cheese factory.

The town is situated in the Neosho Valley eleven miles northeast of Emporia, and is surrounded by excellent farms. A term of the United States District Court was held in Americus in 1858, lasting but two days. The grand jury returned twenty-nine indictments, mostly for trespass on school lands. Americus has three churches—Methodist, United Presbyterian and Free Methodist.

¹The late J. S. Gibson, of Americus, writing in 1919 of early days in Americus, said in part: "My mother died October 28, 1858 . . . . This was the first death in Americus, and there was but one team of horses in the funeral procession, the rest of the conveyances being drawn by oxen."

HARTFORD

Hartford, twenty miles southeast of Emporia on the M. K. & T., was established in 1858. It is in a bend of the Neosho River, near the Coffey County line. It was located in the autumn of 1857, and named by a member of the Town Company, A. K. Hawkes, in honor of his home city, Hartford, Connecticut. Mr. Rice, whom Hawkes met in Topeka, and a man named Woodford, also a Connecticut man, were other members of the Town Company. The town site proper was laid out in 1858 by Judge Graham and D. F. Bond.

The first school in Hartford was taught by Mrs. Hawkes in her home, in 1860. That year a branch of Baker University was located in Hartford, and named the Hartford Collegiate Institute. Work was started in 1862 on a building for this school, and it was completed in 1863. Solomon Lewis taught the first school in the new building, which for many years was the home of the Hartford Public Schools and now houses the primary department. It is the oldest building in Hartford, and the oldest school building in Lyon

County. In 1866 Asa D. Chambers[1] leased the institute building for ten years, and in 1867 opened it as an academy. The substantial brick public school building was erected in 1915, when Hartford became a consolidated school, and this building also houses its accredited High School. There are three flourishing churches—Methodist[2], Christian and Catholic.

Hartford was incorporated as a city of the third class March 12, 1884, and Thomas Campbell was its first mayor. The Emporia Gazette, the summer of 1929, said editorially of Hartford:

"Hartford is going after a system of sewers and a waterworks plant. Already Hartford has the best rural schools in this part of Kansas, and the town has turned out more smart men and women than any town of its size in the county. Highway No. 57 is paved through the town, and lacks only a few miles of being the short line to Joplin—a first-class highway. The principal streets have been graveled since 1921."

A big celebration was held in Hartford on the completion of highway No. 57, in which Emporia and all

[1] A. D. Chambers twice was elected superintendent of the Lyon County Schools—1868 and 1870.

[2] The Rev. Cyrus R. Rice always was called, affectionately, "Elder" Rice. He was the first of the itinerant Methodist ministers in the Neosho Valley, having been sent to Kansas as a missionary in 1855. On horseback, he rode over hundreds of miles of lonely prairie, seeking opportunity to minister to those in need of his services. There were no laid-out roads and no bridges, and often he swam the swollen streams, and followed cowpaths when the road disappeared. He organized numerous churches and Sunday Schools, was presiding elder of the Emporia district, served many churches as pastor, and from 1896 to 1898 was pastor of the Hartford Methodist Church. By this time he was growing old, and in Hartford he bought a home, on the site of the log cabin which had housed the first Methodist organization in Hartford, and named it Rice's Rest. There he and Mrs. Rice were happy in a beautiful and useful old age. Their sons, Edwin and Merton Rice, are ministers of prominence in the Methodist Church.

Southern Lyon County participated. The grist mill on the Neosho north of town, founded and operated by I. A. Taylor, met the fate of many of the mills of the early days—it was burned and was not rebuilt. Mr. Taylor also founded the first bank in Hartford.

PLYMOUTH

The first settler on the Plymouth town site was Charles Humphrey, who took a claim there in 1857. The town, nine miles west of Emporia, was laid out in 1858 and platted in 1859. Daniel Holsinger was president of the Town Company and H. W. Fick, secretary. Other members were David McMillan and Ross Thomas. David McMillan was the first postmaster, appointed in 1858. The original village, on the hill north of the Santa Fe station was not moved when, in 1871, the railroad "took the low road."

Many of the residences built in the early sixties still are occupied. John Carter, a North Carolina Friend and a former president of Guilford College in that state, built the first house in Plymouth, and later added to it on the west a large store building. Here he put in a $5,000.00 stock of general merchandise, and for eight years did a flourishing business. Also he was postmaster. The entire structure of eight large rooms since has been used as a dwelling, and for many years

---

Elder Rice, in traveling over the country often found himself at night many miles from a human habitation, and he lay down under the stars on the blanket he always carried, his saddle for a pillow, his faithful horse his only companion. He was a fluent Greek and Latin and Hebrew scholar, and acquired these languages, largely, by the light of his lonely camp fires on the prairie, while traveling from one preaching point to another. In his later years he found holding a pen difficult, and after his retirement from the ministry, at an age when most men have ceased to labor he took up typewriting, and found it greatly to his advantage. He died in 1919.

has been the home of Mr. and Mrs. Hugh Jackson. Much of the lumber in this building is native walnut.

In the basement of this building, warmed by a huge fireplace and lighted by candles, the first literary society of Plymouth met. The late Malcolm Campbell was its president. Upstairs in the parlor the Friends held religious services. Stage hands used to stop for meals here, and to quench their thirst from the deep well in the well-house, adjoining the residence. The late L. M. Harris, of Emporia, in this old house organized the first Sunday School in Plymouth. The big barn on this place—an entire block—was the first schoolhouse in Plymouth, built in 1864.

The first school was taught in the house afterward the home of Mrs. Barbara Campbell and her sons and daughters, across the street from the Carter house. Miss Mary Hammer was the first teacher, and Mrs. Ella Spencer—now Mrs. Brown—was the second. This house was built by Elisha Parker, of lumber hauled from Leavenworth, and was the second house in the town. Miss Jean Campbell, the last of the Campbell family, lived in the old house until her death a few years ago. Mrs. Hugh Jackson is a granddaughter of Mrs. Barbara Campbell. Malcolm Campbell was captain of the Plymouth Militia during the Civil War, and the Jacksons cherish the beautiful flag made by Mrs. Barbara Campbell and members of her family, of fine soft merino for which she sent to Leavenworth. Also, she paid $200.00 for guns for use of the militia and, like the militia, who got no pay for its services, she got no refund from a grateful government for helping out in its need. Malcolm Campbell afterward lived several years in Chase County, and represented his district in the Kansas Legislature.

"The business district," as the villagers term the Santa Fe station, the O. G. Walker general store, the elevator and garage and filling station, on the railroad and on highway No. 50s, is half a mile from the old town, in which there are probably twenty houses. They love their old houses and their old furniture, and enjoy relating stories of historic interest concerning the town and its founders. In Plymouth village are a well-built schoolhouse and a Woodman Hall, and church services are held in the schoolhouse.

NEOSHO RAPIDS

Neosho Rapids, on the Ottawa Cut-off Branch of the Santa Fe, ten miles east and two south of Emporia, has enjoyed a greater variety of names than any other Lyon County town. The original site, half a mile south of the present town, was laid out in the autumn of 1856, according to the recollections of the late Mrs. John Rosenquist, who came with her parents, the David VanGundys, to that neighborhood in 1855. Its founders, Jefferson Pigman and a man named Cobine, named their town Florence. It flourished but a few months, and in 1857 another town company laid out another town site, of 350 acres, changing its name to Neosho City. The promoters this time were Pigman, Josiah Gregg and Christian Carver. At some time before the town settled down to the name of Neosho Rapids, it was called Italia. Miss Ella Rosenquist has an envelope addressed to Italia, Madison County, Kanzas Territory, but the date cannot be deciphered.

In 1860 Forrest Page, who had come to Kansas in 1856, H. S. Sleeper and G. J. Tallman, laid out the town on its present site, and since that date it has been Neosho Rapids. Forrest Page was register of deeds of Lyon County in the seventies, and was a brother of the late Dr. J. H. Page, of Emporia, who at that time lived on a farm adjoining Neosho Rapids on the north. School District No. 20 bought eight lots from Doctor Page on which to build the town's first schoolhouse, a stone structure, which for many years has been the Rockford Hotel. It is north of the railroad tracks, while the town is on the south side. The railroad was built in 1887, and before long the danger to school children crossing the railroad tracks brought about the building of the commodious brick school in the town. The old building was sold to the late Capt. C. R. Stone, who turned it into a hotel, and it since has had many owners. Jefferson S. Pigman was the town's first postmaster.

The principal industry of Neosho Rapids for several years was the grist mill owned by the late Alfred Roberts, on the Neosho immediately above the bridge, which did a big business. The mill burned, and was not reestablished. The Free Methodists for years maintained a college in Neosho Rapids, but it also burned and was not rebuilt. This denomination, once the strongest in the town, has dwindled. The churches are the Free Methodist, the Methodist Episcopal and the Catholic.

READING

The land on which Reading, twenty miles northeast of Emporia, is situated, is a part of what was the Sac and Fox Indian Reservation, much of which was in Osage County. Records show that, on June 15, 1867, the United States Government deeded to John McManus, a government Indian agent, a tract or tracts of land of 132,310.95 acres, in consideration of his securing certain promises and a treaty from the Indians.

Portions of this land were sold to Seyfert, McManus & Company, of Brooklyn, New York, a corporation. This land later was sold to the Reading (Pennsylvania) Iron Works, also a corporation, which was the owner in 1870, when the Santa Fe, pushing through Kansas, wished to establish a station at a convenient distance between Osage City and Emporia.

The Reading Town Company—the new town was named for the Pennsylvania city of that name—consisted of John McManus, president, representing the Iron Works, and Edwin Wilder, of Topeka, treasurer of the Santa Fe Railway Company, secretary. The Reading Iron Works sold to the Santa Fe a half section of land on which to establish its station, and all of section 3 to the Reading Town Company. McManus, who was a civil engineer, a graduate of an Irish university and an extremely able man, was the active member of the Town Company. He and James Fagan platted the town site tract. McManus also was agent for the Reading Iron Works. Incorporation papers for the town of Reading were filed for record March 19, 1872.

Records also show that name of Seyfert, McManus & Company, a corporation was, January 14, 1878, by legal process in Berks County, Pennsylvania, changed to the Reading Iron Works, also a corporation, and no doubt an amalgamation. All this probably leads to the belief by some persons that Reading was founded by the Reading Iron Works.

Reading was incorporated as a city of the third class September 1, 1890. The first mayor was Eli Patterson, and the present mayor is Samuel Evans. The population is 375. The town has a first-class school system, substantial business and residence buildings, fine old trees, three churches—Baptist, Catholic and Methodist—and is considering a water-

MR. AND MRS. WILLIAM HAMMOND, 1857-1863

works plant. Michael Fagan, a brother of James Fagan, came to the Reading locality in 1868, took a claim adjoining the town on the north, and was there to help survey the town site when the time came. His son, James Fagan, has a shoe repair shop in Reading.

OLPE

Olpe, eleven miles south of Emporia on the Howard Branch, was established in 1879 when the Santa Fe built this line. Bitlertown, a few rods southwest of the Olpe town site, south of the tracks, founded by Daniel Bitler in 1877, made a fight to retain its name. The new founder, a man named Flusche, wishing to please his German neighbors, named the new town for his home city, Olpe, in Germany, and the Santa Fe decided in his favor. Eagle Creek, established probably in the sixties, was a star route post office kept by Mr. and Mrs. F. G. Soule, a mile west of the present town. A stage barn was located on the Soule farm, and horses were changed there on the trip to Eureka. Olpe is a neat and thrifty place, one of the best-kept towns in Lyon County, and has a larger proportion of home-owners than any other Lyon County town. Its most imposing building is the large and handsome Catholic Church—St. Joseph's—and the Catholic parochial school is housed in a substantial building. There is a good public school building and a Methodist and a Lutheran Church.

ALLEN

Allen, sixteen miles north of Emporia, is proud of the fact that it is the direct descendant of Lyon County's first post office, also called Allen, whose first postmaster was Charles Withington, the county's first settler. This post office was at the crossing of 142

Creek on the Santa Fe Trail three and one-half miles northeast of the present town, and was established in 1854.

When the Missouri Pacific Railway Company built its road across Northern Lyon County in 1886, it planned for but two stations in this county—Admire and Bushong. But the people of the Allen neighborhood, many of whom were stockmen whose shipments were large, protested, and demanded a station at this point. They took their troubles to the State Railroad Commission, and got their station. Much of the work of securing this station was done by the late Judge G. W. DeCamp, of Emporia and Allen, who had large holdings in that locality. The post office was moved from its original site, and E. R. Marcy, still of Allen, who had been postmaster and who opened the first store in the new town, looked after the mail until the appointment of John Grimsley, the first postmaster.

The Town Company consisted of John Grimsley, president; George Withington, clerk; R. A. Reaburn, D. W. Leavell, W. E. Rust, E. R. Marcy and Emil Shellack. The first purchase of land for the town was a quarter section, and later another quarter section to the west was added. Most of the lots platted have been sold and are occupied. A strip of land running east and west, south of the tracks, one hundred feet wide and five blocks long, was given the Missouri Pacific as a site for its station buildings, siding and stockyards. Allen is the most important shipping point in Northern Lyon County, and the station was a real need of this grazing and stockraising section. When the Town Company disbanded, about 1895, E. R. Marcy being its last president, the cemetery, which had been owned by the Town Company, was turned over to the city.

Allen was incorporated as a city of the third class in 1909. James S. Barr was its first mayor, and A. H. Smith, of the Smith Lumber Company, Emporia, was the first city clerk. The first newspaper was the Allen Tidings, established by Major Paul, which he moved to Emporia, where it became the Times. The Northern Lyon County Journal, D. S. Gilmore, editor and proprietor, is the largest and most important weekly newspaper in Lyon County outside of Emporia. It serves the entire north end of the county—Allen, Admire, Bushong and Miller. Allen has a population of about 280, good schools and a flourishing Methodist Church, a live and progressive citizenry. Harry Grimsley is mayor of the town, and Bern Davis city clerk.

ADMIRE

Admire, twenty miles northeast of Emporia, on the all-weather highway No. 11, completed in 1929, was established as a station by the Missouri Pacific Railway in 1886. A post office, Waterloo, seven and one-half miles southeast of the present town, had provided mail facilities for the neighborhood since an early day. Major Hicks, a veteran of the Mexican War, was the first postmaster of Waterloo. Later, this post office was discontinued, and the Ivy post office was established, two and one-half miles southeast of Admire. Ivy was discontinued when the post office at Admire was established.

When the proposition for a bond issue for the building of the Missouri Pacific Railway was agitated in Waterloo Township, the west half of the township opposed the bonds, and pulled wires successfully to secure a division of the township. The new township was named Ivy, giving Lyon County eleven townships where had been but ten. Three Osage City men, Jacob Admire, W. E. McElfresh and J. D. Hall, worked in the interests of the railway company to secure the bond issue, and afterward these men were incorporated as a Town Company, were given the privilege of buying land for a station and town site, and naming the town. The site selected, oddly enough, is in Ivy Township, which had opposed the railroad. The town was named in honor of one of the members of the Town Company.

The quarter section on which Admire stands was purchased from B. H. G. Wilbur, and later an 80-acre tract to the west was added, 240 acres in all. This eighty never has been platted, and only a few scattering lots have been sold. In 1894, Fremont Miller and Herbert Miller bought all of the remaining stock from the Railroad Company. Admire was incorporated as a city of the third class July 6, 1896. Its first mayor was George W. McDaniel, then, as now, in the mercantile business in the town. The present mayor is Herbert Miller. Mr. Miller also is president of the Admire State Bank, which office he has held since November 1, 1894. Fremont Miller, his brother, long a resident of Emporia, now lives in California. Mrs. Will Wayman, of Emporia, is a sister of the Millers.

Admire has an excellent new rural high and grade school building, which was erected at a cost of $65,-000.00 following the destruction by fire of the first school building, a frame, 1925. The Rev. J. R. Eubanks is pastor of the one church in the town, and there is an interested Sunday School. The population is about 270. The business and residence buildings are neat and substantial, and the town presents a pleasing appearance.

BUSHONG

Bushong, first called Weeks, was established in 1886, at the time the Missouri Pacific Railway Company built its tracks across Northern Lyon County. Joseph Weeks owned the farm on a part of which the Missouri Pacific wished to build its station, and he donated to the railway company about twenty acres of land. The company built on part of this land, sold part of it as town lots, and still owns some of it, unoccupied. Mr. Weeks platted another twenty acres and sold it as town lots. There was no town company. The name later was changed to Bushong. The town is twenty-two miles northwest of Emporia.

Joseph Fulls was the first postmaster, and the first station agent was R. D. Cottrell, and Mr. and Mrs. Cottrell also built and operated the first hotel. Bushong was incorporated in 1927, and L. A. Grimsley was the first mayor. R. D. Cottrell died in 1896, and Mrs. Cottrell now is Mrs. C. E. Lewis, wife of the postmaster, who was appointed under Taft, and who has held the postmaster job for more than nineteen years. The town, with a population of 150, maintains a two-room grade school, and a four-room rural high school is located in Bushong. The rural high school district has a valuation of $1,600,000.00. The town is proud of the many graduates from this school, who have made names and places for themselves in the world. The percentage of young people who have left the town and attained success, says Mr. Lewis, is unusually large. The Methodist Church and Sunday School are well attended.

MILLER

Miller is the baby town of Lyon County, having been founded in 1910. A store was running in 1907 in what now is a cornfield bordering the town on the west. A Miller post office was established in the early days, and moved to its present location in 1886, when the Missouri Pacific railway was built across Northern Lyon County. The town was named for the Millers of the Miller ranch, of which Clyde Miller, of Topeka, is owner. A Rural High School was established in 1919, and a commodious, modern four-room building erected. The Methodist Church was built that year. The town is lighted by electricity, its residences and business buildings are well kept, neat lawns and brilliant flowerbeds and substantial cement sidewalks add to the attractiveness of the town.

A FEW OF THE FIRST THINGS

FIRST RELIGIOUS SERVICES

Regarding the first preaching services held in Emporia, the recollections of William Hammond and Mrs. Margaret Gilmore are clear and distinct, and their impressions of the events of that day are the same. Mr. Hammond's father, John Hammond, had come alone to Emporia from Ohio in February, 1857, built the hotel and two other houses, and was prevailed upon by the town company to take charge of the hotel as soon as it was ready for occupancy, though still unfinished. Mrs. J. H. Clapp had kept boarders in the first house in town, and she and Mr. Clapp were Mr. Hammond's assistants in running the hotel. There were no chairs in the hotel, and benches had been built for seats at the dining table. The Hammond family arrived in Emporia Wednesday afternoon, June 3, 1857, says William Hammond.

The following Sunday morning John Hammond said to his son, "Will, I wish you would move the benches from the diningroom to the barroom, (never was there a bar in this room) as we are going to have preaching here today, the first we have had, and there are no other seats."

"Well, I'd like to know who there is around here to preach," was the boy's response.

"A Campbellite preacher named Solomon G. Brown lives down southeast a mile or two on the Cottonwood, and he is coming here to preach," said the elder Hammond.

The boy placed the benches as his father had requested, then watched for the coming of the preacher. He arrived shortly in a wagon and his children were with him. Mrs. Margaret Gilmore—11-year-old Maggie Brown—was one of these children. William Hammond distinctly recalls, not that first sermon, but its setting, and the incidents in preparation for it.

Mrs. Gilmore relates how her father told them to get ready to go with him, as he was going to preach that day the first sermon to be delivered in Emporia. "We all got ready," says Mrs. Gilmore, "Father hitched the team to the wagon and we all piled in. As we drove into town, I noticed the green prairie grass on Commercial Street. And I distinctly remember that my father preached in the hotel and that his was the first sermon preached in Emporia."

The Rev. Henry Moyes, an itinerant Methodist minister, preached in the hotel a little later, probably the second sermon in the town. The Rev. J. P. McElfresh was another of the earliest of the pioneer preachers.

"Of the eighteen persons in the town when we arrived—counting my mother and her four children—I am the only one living," says Mr. Hammond. "The Browns did not live in the town, and the David Plumbs, who had come to Emporia in April, had moved on their claim. The Storrses came soon after us, and their daughter, Mrs. G. W. Newman, is another of the youngsters who grew up with the town."

FIRST FOURTH OF JULY CELEBRATION

Emporia's first Fourth of July celebration was in 1858. Two large bowers were built, one near the Watson home, Eighth and Mechanic, where a patriotic program was given, the other between Third and Fourth on Constitution Street, where a big free dinner was served to all comers. Martin F. Conway, Lawrence, was the orator of the day. The evening was wound up with a "grand ball" at Americus, which was attended by many Emporia young people. The bowers were built of long forked poles driven into the ground, across which lighter weight poles were laid, and these, covered with the leafy branches of trees—all brought from the banks of the Cottonwood—provided shade for the large crowd.

THE FIRST WEDDING

The marriage of Joseph V. Randolph and Miss Anna Watson, daughter of Judge and Mrs. J. H. Watson, December 22, 1859, was the first on the town site. The ceremony was performed by the Rev. G. C. Morse. Last year the six sons and daughters of this couple, all past 50, and some of them with grandchildren, assembled in Emporia and while here photographs were made of the group. Three of the six, George H. Randolph, Mrs. Frank Keeler and Miss Lucile Randolph, live in Emporia. J. V. Randolph was an expert orchardist, and planted hundreds of the elms and other trees which beautify Emporia streets, as well as orchards and shrubbery. He and Mrs. Randolph settled at Riverside, adjoining the town on the southwest, a few years after their marriage, and this ever after was their home. It long has been one of the lovely places of the town. The Randolphs and the Watsons were equal suffragists, and shared the obloquy accorded the various national speakers, and others, who came here in the interest of universal suffrage, during the suffrage campaign of 1868-1869. Mr.

Randolph was a member of the State Board of Pardons in the nineties.

HOW TWO MEN HELPED

The History of the State Normal School of Kansas, 1889, on the occasion of the twenty-fifth anniversary of its founding, relates this story of one man's interest in the school at a time when its work was being retarded by lack of room:

"Mr. John Fawcett, a liberal-minded citizen whose children were attending school, was so much interested in the success of the institution that he erected a one-story frame building, fourteen by twenty feet, a short distance south of the main building, and gave the school the free use of it. The buildings were connected by a plank walk, and this building was used the fall of 1865 and all of 1866 for all recitations outside of the assembly room, except an occasional recitation by that first graduating class, which sometimes was crowded into one of the cloakrooms at the east end of the building."

John Fawcett settled first on East Logan Avenue, on the farm occupied by E. A. Bryan. He moved soon to the Rinker neighborhood, having bought the Timothy McIntire claim, and the family lived many years on that place—now the Hoch dairy farm. The beautiful avenue of maples leading from the highway to the house and farm buildings was planted by Max Fawcett, a son of Mr. and Mrs. John Fawcett, says William Hammond. Max Fawcett, wounded in the Battle of Prairie Grove, was home on furlough, and while resting and recuperating, with little he could do to occupy his mind and hands, planted the maple trees forming this avenue. He brought the saplings and seed from the timber along the Neosho, and carefully planted them, where their grateful shade and handsome proportions long have been a source of pleasure to the owners of the farm and the passersby.

JOHN BROWN IN EMPORIA

"One day in 1859," the late Mrs. Elizabeth Storrs related, not long before her death, "we entertained John Brown and his men at dinner. We had left the Emporia House that year, and moved to a house on the present site of the Samuel furniture store. We returned to the Emporia House in 1860, and ran it until 1868. This day of which I speak, Mr. Storrs brought the strange men in the house, told me to ask no questions, and to prepare dinner for his guests. They went into the parlor, pulled down the shades, and were closeted there for a couple of hours, maintaining the greatest secrecy. Mr. C. V. Eskridge and Judge L. D. Bailey also were in the party, and I got a good dinner for all of them. Mr. Storrs told me, after the men had left, that we had entertained John Brown and his men, and that they had come here hoping to raise money to help carry on Brown's expedition into Virginia. I don't know how much assistance they received, but I imagine it was not much, as there was so little money in Emporia in those days. The next we heard of John Brown was of his seizure of Harper's Ferry, and this was followed by news of his execution."

Mrs. G. W. Newman dimly remembers John Brown, as a tall man with bushy whiskers, wearing a Zouave uniform, who took her on his knee and talked to her. She was a little girl, and was in and out of the room during the conference.

FIRST NIGHT IN EMPORIA

The late Mrs. Elizabeth Storrs, telling of the arrival of her family and herself in Emporia, said: "We arrived in Emporia, a town of three houses, on a cold, rainy evening. There was 'no room in the inn' for us, and Mr. Storrs found we could sleep in the little 14x16 up-and-down board shanty,[1] located where the Emporia State Bank now stands. We had come on the stage, which made better time than the wagons hauling our bedding and furniture, so we had no bedding, and few wraps, as it was midsummer and we had not expected cool weather. After we had lain down and tried to make ourselves comfortable on the hard ground—there was no floor—a man came to the door and asked: 'Is that you, Storrs?' When my husband replied in the affirmative, the man—who was Preston B. Plumb, who had lived at our house in Lawrence—asked if we had any bedding. Mr. Storrs replied that we had only a double shawl for the baby and me. 'Here, take my coat,' said Mr. Plumb, 'it will help some.' And Plumb slept that night on the ground without even his coat.

"The next day was bright and sunshiny, but I was lonely and, taking my little girl by the hand we walked what seemed to us far out on the prairie—probably as far as Exchange Street. There we lay down in the

---

[1] Mrs. J. H. Clapp, the first woman resident of Emporia, earlier had kept boarders in this first building on the town site. Mr. Clapp was the first shoemaker. James R. Cox opened the first blacksmith shop, at the corner of Sixth and Mechanic. Horace Bundrem opened the first saddle and harness shop, and Abner Hadley the first queensware store. E. P. Bancroft's large and handsome home at the corner of Fifth and Commercial was the first strictly residence building in Emporia. The Bancroft house later was moved to Merchant Street, between Fifth and Sixth. This lot was sold to the Federal Government when it bought the post office site, and again the building was moved. Joseph Rickabaugh opened the first wagon shop, on Commercial Street, in 1858.

tall, sweet grass, and both of us went to sleep. We were awakened by a sound which startled us—but it was only the mooing of a gentle cow to her baby calf. After our nap we felt better, and never again was I so homesick as that first day. For one thing, I was too busy to be lonely. Our furniture came, and almost at once we took charge of the Emporia House, and there was work enough to keep several women busy. But it was interesting—so many different people, from so many different states, and each one with an interesting story to tell of the adventure of coming to Kansas, and of the hopes and ambitions that brought him here. Those years in the hotel were happy years, and always I have been glad that we could do our part in the work of building Emporia."

The little daughter of Mr. and Mrs. Storrs—Mrs. G. W. Newman—was happy in her new home, and did not realize she was living in the midst of great privations, or that she was a part of the history the town was making day by day. "We played happily in the tall grass," says Mrs. Newman. "There was so much to interest children. My father owned lots running west from the hotel to Merchant Street, at the back were pigs and chickens and a cow, and a horse and buggy. The cow grazed on the prairie during the day, unhindered by fences. We slid down the haystacks in the barnlot, and most of the town site was our playground."

Mrs. Newman attended the first school in Emporia, taught by Miss Watson, and also was a pupil at an early age at the Normal School. She wasn't there the first day, as the Normal School was not supposed to take children, but her father made arrangements with the principal, Mr. Kellogg, for little Nellie Storrs and little Susie Huffaker to attend. They were known as "the Normal's little girls." Susie was Mrs. Newman's dearest playmate. She was the daughter of Mr. and Mrs. T. S. Huffaker, who had charge of the old Kaw Indian Mission at Council Grove. She boarded with Mrs. Van Holmes while attending school in Emporia.

Mrs. Newman was graduated from the Normal School, and always has maintained a lively interest in its growth and progress. She has been one of the most active members of the Alumni Association, and has served it in many capacities.

Mrs. Newman recalls the day the first company of soldiers left for the Civil War. A recruiting station had been established at the Emporia House, and the day the men marched away she sat in her mother's room on the second floor and watched them, and heard the women crying. She watched the lines of soldiers, fascinated, with the flag rising and falling as the ground toward the northeast part of town dipped and rose, in places, until finally, as it went over the rise about Eighth and Union, she saw the stars and stripes grow less and less until the flag had entirely disappeared. Men who were not eligible for enlistment waited a mile or two outside the town and picked up the marching soldiers and took them in wagons to Leavenworth. Just one man, an old man, was left in the town, and the women, fearing always attacks by the Indians on the west, the Cheyennes and the Arapahoes, were greatly alarmed at being left without protection. The Kaws always were friendly.

BLEEDING KANSAS

The men and women who came to Kansas on the opening of the territory for settlement, as well as those who came in later years, largely were actuated by the common impulse of securing homes. It was a marvelous story they had heard—of farmers being able to plow furrows without striking stick or stone, as is done in many sections of the state. The virgin soil[1] had been found by the advance guard to yield abundantly, there was land at low cost for everyone, and prospects were most alluring. Then, too, the urge for the abolition of slavery, for making Kansas a free state, for the prevention of the spread of National Disgrace to States not already under its dominion, brought many of the settlers, who carried with them their Beecher Bibles,[2] determined to die, if necessary, in the cause of Freedom. Among these devoted anti-slavery men were those of the Andover Band,[3] a little group of young men just out of college in Massachusetts, who pledged themselves to the cause of the Negro, and came to Kansas to help to make him free. Also, there came from the South men and women, equally earnest and determined, with their inherent belief in State's Rights, that Kansas should come into the Union a slave State.

After a warfare—bitter as that between the North and the South a few years later—when many lives

[1] On these fertile prairies eighteen to twenty successive crops of corn were grown without fertilization, and crop rotation never had been heard of west of the Missouri river.

[2] Henry Ward Beecher, appealing in his Plymouth Church, Brooklyn, for aid for Kansas, used the money raised to buy rifles for use of members of the New England Emigrant Aid Society, who were going to the new Territory. These rifles were called Beecher Bibles.

[3] Grosvenor C. Morse, of the Andover Band, with its other members, Richard Cordley, S. D. Storrs and R. D. Parker, all ministerial students at Andover Theological Seminary, Andover, Mass., had banded together to come to Kansas to help to exterminate slavery and build a state, and to preach the Gospel. Mr. Morse was a graduate of Dartmouth College as well as of Andover Seminary. In 1858 he organized the First Congregational Church in Emporia. Richard Cordley said of him: "There was no church to call Mr. Morse, so he called the church." His work for education was as important as his ministerial labors. He

were sacrificed on the altar of Freedom and to the belief in State's Rights, when prairie homes in the process of making by sweat and toil were laid waste, when towns were plundered and burned and many of their citizens murdered, when bloody battle after bloody battle gave to to the Territory the name "Bleeding Kansas," she came triumphantly into the Union, January 29, 1861—a free state. And the term Bleeding Kansas has stuck. Her early settlers and their descendants never have forgotten it, nor have wished to forget it. But other States made of it a term of opprobrium, which long since should have ceased to be attached to this State.

Does a high wind strike a Kansas town or neighborhood? Immediately the news is wired to the Associated Press as a "destructive cyclone." Does a season of dry weather in August put everyone on the anxious seat concerning the corn crop? News is flashed over the country that the corn in Kansas is lying flat from heat and drouth, and is "teetotally ruined." The attention of the writer hereof, sojourn-

---

was the first county superintendent of public instruction, and he it was who interested the people, more than any other one person, in organizing school districts and voting bonds for the erection of schoolhouses. He was appointed a director of the State Normal School on its organization, in 1864, was chosen a member of the executive committee and secretary of the board, and held these positions until his death. He secured the services of L. B. Kellogg as principal of the Normal School, he rode on horseback over the State securing students, looked after them when they reached Emporia, and his interest extended through all their student days. He helped to influence legislation in the interests of the Normal, and gave himself unselfishly to his unpaid labors for the advancement of education. He died in 1870. Mrs. Morse was almost equally active in educational and religious work, and lived to see many of their dreams come true, to visit Abigail Morse Dormitory for Women at Teachers College, named in her honor, and died full of years and honors, in 1925. Richard Cordley for several years was pastor of the First Congregational Church in Emporia.

LITTLE NELLIE STORRS
(Mrs. G. W. Newman)

ing in Indiana during August a few years ago, was called to a dispatch in an Indianapolis newspaper, under a Topeka date line, which declared that hot winds had laid low the entire Kansas corn crop. The story was untrue, except possibly for a few square miles, and the corn yield that year was one of the heaviest in the history of the State. Chinchbugs have "destroyed the wheat," which later yielded twenty to forty bushels an acre, so many times that such stories have come to be looked upon as a joke.

A few years ago, when the Cottonwood and Neosho Rivers were rising rapidly during heavy and long-continued rainfall, a message was sent to the Associated Press by a careless correspondent saying both rivers were out of their banks and that water was running across Commercial Street at Eighth Avenue, in Emporia, presumably the overflow from the rivers. Anyone knowing Emporia's location, far above any danger from the rivers, would realize this was a highly improbable story. It was literally true, however, that water was running over Commercial Street at Eighth Avenue, but the water did not come from the overflowing rivers. It drained naturally to that place, across which a ravine had run before the street was filled in. The sewer drain was not of sufficient capacity to carry away the unusual volume of water as rapidly as it reached that corner, and so "water was running across Commercial Street at Eighth Avenue." Numerous other stories, as misleading as this, are believed to be true when sent out by authority so eminent as reputable press associations. Press correspondents are responsible for much of the misinformation regarding Kansas which appears in the newspapers of other states. Much of it, of course, is carried by word of mouth by persons of bad judgment.

Kansas citizens, strong and brave and resourceful and, generally speaking, optimistic—else they could not have "hung on" during the really troublous years —inordinately proud of their State, seem possessed by a desire to excel in everything. During seasons of storm and dry weather and crop pests—common to all States—Kansans are inclined to think the worst of Nature, and frequently talk and write too freely of their State's caprices. Kansans, the greater part of the year when "every prospect pleases," forget their seeming troubles, and yell louder and longer for their State than do the inhabitants of any other commonwealth. But the residents of other States do not forget, and many of them look on Kansas as a place of freak weather demonstrations, of uncertain crops, of a peculiar citizenry. Crops are no more uncertain than in any other agricultural State, cyclones are no more frequent or destructive, the snow and the mud are no deeper and the rains no heavier, and the rivers rise no higher. The people rank high in citizenship, in patriotism and loyalty to their State and Nation, in culture and righteousness. Industry and ambition are certain of reward, and Kansas citizens measure up with those of any place in the world.

EARLY-DAY TABLE DELICACIES

The first few years in Lyon County there was a scarcity of what had been, in the old homes, necessary staple foodstuffs. Nature supplied many of these deficiencies. Flour, until crops of wheat were raised, was scarce and so high in price that most of the settlers, as soon as a corn crop was raised and a part of it could be ground into meal, and for the next two or three decades, ate chiefly cornbread. Sugar was high, was used only on special occasions, and after the first crop of cane had been turned into sorghum, still less sugar was used. There was little good beef and fresh pork at first, but the woods along the Neosho and Cottonwood were full of wild turkeys, great flocks of prairie chickens[1] and quail inhabited the prairies, there were wild ducks and geese in their season, rabbits and squirrels in abundance. Venison and buffalo meat were not so easily available, but frequently appeared on the settlers' tables.

Wild plums, grapes, gooseberries,[2] strawberries, elderberries and mulberries all were to be had for the picking, in the woods along the streams, and when sweetened with sugar, were highly palatable, but old settlers say they wearied of the everlasting sorghum sweetening. Elderberries and mulberries, sweet and insipid, were mixed with sour fruit. Mincemeat for pies was made with rabbit and squirrel meat instead of beef, green tomatoes took the place of apples, and some of those who ate these mince pies say they were good. Pie "timber" was scarce, and vinegar pies are mentioned longingly by old settlers, as well as the

[1]Occasionally so many prairie chickens would be brought home that they could not all be eaten. It wasn't easy to divide them with the neighbors, as usually the neighbors had all the prairie chickens they wanted. This was long before the day of home-canned meats. But the resourceful housewives "salted down" the breasts and thighs of surplus prairie chickens, and used them later in the season, when the fowls were not so plentiful.

[2]An early-day housekeeper's recipe for wild gooseberry pie included—if she had sugar for her pie—"Put over the berries all the sugar your conscience will allow, then shut your eyes and put in a handful."

An early-day substitute for coffee was made by slicing sweet potatoes very thin, and roasting them, with corn and wheat, until all were a rich coffee color. Sometimes sorghum was boiled until it became a hard, brittle candy, and pieces of this were put in the pot and boiled with the other ingredients. It really looked and tasted like coffee, say those who drank it.

mock-apple pies made by flaking ordinary soda crackers, sweetening them and moistening them with water well flavored with lemon extract or tartaric acid. This substitute was so convincing that many persons, eating of the pies, wondered where the green apples with which to make them had come from, in this new country. Dried apples were sent from States further east, and were highly prized. Another makeshift was the sheep sorrel pie which, according to most housekeepers, "required more sugar than it was worth," but the "men folks" and the children liked it, and it usually was the children's job to pick the great quantity of sorrel necessary to make a couple of pies. Green and ripe tomatoes made acceptable pie filling, as well as helping to fill the preserve jars. Big jars of plum, grape and pumpkin butter were made up each summer, with sorghum, and constituted the "spread" for the children's bread in the school dinner pail. Sorghum cookies frequently went to school along with the wild fruit butter and corn bread and ground cherry preserves. Watermelons and muskmelons—not the cantaloupe of today—grew to huge size on the newly turned sod, and their meat was made into marmalade, and their rinds into pickles and preserves. Citrons, which apparently have gone out of fashion, made delicious preserves. The sod yielded bountiful crops of pumpkins and squashes, and they almost never failed. Two men often were required to load a pumpkin into a wagon—they weighed from 100, 200 to 350 pounds. "Egg butter," a spread which most children enjoyed, was made of a mixture of water and sorghum, thickened with flour and an egg or two beaten in. "Vinegar butter" was made about the same way, using sorghum and vinegar in about equal parts, and without the egg. Black walnuts were plentiful along the creeks and rivers, and every family tried to get a supply in the fall.

"We were like Peter Cartwright's backwoodsman, who took this famous itinerant Methodist preacher home to dinner one day. 'Now set right up and eat, we've got a-plenty, sich as it is, and good enough, what there is of it,'—and that was our situation exactly," says an early-day Emporia Methodist.

RELIGIOUS BODIES

PROTESTANT CHURCHES

The first church in Emporia, the Christian, was organized in 1857 by the Rev. Solomon G. Brown,[1] with six members, in his cabin on the bank of the Cottonwood, a quarter mile south of the frame house he built in 1858, which still stands, a stanch and sturdy farm home. A meeting to discuss building was held February 19, 1859, and the members decided to build, "way out in the country"—Seventh and Exchange. The building was completed that year, and was dedi-

---

[1] The Rev. Solomon G. Brown came with his family to Emporia the spring of 1856. They had moved to Fort Scott from Morgan County, Indiana, in 1855. Mr. Brown built a cabin in the timber on the Cottonwood, south of Logan Avenue, on a claim, and divided his preaching with farming. When the Town Company —Brown, Deitzler, Allen, Hornsby and Plumb—finally decided on the location for their new town, the nearest house to the town site, and the only one within their vision, was the Solomon Brown cabin. To this cabin they went, and Mrs. Brown and her daughters cooked dinner for them. They returned to supper and stayed all night, sleeping on the puncheon floor.

Mrs. Brown died late in February, 1857, leaving a tiny three-and-one-half pound baby girl to the care of her 13 and 11-year-old daughters, the late Mrs. Sarah Staley, and Mrs. Margaret Gilmore, 423 Union. They cared for the baby several months, and Mrs. Gilmore tells how they fed her. "We filled her bottle with plain cow's milk, warmed, wrapped a goosequill in a piece of old soft rag, and stuck it in the neck of the bottle. We would hold the baby in front of the fireplace to feed her, spreading our laps with a blanket under the baby to keep her warm. She was sick a good deal, but we pulled her through that summer. In the fall, Sarah Ann Hinshaw—Steve Hinshaw's mother—kept the baby a few months, and then Mr. and Mrs. S. E. G. Holt—the 'Gib' Holts—took her, and they brought her up. They had no children, and wished to adopt her, but Father would not consent to that,

cated October 2, 1859. This building, of native lumber, ever since has been used as a house of worship, having been sold to the colored people of this denomination when the First Christian congregation built its first brick church, on the site of the original building, in the eighties. The colored people moved the church to Eighth and Congress, and have kept it in repair and constant use. It is seated with the first pews used in the First Congregational Church in Emporia, which was the second church building in the town. It is the oldest church in Lyon County, and probably the oldest in the Fourth Congressional District.

Mr. Brown was a leading spirit in his denomination, and was pastor of the church many years. He did a great work in other settlements, walking long distances over the country to keep his appointments. When a horse could be spared from the work of the farm, he rode, and often drove a horse and buggy. He built an enduring foundation for his church in this section of Kansas.

The Rev. G. C. Morse held preaching services in the hotel office and diningroom in October, 1857, and he organized the Congregational Church August 19,

---

and said they might keep her only on condition that they did not leave this county. They were all that any parents could have been to her, and frequently brought her home for visits. That tiny baby is Mrs. Martha Matilda Wilson, and her home is in Hartford, which was the home of the Holts for many years."

Mrs. Gilmore frequently accompanied her father on his preaching trips over the prairie, and to weddings and funerals, and sang on many of these occasions. Cooking extra meals was so common an occurrence that the little girls did not mind the work at all, but enjoyed the company. Mrs. Gilmore rode among the settlers and raised the money to buy a bell for the new church. John Fowler hauled the bell to Emporia from Leavenworth. Rice Brown, principal of the Emporia Senior High School, is a son of Solomon Brown.

1858, with five members. Theirs was the second church in Emporia, on the site of their present building, Eighth and Mechanic. The town company gave the lots to the church, and the building was accomplished under great difficulty. It was dedicated July 8, 1860. Mr. Morse was its pastor several years, and its leader until his death. The cost of the building was $840.00, and served the congregation until the erection of the present building, in 1881. The first little white church was sold and moved to Sunny Slope, and only this year was razed. "The pews, of which we were so proud," said Mrs. Morse, "we were glad to give to the colored people for their church." Mr. and Mrs. Morse[1] not only did the pioneer work in the founding of this church, but had important parts in the educational progress of the town and county. Their labors were those whose influence lasts from generation to generation.

The first services of the Methodist Episcopal Church were held the summer of 1857, in the Emporia House, conducted by the Rev. Henry Moyes. Later the Methodists held services in McElfresh's Hall, and started to build a church in 1860. The work was delayed when almost all of the men of the church enlisted

---

[1]Their son, Park L. Morse, lives on the farm which was settled by his father and mother, two miles southeast of town, in 1857. Mr. and Mrs. G. C. Morse, having come to Kansas as missionaries from the Congregational Church in Massachusetts, hesitated about taking up land, fearing the Home Missionary Society might not approve of their being land-holders. Also, said Mrs. Morse, they feared the people of the community might think they were only land-seekers, instead of missionaries. The Morses considered that ten acres would be ample for their needs, but some of the young men of the town who were advising them to get land, told them it was easier to secure a quarter section by occupation than to get hold of a ten-acre tract. When the news of their being landowners reached the Home Missionary Society, the Morses received a letter from that body, congratulating them on their good fortune.

for service in the Civil War, and the building was not completed and dedicated until June 26, 1864.

Mrs. Ella Pemberton's recollections of the Methodist Church of the sixties are especially clear. Her father was a "local" minister of this faith, and Judge John H. Watson was the first Sunday School superintendent. "The Civil War stopped work on the first church building," says Mrs. Pemberton. "It was at Ninth and Merchant, our present location, and the walls, of native stone, had been laid. There was no roof, no floor, and no inside finishing. The building was completed after the war, this being one of the first tasks undertaken when the men of the church came home from the army. Some money—not much—was subscribed, but mostly the subscriptions were in terms of days' work, and stone and lumber and other materials. A cupola was added to the church after several years.

"The dedication of the church was a great day for Emporia Methodists," says Mrs. Pemberton. "On the platform were the Rev. Daniel P. Mitchell, of Leavenworth, probably the presiding elder; our first stationed pastor, the Rev. J. C. Fraker, and my father. I was a proud and happy child, and as interested in that dedicatory program as any grown person present."

Mrs. Pemberton related how, stirred by the appeal for money with which to complete the payments on the church, the wonderful thought struck her that she might help—that she could give five dollars. She tiptoed to her mother and in a whisper asked if she might give to the church this enormous sum. She was told to ask her father, his consent was given, and the little girl—called "Puss" instead of her real name—gave her five dollars happily and freely.

"How did I happen to have five dollars? It was a

happen-so. One day during the war, while hanging around the News office—my brother-in-law, Mr. Stotler, was editor of the News—I picked up in the street two five-dollar bills. No one could imagine how anyone could be so careless as to lose all that money. We inquired of everyone, but no one claimed it. Mr. Stotler advertised the find in the News for several weeks, with no response. It was recalled that, about the time the money was found, a government paymaster and his gang, on the way to a reservation to pay off the Indians, had stopped a short time in Emporia, and it was supposed some member of that group must have dropped it. Anyway, my parents said the money should be mine, as no one claimed it after all our efforts to find an owner. Feeling I owned most of the riches of the world, I was only too happy to give half of my wealth to our beloved church.

"It was a red-letter day for the Methodist Church when the Holderman family came to Emporia, from Ohio," says Mrs. Pemberton. "The family filed into the little church the first Sunday of their residence here, the men six-footers, the women large and handsome and well proportioned and beautifully gowned, their hoop-skirts hitting the pews as they walked down the aisle. They filled the longest pew. There was the widowed mother of Jacob[1] and Dan and El Holderman, and their sisters, Miss Madeline, Miss Elizabeth

---

Mrs. Fred Baird, of Emporia, is a granddaughter of Jacob Holderman, and Miss Mary Patty, of the Newman Memorial County Hospital, is a granddaughter of Mrs. John Patty, who was a sister of the Emporia Holdermans. She married in Ohio, and did not come to Kansas with other members of the family. Jacob Holderman was a farmer and stockraiser on a large scale for many years, owning much valuable Verdigris Valley farm land a few miles east of Madison, and large areas of prairie pasture land. Dan and El Holderman were leading business men in Emporia for several decades.

and Miss Harriet, afterward Mrs. Kemp, and their niece, Josephine Patty, who many years later married Alexander Crowe. The Holdermans had some money, they could sing, they were interested in church affairs, and they were a distinct acquisition to the community, as well as the church, soon becoming prominent citizens.

"The Methodists sponsored the first community Christmas tree in Emporia, though they didn't call it by that name. It was the first or the second Christmas following the war, and the church was greatly in need of money. A two-day bazaar was put on at the Normal, with dinner and supper served to the public. Wild turkey was a part of the menu, and roast pigs with red apples in their mouths took my fancy. The Christmas tree was a gorgeous affair, and no child who saw it was without a gift from its branches. The affair was a social and financial success."

The First Baptist Church was organized in October, 1859, by the Rev. J. C. Brant, with seven members. It was reorganized in 1870. The first and second buildings were at Fourth and Merchant, and the third, the handsome new structure at Eighth and Constitution, was dedicated in 1929.

The Society of Friends established a monthly meeting October 6, 1860, with sixty-one members, at the John Moon home, five miles west of town, though they had been holding services in their homes since the first members of that faith arrived in 1854. A quarterly meeting was established in 1868. Often the Friends drove long distances to attend quarterly or yearly meetings, and many members from a distance attended the meetings in Emporia. In 1862, at the quarterly meeting of Friends at their new meeting house five miles west of town—the Cottonwood neighborhood—

it was estimated that one thousand persons were in attendance. Robert and Sarah Lindsey, of England, ministers of this society, held appointed meetings at the home of Curtis and Sabina Hiatt, half a mile west of the Soden bridge, in April, 1858.

The Bethany Congregational Church was organized in 1866 by the Rev. G. C. Morse, with thirty-seven members. The congregation was made up largely of Welsh settlers.

The First Presbyterian Church was organized by the Rev. James P. Gordon, November 9, 1867, with eleven members. Caleb Beckes was the first ruling elder. The Rev. Robert M. Overstreet became pastor of the church in 1869, and sixty-eight members were added in a little more than a year. Church services were held the first few years in down town rooms, and in December, 1871, the first church building was dedicated. It stood on the rear of the lot on the present site, and served the church until the erection of the present building, the cornerstone for which was laid in October, 1895. The dedication was May 16, 1897, and since that date the building has been enlarged and improved. Dr. W. S. Dando is pastor of this church, which has one of the three largest congregations in Emporia, those of the First Methodist and the First Christian being larger.

The Second Presbyterian Church, another Welsh congregation, was organized by the Rev. John Jones, in 1871. About twenty members made up the first congregation.

The Salem Presbyterian Church—Upper Dry Creek —also largely Welsh, was organized by the Rev. R. M. Overstreet, in 1869, with eighteen members.

The United Presbyterian Church was organized

with thirteen members by the Rev. J. A. Collins, in 1869.

St. Andrew's Episcopal Church was organized in 1870 by the Rev. L. R. Holden. The beautiful new church building, considered the handsomest in town, was dedicated in 1928.

The Church of the Sacred Heart—Catholic—was organized in 1874 by the Rev. Father Perrier, with twelve families.

St. Paul's Reformed Church—the building now the property of the Evangelical Church—was organized in 1878 by the Rev. J. G. Shoemaker.

The Free Methodist Church was organized by the Rev. J. P. McElfresh in 1879, with seven members.

The Lyon County Sunday School Association was organized in 1868, and was continued intermittently for many years. For four years during the World War there was a complete lapse. In 1923 the association was reorganized as the County Council of Religious Education, U. S. Wolfe was elected president, and has served ever since in that capacity. Fifty-four Sunday Schools, in addition to those in Emporia, make up this organization. Lyon County is divided into five districts, each of which holds conventions, and an annual convention of all the Sunday Schools of the county is held. Vacation Bible schools are held each summer in Emporia.

Following is, it is hoped, a correct and complete list of Emporia churches and their locations:
First Ward:
First Methodist, Ninth and Merchant.
St. Mark's Lutheran, Seventh and Constitution.
Second Christian, (colored) Eighth and Congress.
St. James Baptist, (colored) 917 Commercial.

Arundel Avenue Presbyterian, Seventh and Arundel.
United Presbyterian, Sixth and Neosho.
Calvary Evangelical, Ninth and Constitution.
Mount Olive African Methodist Episcopal, Sixth and Congress.
First Baptist, Eighth and Constitution.
Church of Christ Scientist, Ninth and Commercial.
Church of Christ, Sixth and Arundel.

Second Ward:
First Friends, Sixth and Sylvan.
Sacred Heart—Catholic—First and Exchange.
Second Presbyterian, Fourth and Market.
Primitive Baptist, (colored) 201 South Market.
Salvation Army, 322 Commercial.
Church of God, 205 South Exchange.

Third Ward:
Grace Methodist Episcopal, South and Neosho.
St. Catherine's Mission—Catholic—West Randolph and South Pine.
Mexican Mission—Methodist—22 South Arundel.
Evangelical Lutheran, South and Constitution.
Church of the Nazarene, First and Constitution, northeast corner.
Seventh Day Advent, First and Constitution, southeast corner.
Bethany Congregational, Second and Merchant.
Foursquare Gospel, Randolph and South Commercial.
Free Methodist, South and Commercial.

Fourth Ward:
First Christian, Seventh and Market.
First Congregational, Eighth and Mechanic.
First Presbyterian, Eighth and Commercial.
Miles Chapel, Colored Methodist, 808 East.

St. Andrew's Episcopal, Ninth and Commercial.
Church of God in Christ, 1112 Sylvan.
Young Men's Christian Association, Fifth and Constitution.
Young Women's Christian Association, Sixth and Union.
There are about thirty churches of various denominations in Lyon County, in the smaller towns and in the country, outside of Emporia.

CATHOLIC CHURCH AND CONGREGATION

The first Catholics in this community were the late Mr. and Mrs. Thomas L. Ryan,[1] who came to Emporia in 1869. In that year came also the P. F. Kings, and in the seventies Casper Ellison, the Michael Maloneys, the Thomas F. Byrnes family, Mr. and Mrs. John Perrier, Mrs. John Atyeo, and Mr. and Mrs. O. Pfefferle. Two Kowalski families came in the eighties, as did Mr. and Mrs. Carl Ballweg,[2] Mrs. J. Harvey

[1] Mr. and Mrs. Thomas L. Ryan were among the leaders of their church in Emporia, and held an important place in this community. Their hospitable home at the corner of Sixth and Exchange was open to friend and stranger. Mr. Ryan for two terms was treasurer of Lyon County, and for many years he operated a carriage and wagon factory on East Sixth, between Mechanic and Market. Mr. and Mrs. Ryan were of the town's dependable, substantial citizens. Dr. Louis D. Ryan, and Charles E. Ryan, of the Mutual Building & Loan Association, are their sons.

[2] Mrs. Carl Ballweg—Maggie Byrne Ballweg—for many years was the most outstanding Catholic laywoman in this section of Kansas, as well as one of its most successful business women. She came to Emporia in 1883, only a year out of Ireland, and started a millinery store of which she made an early and unqualified success. Her business career ended only with her death, which occurred September 15, 1927. During her almost forty-five years in business in Emporia, always she took an important part in the town's activities. Her church came first—she was a most loyal churchwoman—then her family, her business, and her town. And she put into all of these interests her lightness of heart and beauty of spirit, her buoyancy, her scintillating Irish wit, her best

Frith, Mr. and Mrs. Michael Roach and Mr. and Mrs. Martin Grosz.

In 1870 the Rev. Father Penzaloni said the first mass, in the Ryan home, and on his periodical visits to the Indians of the Osage Mission, always he stopped at the Ryans' to celebrate mass. Other priests came during 1871 and 1872, and in 1873 the Rev. Father Perrier[3] began coming regularly to Emporia from Topeka. Services were held a few times in the courthouse, and finally a regular place of worship was secured in the upper rooms of a restaurant on West Sixth Avenue. In 1874 a small brick church was built at the corner of Second and Cottonwood. Father Perrier was succeeded in 1880 by the Franciscan Fathers, and Father Dominic was the first Franciscan priest. A two-story building, the second floor

---

and highest thought; her time and her money, as well as the work of her brain and hands. With Mr. Ballweg, who died in 1918, she gave generously of her substance to their church and to every civic need. Her gayety was saddened by the passing of her beloved companion, but she did not allow this sadness to distress others. To many girls and women she taught the millinery trade, fitting them for useful places in the business world. She was an interested member of the Business and Professional Women's Club, took part in the activities of the Young Women's Christian Association, was liberal in her attitude to all churches and to all agencies for good. Her son, Ernest Ballweg, and Mrs. Ballweg and their children, Carl and Margaret, live in Emporia.

'Father Joseph Perrier often was called "the Marquette of the Kansas prairies." Born in Savoy, France, in 1839, he was confirmed in 1851. At 18 he was a university graduate, and at 23 a professor of languages in a college. He was ordained at 24, in 1863, and in 1866 came to America as a missionary, with Kansas for his field. He was the first regular pastor of the Emporia church, coming here in 1873, when his pastorate covered the state west from Topeka to the Colorado line. Many were the thrilling experiences he used to relate, and many were the hardships he endured. He rode over trackless prairie and forded swollen streams, slept on the wet ground without shelter, often was hungry and cold, with no immediate prospect for food and shelter. He related these and other stories as good jokes, and got many a chuckle out of the telling. He organized churches at Hartford, Eagle Creek, and Osage City while in this section of the State.

serving as temporary church and the first floor as a priest's residence, was built in 1881.

Always the congregation and its leaders had dreamed of a handsome building as a fitting place for its permanent home, and in 1910 work was started on the new building, which was dedicated September 5, 1912. This building, with its furnishings, cost a little more than $45,000.00, and is a distinct asset to the community as well as to its membership. To the Rev. Father Berthold, who died in 1917, is due much credit for this church, which was erected during his pastorate. This church is located at First and Exchange.

Among other activities of the Catholics has been the maintenance of a hospital against tremendous odds. St. Mary's Hospital was built by the Sisters of St. Francis in 1883, and rebuilt, later, with additions. As an example of the unselfish devotion of these Sisters may be mentioned a year in which a smallpox epidemic found the town with no adequate preparation for caring for the patients—at a time when smallpox was a much more dreaded disease than now. Dan Dryer, city marshal, went to the hospital and asked the Sisters to care for the smallpox patients. The hospital was full, but two Sisters who were teaching in

---

In 1888 he was sent to the church at Concordia, as its first resident pastor, and while there celebrated his silver jubilee, and later, his golden jubilee, October 12, 1911. At Concordia his work included the building of the cathedral, the school, convent, hospital and the beautiful St. Joseph's Church, near Concordia, of which he was monsignor. Fourteen churches in all are to his credit, and seventy-five missions. He retired in 1913, and became chaplain at Nazareth, La Grange, Illinois. He died in 1918, in California, and his funeral services, in Olpe, were the most impressive ever held in St. Joseph's Church. John Peter Perrier, Olpe, is a nephew of Father Perrier, and the late John Perrier, of Emporia, was a cousin. Mrs. T. Jensen is a daughter of Mr. and Mrs. John Perrier. A sister, Sister Mary Joseph, is Mother Assistant of the convent at Concordia.

the Catholic school were sent to the town's temporary pesthouse, and nursed the patients back to health, the school being closed meanwhile.

When the new St. Mary's Hospital, at the head of State Street on Fifteenth Avenue, needed the town's help, the town remembered, help came spontaneously, and Emporia non-Catholics contributed $35,000.00 to the hospital. The beautiful new building was dedicated November 21, 1928, the cost of erection and equipment having been $250,000.00. Sister Aquilina is Mother Superior, and has held this position the past twelve years in Emporia.

The Sacred Heart School was established in 1882, and a building erected, which served until it was replaced by the new building, Second and Cottonwood, in 1927. A handsome and commodious parish house is at First and Cottonwood, in easy access from the church. The Rev. Father Steman Prosper is pastor of this congregation, which is one of the most active in Emporia.

Albert Atyeo, a son of the late Mr. and Mrs. John Atyeo, was the first child's name entered in the baptismal record, 1874.

IN THE GOOD OLD DAYS

EARLY-DAY HOSPITALITY

In the early days every traveler over the prairie, with team and wagon or buggy or on horseback, was certain he could secure "entertainment for man and beast"—as the old-time tavern signs used to read—at the homes of the settlers. There was little room in their houses, no extra beds or guest rooms, but seldom was anyone turned away. Most housewives kept two strawticks on one or more beds, and when extra beds were needed it was an easy matter to transfer the extra strawticks to the floor, and build the beds on them. Sometimes there would be two or three beds on the floor, in the one big room which held the family sleeping places. Immodest? Not at all. When bedtime came the men went outdoors until the women got to bed, and when they came in they were told where to sleep, blew out the light and undressed in the dark. Usually the men were up and outdoors in the morning before the women. But if a man happened to be in the house and a woman wanted to get up, it was easy to conceal her dressing operations. She sat up in bed, pulled the top sheet over her head, and dressed in the strictest privacy. Women who never traveled in a sleeping car until late in life, found dressing in a Pullman berth not so different from, and no less difficult than dressing under a sheet in a roomful of people.

Entire families piled into the lumber wagon and drove eight or ten miles to "stay all day" with a neighboring family, without special invitation or sending word they were coming—no telephones. They were welcomed as warmly as if extensive preparations had been made. It wasn't expected they would send word of their proposed visit.

Children playing in the prairie grass always were on the lookout for travelers, and ran races to the house to see which would be first to tell Mother that a covered wagon was coming over the hill. If near the end of the day, the travelers were almost certain to stay all night, if nearing noon, to stop for dinner. Often travelers were prepared for camping, and frequently, if the weather were cold or rainy, the man would ask if the women and children might sleep in the house, and he would sleep in the wagon, or under it. Sometimes the men of the house would sleep outside, giving up their beds to the women and children. Always the travelers were welcomed, as they brought news from other places—and the settlers got as hungry for news as for fruit and other food they missed on the claims.

Often warm friendships were formed between travelers and the people whose hospitality they enjoyed. In October, 1887, a family named Snyder, moving from Elmdale to Golden City, Mo., with two teams, a wagon and buggy and several extra horses and twelve head of cattle, besides Mr. and Mrs. Snyder and their four small sons, stopped one rainy Saturday night at the home of Mr. and Mrs. W. B. Willis, who lived south of the Cottonwood near the Columbia Bridge. The Snyders were rained in until Tuesday, but everyone enjoyed the visit. Both Mr. Willis and Mr. Snyder were Civil War veterans, and had much in common.

Not long after the Snyders left, Mrs. Willis received a letter from Mrs. Snyder, again thanking the Willises for their hospitality. Mrs. Willis answered the letter, and ever since the two women have kept up an interesting correspondence. Christmas and birthdays are remembered, and there are frequent letters in between. The Snyders have lived for years in New Plymouth, Idaho. These women never met but the one time, yet they cherish for each other a real and affectionate friendship. The Willis home is at 910 Neosho.

Agents selling all sorts of merchandise—fruit trees, patent rights for churns and washing machines and the machines themselves, lightning rods, books, tinware and crockery and glass, dress goods and men's suiting, blankets and curtains and coverlids, and almost every tool and implement used on a farm, "made" every neighborhood several times a year. They depended entirely upon the farmhouses for food and lodging, as the distance to town was too great to go back and forth, before the days of motor cars. Besides, what was the use? The farmer family with whom the "peddler" stayed would take out the board and lodging bill in trade, and each was satisfied with the exchange.

DEFUNCT TOWNS AND POST OFFICES

Elmendaro, county seat of old Madison County, was located in 1855, ten miles south and seven miles east of Emporia, south of Little Eagle Creek. George H. Lillie was president of the Town Company. There were several stores and dwellings, a post office, a big log schoolhouse in which church services and Sunday School and court sessions were held. The town was ambitious, but it had no incentive to live after the elimination of Madison County by the State Legislature, and in a few years was known no more as a town. Its name is perpetuated by a township, a church and a school.

Orleans post office, on the Neosho west of Americus, was moved to that town soon after it was started. E. Yeakley was postmaster at Orleans.

Waterloo was laid out in 1858 by W. H. Mickel. Mr. Mickel built a hotel which he kept going several years after the town was disbanded. Waterloo was fifteen miles northeast of Emporia. It was a popular stopping place for travelers on the Lawrence and Emporia road. It consisted of not more than half a dozen houses, at its best.

Fremont, which was laid out in April, 1858 by Dr. Thomas Armor, S. G. Elliott and W. B. Swisher, was a thriving village of twenty-five or thirty houses, with post office, stores and blacksmith shop. It had county-seat aspirations, and when these failed, the town dwindled and soon was gone, leaving its name to a township and a school district. It was three miles north of Emporia on the west Allen road, on the farm now owned by L. A. Trumbull.

Forest Hill, eight miles east of Emporia on Sixth Avenue, was located in 1858, on a sightly hill without a forest but, as one of its promoters, Timothy McIntire, said, they had the hill and it was a fine location for a forest. A stone building on the farm belonging to Mrs. Charles Galt remains of what was the town, and the school district retains the name. A post office was established at Forest Hill.

Chicago Mound, from which the church, the neighborhood and the school, ten miles southeast of Emporia get their name, was, according to an article printed in the Gazette September 16, 1909, and agreeing with the version of several old settlers, founded the autumn of

1857 by Vinegrave, an Englishman, and Webber, a Maine man. Stakes were driven and town lots divided off. Hundreds of these lots, according to the story, were sold to unsuspecting Easterners. A more recent story printed in the Gazette gives credit for the founding of the town to Henry Pratt and J. J. Campbell, for many years Lyon County citizens. No houses ever were erected on this town site—it was purely a paper town.

Columbia, three miles southeast of Emporia on the Cottonwood, was laid out early in the summer of 1855 by promoters from Council Grove—T. S. Huffaker, Seth Hays, G. M. Simcock and Christopher Columbia. There were several houses, a store and postoffice and blacksmith shop. Columbia ceased to exist soon after Emporia was founded.

Hortonburg, the first station on the Santa Fe northeast of Emporia, was established in 1882, but soon the name was changed to Lang.

Attica, adjoining Hartford on the west, was the site of the first M. K. & T. station, which afterward was moved to its present location and Attica abandoned.

Many star route postoffices were discontinued when rural mail delivery was established. Among these were Ivy, Waushara, Agnes City, Foster Springs, Plumb, Elco, Eads, Badger Creek, Verdigris, Wyckoff, Trail, Waterloo, Fourmile, Menda.

The post office at Agnes City was moved to Bushong after that town was started. Agnes City was three and one-half miles north of Bushong, on the Santa Fe Trail, and became a post office in 1857, or possibly 1858, says John McMillan, of Bushong. Agnes City earlier had a store, and did business with the trekkers over the Santa Fe Trail, and the settlers on the claims. Trail was another post office, further east, which was discontinued when Bushong was established. Agnes City was named in honor of a young woman named Agnes Baker, probably a daughter of Judge A. I. Baker, who was murdered by the Anderson outlaw gang.

OUTLAW RAIDS AND VICTIMS

Outlaws, calling themselves Free State men, in 1856 visited this section of Kanzas Territory. The night of September 14, after looting the Gregg general store, near the present site of Neosho Rapids, they went to the home of Christian Carver, in the same neighborhood, and demanded admittance. The Carvers had retired, and refused to allow the outlaws to enter their home. The outlaws fired into the cabin, through an opening which had been left for a window, and shot Mrs. Carver, from the effects of which she died the next day. Mrs. Carver was a daughter of Mr. and Mrs. David VanGundy, who had settled near the junction of the Cottonwood and the Neosho in 1855. Next day, the outlaws went north to the old Santa Fe Trail, where they robbed the store belonging to Charles Withington. They carried off and destroyed property to the value of $3,000.00. The settlers had no recourse from the depredations of these outlaws. It was the belief of the settlers that this gang was led by Capt. John E. Cook, who was hanged at Harper's Ferry.

Many of the settlers brought with them considerable sums of money and other valuables, and when news of raiders in the vicinity reached them, they concealed this property. The story is told of Jonathan Pierce having buried $1,000.00 in gold at the foot of a tree in the heavy timber on the north bank of the Cottonwood near the old Humphrey grist mill, seven miles southeast of town, which he never thereafter could locate. Many persons spent valuable time digging up the earth searching for this gold, though some of Pierce's acquaintances declared their belief that he recovered the gold and told the story of losing it to avoid further attention from robbers, and others believed he never had owned the gold, but told the story of losing it to gain sympathy. Still another theory was that Pierce was watched while hiding the gold, and when he had completed the job and gone home, the watcher dug up the gold and disappeared. Pierce was considered a miserly man, and most people believed he had owned the gold.

Charles H. Withington was Lyon County's first settler, having located on the Santa Fe Trail in June, 1854, where he established a store, the first in this county and the first in Southern Kansas not connected with an Indian post. Withington's, during 1855 and 1856, was headquarters for most of the immigrants who came to this section of the Territory. Mr. Withington helped the new people to find claims, acted as guide, and often neglected his own business to assist a newcomer. He came to Kansas in 1853, settled at Council Grove, where he was a gunsmith for the Sac and Fox Indians, and ran a store for the Santa Fe Trail and Indian trade.

An interesting story is told of how Mrs. Withington saved the family's money from the notorious Anderson gang of robbers. Mr. Withington, before leaving home one morning on business, told Mrs. Withington he disliked to leave her alone, as he had heard the Andersons were headed in their direction, and no telling what day they would swoop down upon them. Mrs. Withington said she could manage them, and that she wasn't afraid. She was washing that day, her washtub in the narrow strip of shade made by the cabin, when she saw the little band of men on horseback coming over a hill. She knew them, personally, and when the leader ordered her to prepare dinner for them, she replied: "Mr. Anderson, you have eaten many a good meal in my house, to which you have been welcome, but I take no orders from you or any other man. When you ask me, respectfully and decently, to get dinner for you, I'll do it, and not before." The leader apologized, and politely asked Mrs. Withington if she would prepare dinner for him and his men. She got up the best dinner she could, and after the meal the leader said:

"Now, Mrs. Withington, we'll have no more fooling. I want that bag of gold that is hidden somewhere about this place, and I am going to have it, and the quicker you get it for me the better it will be for you."

"Help yourself," said Mrs. Withington, "but don't expect me to assist you in your search."

For a long time the robbers searched, ripping open featherbeds and pillows, emptying trunks and drawers, tearing up the carpet, while Mrs. Withington calmly went on with her washing. Finally the men threatened her, telling her she would have to tell them where the gold was hidden or they would not be responsible for the consequences. She looked the leader straight in the eye.

"You call yourself a brave man," she said, "yet you threaten a defenseless woman. Go ahead—shoot me if you will, but I will not tell you where to find that gold."

It was getting late and the robbers feared that Mr. Withington might come, accompanied by other men who would put up a fight, so they left after Mrs. Withington defied them. After Mr. Withington arrived, Mrs. Withington lifted the bag of gold from the bottom of the washtub, where it had reposed all this time under dirty suds and soiled clothing.

Following these raids the people organized for protection against further visits from the Border Ruffians and other outlaws. In almost every town, companies of militia were formed and every man of the required age was expected to enroll. Streets were patrolled at night for weeks at a stretch, but no further raids occurred.

Always the settlers in town and on the claims were on the lookout for Indian outbreaks, but they were spared this. The Kaws who lived on a reservation between Americus and Dunlap, were lazy, and most of them would steal anything they could get their hands on, but they were not fighters. The warring tribes, further west, never reached this section of the Territory after settlement was started.

In 1862 an invasion of half-breed Indians and white men came into Kansas from the Indian Territory, and the people of the Neosho Valley were thrown into a state of wild excitement. The marauders reached Humboldt, where they robbed and burned many houses. P. B. Plumb headed a small company of men who went to the defense of Humboldt, but the invaders had turned back when the Emporia men reached the town. The Emporia company went on to Fort Scott, however, and joined the expedition which captured Matthews, the leader of the raiders, and much of the property he had stolen was recovered.

July 3, 1862, Arthur I. Baker, who ran a store on the Santa Fe Trail in the northwest part of Lyon County, was murdered by members of the Anderson gang, who were a part of Quantrill's organization.

Baker was shot as he was descending the steps to the cellar under his store, and the store and its contents burned over his body which, when recovered, was charred beyond recognition. Baker had taken a prominent part in the affairs of the county from the first, and was a strong Free State man. He was elected probate judge in the territorial election of 1857, and was one of the members of the Americus Town Company.

In 1864, when the Confederate General Price and his army came north with the avowed intention of taking the State, the Lyon County Militia, which had become the Eleventh Kansas Cavalry was called out, and three hundred men went to the eastern border of the State, where they did valuable service, holding back the marauders until, discouraged and disheartened, Price withdrew his army.

CARRYING THE MAIL

Mrs. George Plumb carried the mail for one day, in 1863. She was 16-year-old Ellen Cowles then, and took the place of the regular carrier, who was sick. She went on horseback, of course, and her route took her first to Elmendaro, southeast of Emporia, along a little traveled prairie road. From Elmendaro she went southwest to Madison, and the road grew fainter, and sometimes was almost hidden by the tall grass. From Madison she went down the Verdigris to Shell Rock post office, and home by way of Elmendaro. At the Elmendaro post office and general store, seven women sat waiting for the mail, in the hope of receiving letters from their husbands, who were in the army. One woman said not a word to anyone, but when her turn came and the postmistress said, "I am so sorry, Mrs. Quimby, but there is no letter for you today," she threw back her head and walked out of the office with her cruel disappointment showing in her face. "She has been here every mail day for seven weeks," said the postmistress, "and has had no letter. I do hope her husband hasn't been killed or wounded." And this hope was fulfilled, as the man returned safe and sound from the army.

When Mrs. Plumb left Madison it was late, and night was approaching as she neared Shell Rock. She stopped in front of a house on a hill—one of the Long families lived there—and asked the woman who came to the door the way to her destination. Mrs. Long said her husband had just started, on foot, to the post office, and that Mrs. Plumb probably would overtake him in the timber, and he would guide her to the post office. Mrs. Plumb overtook the man, and as he walked alongside her horse, on the side on which were her feet—no woman rode astride in those days—Mr. Long said to her, "I should think you'd be afraid of me, walking along here with you all alone." She replied, "Well, if I were afraid, I couldn't help myself." "And all the time," says Mrs. Plumb, "I was shaking with fear, and kept a tight hold on my rawhide whip, to be used as a weapon if I needed one. But I did not need it." Rendel Brown was postmaster at Shell Rock, and Mrs. Plumb stayed all night at the Van Horn home. After she had gone to bed, she heard someone come into the next room and inquire, "Did the mail come?" "No," was the reply, "but the female did." She was up early next morning and reached home without mishap.

ORCHARDISTS AND OTHERS

EARLY-DAY ORCHARDISTS

What was considered an essential improvement on every early-day claim was the planting of an orchard. Many settlers and their families denied themselves other necessities that they might scrape together money to pay for fruit trees. Peach trees, plums, cherries, all were early yielders, and in a few years these fruits were plentiful. Pioneers say the springs were earlier then, and seldom were the fruit buds killed by a late freeze, or by frosts, as so often is the case in later years. Apple trees, not coming into bearing so early, were planted and the young trees carefully wrapped each autumn to protect them from the depredations of the rabbits, which enjoyed meals of the tender apple-tree bark. There were few, if any, fruit-tree diseases, and spraying was unnecessary and unheard of.

Among the early orchardists were Mrs. J. H. Slocum, Emporia; L. M. Harris, Plymouth; P. G. Hallberg, who owned the first nursery in Emporia; J. V. Randolph, Emporia; N. F. Ames, Neosho Rapids; James H. Doile and J. W. Weaver, Emporia; W. M. Nelson and Robert Logan, Emporia; Simon Bucher, Eagle Creek; the Hill Brothers, in later years, north of Emporia; Asa D. Chambers, Hartford; William Grafenstein, Center Township. Thomas H. Stanley, southwest of Americus, was a government agent and missionary to the Indians, and spent much time at this work, yet in his first years on his farm he planted a large orchard, the fruit from which for many years not only supplied his own family, but many fruit-hungry new-comers as well. Also, he instructed the Indians on various reservations in farming and fruit-raising. No fresh or canned fruit, of the domesticated varieties, was available, and often the dried fruit brought from other States was of poor quality—it was likely to be wormy, and often unfit for use.

Isaac Wright, who lived west of Americus, was a fruit grower on a large scale, and his orchard was a paying investment for many years. So many of the Friends who settled west of Americus put out large orchards and raised so much fruit, that they named their school district and neighborhood Fruitland. On every new farm until the nineties, perhaps, an orchard was planted. Since that time, orchard pests have made necessary much hard work in spraying, or a poor quality of fruit would result. The old orchards have died and comparatively few new ones have replaced them. Farmers who raise fruit find a ready market for it, at good prices. Refrigerator cars bring to every railroad station fresh fruit at all seasons of the year, the commercial dried fruit and canned fruit is of good quality, and a majority of the farmers do not consider it worth while financially, to "bother with fruit." During the World War there was a revival of fruit canning and drying, and many women who never had canned fruit got the habit at that time, and still do their canning. Others, of course, always had "put up" fruit for their winter's use.

Every farm woman in the sixties, seventies and eighties felt she must have several floursacks full of dried peaches each year, and the drying was done by the sun. The small seedlings—that was a job for the children, and at first it was fun, but soon it got old— were halved and dried with the skins on, but for especially nice fruit, the larger peaches were peeled and dried, and made a delectable dessert, either as sauce or in pies. Women added to their incomes by drying every peach they could get hold of, and selling them to the grocers, or sometimes to their neighbors who had no fruit. Unpeeled peaches brought three to five cents a pound, the peeled ones seven to ten cents. At the stores the women had to take their pay in groceries. Farmers in the fall often drove in their wagons with the sideboards on to Missouri, or to Eastern Kansas counties, and brought home loads of winter apples, a part of which they sold to their neighbors to help defray the expenses of the trip.

Berries and almost all varieties of small fruit do well, usually, and are raised by many people in this county, as being a more certain crop and less work than the larger fruits, and a smaller investment in getting them started.

Fruit tree agents, representing nurseries in different localities, traveled over the country, sometimes on foot, taking orders for trees, shrubs and vines. Sometimes the trees were delivered in bad condition, and the farmer might lose an entire order. Often a fruit tree agent would stay at a farmhouse for a week at a time, while working the surrounding territory, and his entire bill for board and room would be taken out in fruit trees.

DIVERSIFIED STOCK-RAISING

While cattle raising always has been of greatest importance in the livestock industry in Lyon County, hogs and horses and sheep, in addition to those raised for use on the farm and the farm table, have added each year to the farm revenues. In the seventies N. A. Stevenson, of Forest Hill, raised Berkshire hogs, as did E. S. Crippen and W. J. F. Hardin, of Hartford. B. F. Myers, east of town, also made swine a specialty. A. C. Ames, of Neosho Rapids, kept Highlander horses, and later on the DeLongs dealt extensively in thoroughbred horses. Many farmers kept only well-bred horses, and many raised a few colts for sale each year. Malcolm Campbell was a shorthorn breeder, as were William L. Hughes, Matthew Kirkendall and Andrew Hinshaw. Many farmers combined somewhat extensive stock-raising with their farming, and among these in the earlier decades were T. J. Price, Reading; Nicholas Lockerman and Patrick Manning, southwest of town; D. L. Ward, Luther Severy, Reading; D. A. Hunter, Forest Hill; J. G. Klock and S. D. Allen, Emporia; J. W. Loy, Americus; Robert Best, Charles E. Paine, Admire; Daniel Bitler, Olpe, raised and sold large shipments of hogs and cattle, and Henry Stratton, several miles down Eagle Creek east of Olpe, was one of the earliest of the Eagle Creek stockmen. Later, the Brewers, N. W. and W. M., for several decades did a large business in cattle and hogs, and some of their sons are in this business in the same neighborhood. L. O. Priest, Olpe, and M. O. Abraham, of Dow Creek, raised stock along with farm crops and fruit. V. A. Gossett ran one of the first dairy farms near Emporia.

George Plumb was the most extensive sheep-raiser in Lyon County, at his ranch on Badger Creek, having sheared in one season five thousand head. The Weavers brought fine-wool sheep—merinos—to this county, having paid a big price for them in Wisconsin. After financial reverses they sold the sheep to George

Plumb for $3.00 a head. Sheep were a paying proposition to Mr. Plumb. The Snedekers—three brothers of them—located on raw land twelve miles southeast of Emporia in the late seventies and for ten or a dozen years kept large flocks of sheep. Judge M. M. Mason for several years kept sheep on his farm, and W. T. Starr, of Elmendaro Township, was another sheep-raiser.

In the first two decades of the settlement of Lyon County, scores of farmers kept a few sheep—a dozen or more, sometimes less. These were strictly for home use. Several times during the summer sheep would be slaughtered by different farmers, and divided among neighbors, and in this way fresh mutton was secured for a considerable portion of the summer at little cost. The wool was sheared and spun, and made into yarn for stockings or into thread for cloth. Many women spun, and wove cloth, and knitted the stockings and socks for their families. They wove the only carpets they owned, and linsey-woolsy—a mixture of cotton and wool—for dresses and shirts. Often the farmers took wool to a woolen mill at Burlington, where it was made into blankets and into jeans for men's wear, into linsey for women and children's dresses and petticoats. The women cut and made the suits for the men and boys, their own and their daughters' dresses, and underwear for the entire family. German settlers in the Rosean neighborhood, who had no sheep, often bought wool of their neighbors to make up into clothing and blankets. Many of the settlers along the Cottonwood and Neosho kept sheep and from the wool made all their clothing.

Some of the settlers raised cotton, and made cloth and yarn from it. The outlay of money was little, and the women counted their hard work as not amounting

HISTORY OF EMPORIA AND LYON COUNTY 187

to much, but they almost clothed their families by their industry. Sheets and pillowslips made of home-raised, home-carded and home-spun cotton, and wool blankets of home manufacture, wore for years, and when a woman once got the necessary changes in bed linen, it was long before she had to renew them. But the knitting kept her everlastingly at it. Women seldom sat with idle hands for as long as half an hour, and knitted by the light from the fireplace to save candles. So expert were many of them that they seldom looked at their work, except to turn a heel or in narrowing. Knitting saw such a revival during the World War that many women who never before had seen a knitting needle became experts at what had been almost a lost art.

FOREIGN IMMIGRATION

While much of the settlement of Lyon County was made by immigrants from other States, as early as 1857 many Welsh[1] were arriving, and they continued

[1] L. W. Lewis, during his long residence in Emporia, became its most outstanding Welsh citizen. He had more important railroad contracts, and other big jobs, than any like firm in the Middle West. Mr. Lewis started as a Santa Fe bridge contractor in October, 1869, and his sons, L. H. Lewis and W. J. Lewis, still carry on the business. Mr. Lewis, from 1896 until 1910, often employed 1200 to 1400 men at a time. He took his men and equipment to the Southwest, having many contracts in New Mexico and Arizona, and in 1887 had a Santa Fe contract in California. His work to the northeast extended almost to Chicago. He erected the old Santa Fe roundhouse, and the stone station building in 1882. When preparations were begun for the new station building, the walls of the old building were found so solid and substantial that they were incorporated as a part of the new building. L. W. Lewis was of the same solid, substantial character. He gave generously to every need, he was deeply religious and lived his profession every day, he hunted up every Welshman who came to this country, and if he needed help, financially or otherwise, Mr. Lewis stood by till he got on his feet. L. W. Lewis was affectionately called by his countrymen, "The father of all the Lyon County Welsh."

to come in large numbers throughout the sixties, seventies and eighties. French, Swiss and German settlers began coming in the sixties, and continued to arrive during the seventies and eighties. The Welsh came in the largest numbers, the Germans next and the French third. A smaller proportion of the descendents of the French settlers, compared to the early settlement, lives in Lyon County than either Welsh or German.

The Welsh settled chiefly in the Neosho and Cottonwood Valleys, along Dry Creek and Coal Creek, securing bottom land whenever possible. The Germans, coming later, took the high prairie land in Center and Elmendaro Townships, mainly, and by their thrift and industry have made of this land—only a decade or two earlier condemned as worthless—excellent farms. Many French settled along the creeks of Southern Lyon County and on the adjoining prairie, in the Reading neighborhood, and numbers of them in Emporia. The Irish, too, though they ran less to settlements of their nationality, came and helped materially in the building of the county. At Hartford were the Brogans, the Carolans, the Mundys and the O'Conners, and others, at Neosho Rapids the O'Tooles and O'Maras and Mulconnerys. A few Italians came with the French settlers, and both these nationalities displayed the same thrift and industry as the Welsh and Germans. There were business men and mechanics among these people, and many of them at once became residents of Emporia, and many others moved to this town later.

The majority of these settlers and those from other European countries became naturalized American citizens at an early date, but some of them hastened to attend to this important business only when made necessary by the World War, and the imminent danger of being called to their native land for military service. If they were to fight, they wished to fight for their adopted country, and not for their fatherland. The foreign settlers and their descendents display the same pride in the achievements of their county and State as do the native-born Americans. Most of the original settlers have gone on to another New Country.

FLOODS IN LYON COUNTY

Floods at various times have damaged farms and crops in the Neosho and Cottonwood Valleys and in the valleys of their tributaries. Water, pouring down from the hills from southwest to northeast after heavy rains, many times overflowed the clogged and narrow and crooked stream-beds. Drainage meetings have been held and drainage and straightening projects discussed for years, but little definite work to that end has been accomplished. Beginning with 1857, engineers in 1926 making a survey for the proposed Lyon County Drainage District No. 1, found record of forty-seven more or less destructive floods in Lyon County. This flood history, published in the Emporia Gazette June 24, 1926, with the Gazette's record of floods the three succeeding years, follows.

The first flood on record was in 1857 when, according to reports made at that time, "A destructive flood swept down the Neosho, carrying with it wigwams, houses and crops." Another time in 1857, and again in 1859, high water was reported. Water stood two and one-half feet deep in the Soden mill in August, 1866, according to stories told by early settlers. Outside business and communication were cut off in 1866 when the water was within a few feet of the second floor of Soden's mill. Much corn and wheat were destroyed by this flood. Many land-owners recall a flood in 1870, but no written record of this flood has been found in newspapers or other sources.

Many farmers living near Neosho Rapids moved out of their homes in June, 1873, and the river at its crest was within ten inches of the iron bridge across the Neosho at that town. Cribs of corn, livestock, haystacks and sawlogs were swept away. A flood of almost equal proportions came four years later. In June of that year the water was two inches higher than ever before, doing great injury to crops and damaging the Soden Bridge across the Cottonwood. The highest known mark was reached in 1877.

Crop damage amounting to $300,000.00 in Coffey County as a result of floods in the Neosho Valley was reported by the Emporia Republican in 1885. Train service on the Neosho Valley Branch of the M. K. & T. was suspended several days. May 30, 1889, the water in the Cottonwood was within two feet of the railway bridge on the Howard Branch.

Another bad flood came in 1891 when, on June 27, the water rose to within three inches of the high mark of 1877, covering roads and fields and almost touching the bridge floor at Soden's. Grain, implements and livestock were washed away. Again, in 1896, a heavy rain in Chase County swelled the Cottonwood River until the water ran over the bottoms from the Cottonwood to Dry Creek, south of Emporia. Cordwood and fences were washed away, as well as crops, and several horses were drowned.

After two small floods in intervening years the Cottonwood River south of Emporia was reported to be one mile wide on April 13, 1901. The Neosho was up twenty-two feet, and trees, fences and stock floated down both streams. Farmers who were warned moved their stock to higher ground. The next year the Neosho reached the highest point in thirty years, water standing thirty-one inches on the floor of the pumping station. Water covered the farms in the valleys north of town. Five lives were lost by drowning, and a rescue party saved the lives of thirty others. A mile of track on the Howard Branch was submerged, the water rising high enough on June 7 to put out the fires in the engines. One farmer reported a loss of $5,000.00.

In June, 1903, the water rose higher than any white man ever had seen it, but this mark was surpassed the following year, when there were four floods, the first reaching its crest June 3. Crops were destroyed and many cattle drowned. June 11 the rivers rose again, and on June 21 the Columbia bridge, on the Cottonwood three miles southeast of Emporia, went out, having been damaged by the two previous floods. On July 7 the water on the Eggers farm, near the junction of the Cottonwood and Neosho, was fourteen inches higher than ever before. Practically all crops on the bottoms were ruined, and it was too late to replant. Water flowed over everything from the bluffs north of the Neosho to the bluffs south of Dry Creek, for several miles west of the Junction.

June 9, 1906, the Cottonwood went out of its banks, destroying about 40 per cent of the corn on the bottoms and doing much damage to wheat. May 12, 1908, the Neosho was thirty-two inches above the floor of the engine room at the pumping station, and the Cottonwood lacked only a few inches of reaching the floor of the bridge at Soden's mill. On the Ptacek farm, a mile north of town, the Neosho was a few inches above previous marks, destroying about half the wheat.

The greatest flood known so early in the season occurred in January, 1910. Most of the damage done was to buildings and fences by floating ice blocks. The bottoms were almost cleared of fences, small houses and haystacks. The next big flood was in May, 1915, when water stood twenty-one inches over the floor of the pumping station. At Soden's mill, the water reached a stage of twenty-two and one-half feet.

Wheat was damaged June 14, 1916, when the Cottonwood reached a stage of twenty-three and six-tenths feet, and the Neosho was eighteen inches over the pumphouse floor. In 1922 the Neosho went out of its banks, flooding Lyon County bottoms. Coal Creek also went on a rampage because the Cottonwood could not carry off the surplus water. May 24, 1923, both rivers went out of their banks. June 9, that year, a heavy rain in Lyon County caused the Cottonwood to reach a stage of twenty-four and eight-tenths feet, and two days later the Neosho rose to twenty-one and one-half feet.

The engineers' report states that floods as destructive as that in 1904 may be expected every fifty years, while those as great as in 1923 may come every ten or twenty years. Drainage districts are expected to prevent most of these floods, especially the small ones, which come every two or three years, and those as large as in 1923.

The files of the Gazette show that in June, 1927, the Cottonwood rose to twenty-two and two-tenths feet. Water stood over a considerable section of the pavement south of the Soden Bridge, and was over the pavement for several miles near Plymouth. Much wheat was destroyed, and corn washed out, which necessitated replanting. Wheat was ready for harvest, and much of it in the bottoms was a total loss. In November, 1928, Santa Fe service was crippled for several days, and many trains were annulled for from one to five or six days. The tracks from Plymouth to Saffordville were under a foot of water. The loss to crops in Lyon County probably did not exceed $40,-000.00, and the loss of livestock was light.

A flood in July, 1929, was one of the most harmful in all the long record of high water in this county. The Cottonwood at Emporia July 12 reached a stage of twenty-five feet and seven inches. Railroad tracks were covered and trains put out of business temporarily. Crops, for a mile and more wide in the Cottonwood Valley from Peabody, in Marion County, to the Junction, in Lyon County, were ruined. Many miles of paved roads were under water several days.

MANNERS AND CUSTOMS

THE HORSE-AND-BUGGY DAYS

A news item in the Gazette the summer of 1929 said: "Lyon County has 7,601 licensed automobiles and 634 trucks, the highest number in its history. The total number of pleasure cars exceeds last year's high mark by 151, and the excess of trucks is 57."

And that is what happened to the livery stable industry! Time was when the livery stable was an important and essential part of the town. Hacks made the trains regularly, were in service at funerals, and one Emporia woman attended every funeral in town when she was at all certain hacks would be used, "just to get the ride to the cemetery, as that is the only time I ever get a chance to ride in a hack," she declared. A gallant bridegroom, whose fiancee lived only a block from the home of the minister who was to perform the marriage ceremony, ordered a hack to call for him and his bride at her home. In his zeal to be on time, he gave his order for an hour earlier than the time set, and the patient hack-driver waited. The bridegroom was game, however, and made no complaint at the extra charge for the long wait. Hack fares were 25 cents, and an Emporia sporting youngster, on going to Kansas City for the Missouri-Kansas game, chartered a hack at the old Union Station to take him and his girl to the football field. The charge was two dollars, but this young sport was not game. He "hollered" long and loud, but in vain, and the driver only laughed when told that hack fares never exceeded 25 cents in Emporia.

A "livery team and buggy" to take his girl out riding was the highest compliment a young man could pay to a young woman. Livery stable proprietors often kept a pair of high-stepping spotted ponies for use of the young men "going sparking," and girls who got rides behind them were the envy of their less fortunate associates. Also, the "slow and safe" horse was popular, as the lines could be tied round the whip socket and Old Slow-and-Safe be depended upon to keep the road without further attention. Often young men were condemned by their elders for "fooling away money on livery teams," but the youngsters considered it worth while. Land speculators driving over the country often hired a team and driver, and the driver frequently could give the speculators valuable information concerning the land they wished to see. The smallest town had at least one livery stable.

Early-day livery stable proprietors in Emporia were Tom Fleming, who also was a popular city marshal; James Davis; the Central Stables, A. M. Fritz, proprietor; the Seventh Avenue, G. T. Barwick, proprietor; W. H. Gilchrist, H. B. Lowe, later the Newtons and Fleming & Potter, and others.

RATTLESNAKES AND "ROSUM" WEEDS

Rattlesnakes, in the early days on the prairie, were dangerous and numerous. They throve along the rocky ledges which crowned many of the hills, and seemed ever on the alert to get in their deadly work. Children, roaming the prairie in search of the succulent "rosum," the gum which grew on the weed of that name, which they chewed as present-day children chew the manufactured article, went armed with clubs to kill the rattlesnakes they were almost certain to encounter. "The old snakes always rattle their warning," an old-timer used to relate, "but the little fellows are 'sassy' and seldom sound their rattle. They get hold of one before one knows they are near."

A family of children who used to hunt "rosum" always took with them their dog, "Cash"—and "Cash" was death to rattlers. He hunted them out of their stony retreats, and killed hundreds of them before they got him. He was bitten many times, but with properly administered antidotes he recovered. One day he stirred up a nest of especially vicious rattlers and was bitten several times about the head and throat. He was taken home at once, but the poison could not be controlled, and he died from the poisoning and suffocation. Many valuable dogs died from rattlesnake bites.

Two men, prospectors, riding over the prairie inspecting wild land, saw a rattlesnake and got out of their buggy to kill it. They had no weapons, and one of them suggested stoning it to death. The other said he had a better way. With his pocketknife he attempted to cut off the rattler's head, but the snake was too quick for him, and bit the man's hand. He was taken at once to a doctor, but lost his arm as a result of the snakebite.

Whisky was an almost unfailing antidote for snakebite—the poison of the liquor counteracting that of the snake. And that was one of the thousands of arguments urged against prohibition—"What will we do in case of snakebite?" But there were other remedies equally effective, and fatalities from snakebite did not increase noticeably after the enactment of the prohibitory law.

PRAIRIE FIRES

Prairie fires, of annual occurrence, were a source of fear and dread, and frequently of heavy financial loss to the early settlers. Usually no one knew how they started, but once started, they swept over the tall prairie grass, driven by high winds, with amazing speed. Many times livestock was burned, together with hay and corn and other feed, the fires coming in the fall after the crops were matured. Occasionally, human lives were lost in the fires, and many times the hands and feet and faces of fire-fighters were burned and blistered by contact with the fierce heat. Children on the prairie claims, realizing the danger from prairie fires, would scan the horizon, and at the faintest sign of smoke or flame, would hasten to report it to their elders. Often the result of a summer's work on a farm went up in the smoke of prairie fires.

Early in the fall, every farmer was supposed to burn fireguards around his land, on days or evenings when there was little or no wind. A burned strip a quarter of a mile wide often would stop, temporarily at least, the advance of a prairie fire. Often, too, furrows were plowed alongside the burned strips, in further efforts to ward off the dangerous enemy. But, given a good start and a high wind, a fiendish prairie fire could and did jump almost any kind of a fireguard, no matter how wide it had been burned nor how deep the furrows plowed. Prairie fires constituted just another of the many hardships with which the early settlers had to contend. Several times Emporia was threatened, but the fire either was got under control, when everyone turned out to fight it, or the wind changed and the path of the flames shifted away from the town.

If one were a safe distance from a prairie fire, and not personally concerned as to the damage it might do, a raging prairie fire was a beautiful and fascinating sight. Far away in the Flint Hills often the fires had their origin, and their progress was a series of leaping flames and smoky spires, and when a haystack or prairie hay stable caught, great bursts of flame filled the vision. But the settlers paid little heed to them except as to their danger.

Many families, "burned out" on claims as far to the southwest as Butler County, came to Emporia for the winter, the first few years. Nothing was left of their year's labor on the claims after the fires had passed over them, and here the men came hoping to get work whereby to support their families.

PLAYTIME AND PLAYGROUNDS

The pioneers, with all their work and anxiety and their numberless privations, enjoyed life and found recreation in many ways. The old-time camp meetings were looked upon by many "worldly" persons more as social affairs than as religious gatherings. They were held in Soden's Grove, in Bruner's Grove, and in many other lovely timbered places along the creeks and rivers. They were more universally attended than any other function, social or religious or educational. Saints and sinners alike went to camp meeting, but for vastly different purposes.

Sometimes it became necessary to maintain guards at the outer edge of the campgrounds, as gangs of "toughs" occasionally rode into a camp to have a good time and often broke up the meeting for the day. The one big tent, in which services were held, was flanked by smaller living tents, in which the regular work of housekeeping was carried on. Sometimes half a dozen ministers preached at different hours of the day or week, and sometimes three or four sermons a day, or more, were delivered. And they were sermons from an hour to two hours in duration, through which the older people sat at attention. The boys and girls often managed to slip away, and indulged in the sinful pleasures of wading in the creek, hunting birds' nests and eating wild berries until the meeting was dismissed for dinner, when they were certain to be on hand. Often families drove forty miles in their covered wagons, carrying tents and bedding and other supplies, to attend a camp meeting. It was a season of refreshment—though not always of the spirit—to all who attended.

Preaching services and Sunday School in the prairie schoolhouses were a sort of social clearing house, where the people of the community met once a week, went with one another to dinner and to spend the remainder of the day, and there might, perhaps, be no further social intercourse until the next Sunday. The literary[1] societies and spelling schools, singing schools and sometimes writing schools and magic lantern shows during the winter were favorite forms of recreation— more social, it has been charged by a later generation, than cultural. Those who danced enjoyed this world-old pastime, often at the homes of some of the dancers, while those whose training and belief taught them that the dance hall was the road to ruin, looked ask-

[1] "A very successful lyceum is maintained in the new city this winter," says the News in an issue in 1859.

ance at such pleasures. However, the straight-laced fathers and mothers who were convinced that the devil lurked in every fiddle, allowed their children to play "party games," which are no more and no less than dancing, in which the feet move to the rhythm of untrained voices which sing lustily of "Marching Down To Old Quebec," "Jersey Boys," "Skip to My Loo," and dozens of other "harmless plays," while the regular dancers moved to the droning of a fiddle whose player might be equally untrained—and saved their breath.

Authors and dominoes in the sixties, seventies and eighties, rook and crokinole and parchesi in the nineties and the first decade of the present century, took the place of the "re-galer cyards," condemned by an old-time minister. Those who played cards were foredoomed to destruction along with those who danced to fiddle tunes. The violin and the pack of cards were looked upon as instruments of evil by men and women who, sincere and earnest in their belief, sought in every way possible to banish these forms of entertainment. Along about 1900 a group of young Emporia married couples, mostly members of the Methodist Church, formed a club whose avowed object was to entertain the members without resorting to card games. They played rook and parchesi and crokinole and the club flourished several years. There is no doubt that, today, most of these men and women play the "regular card" games. Church members today dance and play cards without thought of the harm their forbears were certain lurked in these diversions.

Horse racing at the county fairs was condemned by some of the straight-laced people, who attended the fairs and got their pleasure in looking at the exhibits and visiting with their friends. Many men and women no more would have watched the races than they would have cut off their right hands. It was the same with circuses—many persons were first on the streets in the morning to get good places from which to see the parade, but would not contaminate themselves by paying their money and going inside the big tent. Bicycle races became popular in the nineties, and the old highwheelers often were used on the track of the old fair grounds west of town. A race of the nineties is recalled when the bicycle riders started at Sixth and Commercial to ride the four miles around the original town site—and there were no pavements, and this was before the day of the road drag. Some of the riders fell out by the wayside, some made the entire trip, and these were acclaimed as heroes by the crowd assembled at the starting place, which awaited their return. Croquet, lately revived, was a favorite outdoor diversion, and the young people would play Sunday afternoons, to the scandal of their Sabbath-keeping elders.

Buffalo hunting was a popular sport in the first three decades of the life of the town, organized groups going perhaps two or three counties west and sometimes bringing home several carcasses. Many buffaloes were roaming the prairie in the vicinity of the Walnut and the Arkansas Rivers, which could be reached in a hard day's drive from Emporia. Buffalo meat was frequently on the tables in those days. Early members of the First Presbyterian Church used to tell of a buffalo hunt by the men of the congregation as a means of raising money to meet the church budget. They sold enough buffalo meat that, with the money obtained from the sale of the hides to be made into robes, they realized more than the sum they started out to raise.

The old skating rink at Eighth and Commercial— the site now of a filling station—later located in the old Tanner building on Merchant between Sixth and Seventh, was a popular playground for the young people. Flat Rocks, three miles southeast of Emporia on the banks of the Cottonwood, was a favorite picnicking ground for old and young. Added to its desirability in every other way, it is near town, and in the horse-and-buggy days always distance must be considered. Soden's Grove, on the Cottonwood, and Bruner's, on the Neosho, were standbys for picnickers. Chicken dinners and watermelon feeds, at the home of "Aunt Martha" Wright, east of town, were social events of importance, attended by surrey-loads or hay-wagon loads of young people, and by their elders. Swimming and ice skating on the rivers added to the gayeties of the boys and girls.

Singing schools, from the earliest days of the town, were well attended, and were enjoyed and appreciated. Boys and girls and men and women, who had had no such opportunities before, learned a little real music, which ever after was a joy and satisfaction to them. Mrs. G. W. Newman recalls Mrs. A. G. Proctor and Mrs. Dudley Haskell as two of the early-day music teachers, probably the first in town. Later were Mrs. Wyatt Clarke, Mrs. Emma Jones, Mrs. Noyes Spicer and Mr. Stimson. In dozens of country schoolhouses singing schools were taught on winter evenings, and many of those in attendance there received their only instruction in music.

The Welsh settlers, almost all of them singers, added much to the musical life of Emporia. They organized music clubs, and in state music contests for years they took all the prizes until, finally, they were barred from entering the contests, that others might have opportunity to win. The late Thomas H. Lewis, for more than fifty years leader of the choir of the Second Presbyterian Church, received many honors from music organizations outside Emporia.

The music festivals put on annually by the State Teachers College and the College of Emporia are among the important musical events of the year, and are attended by hundreds of persons outside Emporia and Lyon County. The town, from its first early efforts, has advanced steadily in musical culture, until it stands second to none in the State.

Street band concerts, in the early and middle life of the town, were interesting and entertaining, though not particularly cultural. The proprietors of traveling medicine wagons used to hold forth on the street corners, often carrying shows of a sort, sometimes giving concerts which thrilled the youngsters. An Emporia woman who grew up in the halcyon days says the Wizard Oil concerts were the best of these shows, that young and old turned out to them, and that they were real social events.

Baseball is a favorite diversion of Emporia people. The two State schools, Teachers College and the College of Emporia, each year bring many games to the schools' athletic fields. The most important sport event of the year is the annual Thanksgiving football game between the colleges, which attracts people from all parts of the State and from other States, as well as at least half of the population of the town. These games are played alternately on the two gridirons, and never fail in their interest to the friends of both schools, as well as to the schools themselves. The Emporia High School has had many winning teams in baseball and football. There are town teams which play out-of-town teams, on their home fields and in other towns.

The Country Club, situated on the most beautiful

location in the county, overlooking the Neosho Valley, provides a great deal of indoor entertaining, and its golf links have many devotees. The municipal golf links, in Dryer Park, also are popular, and golf has become a favorite sport for hundreds of Emporia men and women.

Today the city owns Soden's Grove, the most beautiful natural picnic ground in the State, which throughout all the years of its ownership by the Sodens, was open for the free use of Emporia and Lyon County people. Always it has been a delightful place, and with the city's improvements, will be more and more desirable. Dryer Park, also city property, a part of the waterworks tract, provides ample room for dozens of small picnic parties at the same time. [1]Peter Pan Park of fifty acres, extending from Congress and Kansas Avenue west to Neosho Street, then jogging up to Randolph Avenue, and south across the Cottonwood, when improvements are completed, will afford playground for hundreds of children. Emporia's two city parks, a block each, Fremont in the Second Ward and Humboldt in the Third, are well kept up, are all-the-year beauty spots, and band concerts are held in them alternate Friday nights during the summer and autumn months.

[1]Peter Pan Park was a gift to the city from Mr. and Mrs. W. A. White, as a memorial to their daughter, Mary, who died May 14, 1921, the result of a blow on the head from an overhanging limb of a large tree, when the horse she was riding turned unexpectedly into a parking. The rest room for colored girls, at the Senior High School, also was fitted up in Mary White's memory by her father and mother.

CHANGING CONDITIONS

With the increase in the price of labor has come better living conditions and larger cultural opportunities for all of the people. In 1890, of the twenty thousand inhabitants of Emporia and Lyon County, only about twelve hundred subscribed to the two daily and three weekly newspapers in Emporia—the Gazette, the Republican and the Tidings, later the Times. Few farmers read daily newspapers, and there were but a few hundred subscribers to the dailies in the smaller towns of the county. The Emporia Free Library was housed in a small room in a business building, the libraries of the College of Emporia and the State Normal School found ample space in rooms in the administration buildings, and comparatively few books and magazines were read by the farmers and their families and other working people. Rural free delivery of mail, established in 1900, put the daily newspaper in reach of the farmers, and the large majority of them are, and have been for many years, readers of the dailies. The telephone is valuable in the spread of information, and is a convenience in a thousand ways.

The telephone, rural mail delivery and the traveling library have dispelled the loneliness of the farm, and the automobile has put farmer families within easy reach of all public entertainments and lectures and shows that come to Emporia, or to other nearby towns. The rate of increase in the attainment of general knowledge—not in native intelligence—in the past twenty-five years has been so great that it would be considered phenomenal were it possible to put such an intangible thing into facts and figures. The radio is an every-day convenience and pleasure in many farmhouses, as well as in the towns. Labor-saving machinery and gasoline and oil cookstoves in the farmhouses have eliminated much of the drudgery for the farm women—and the everlasting problem of whether or not enough wood is split to get dinner or to finish the ironing—and they have more time for pleasurable and intellectual pursuits.

In Lyon County outside of Emporia, forty or more clubs are attended every week, or every two weeks, by 700 to 800 farm women.[2] The products of the farm have increased in value and in quality—the farm woman reads her poultry and dairy journals, and she and her customers profit thereby. Pure-bred poultry brings much more money than the small, rangy, hit-or-miss stock of the earlier days. Eggs are uniform in size and color, unlike the twelve sizes and tints to the dozen of the mongrel flock. The cream check at the end of the week takes the place of the groceries the farm woman formerly was compelled to take in exchange for her butter, which often she made from cream kept without ice or a good cellar, under the most trying conditions. She drives the family car, and waits for no man to hitch up the team when she is ready to come to town. She meets the women of the town on the basis of their mutual interests in the home and school, the church and clubs and politics, and no longer is looked down on by the self-styled "superior" women of the town. There are, fortunately, few "superior" women in Emporia, and they count for little. The advantages of some women have been greater than those of others, but they, too, meet on the basis of their mutual interests.

The men's service clubs—the Rotary, Lions, Kiwanis, Cooperative, and others, are actively interested in the civic and moral welfare of the town, and assist materially in the development of its high standards. Also, half a dozen or more men's study clubs add to the cultural tone of this community.

The Welfare Association, housed in a beautiful

$10,000.00 building, a gift to the city by Mrs. Margaret Warren, an Emporia woman, functions every day of the year. Its capable superintendent, Mrs. Margaret Randolph, looks after the needy, both resident and transient, maintains a labor bureau, and administers money and supplies and the "milk of human kindness" to the best possible advantage. A twice-a-week market is held at the Welfare Association grounds during the summer and autumn months, at which products fresh from the farm are sold to Emporia householders. The Good Fellows, at the Christmas season, assure every child in Emporia a full stocking, and every family a real Christmas dinner.

Much building is in progress in Emporia, and has been since the close of the World War. Residences are noticeable for their small size, compared to those of an earlier date. Several reasons are apparent for the change in taste regarding large residences. The rising wage of men and women has set so high a price on domestic service as to make it almost prohibitive to the average family which, in the eighties and nineties, always kept "help." Now, with wages for a girl in the kitchen doubled and trebled and more, with yard men getting 50 cents an hour, people have cut down on the amount of work to be done in the maintenance of comfortable homes. The house is smaller—just large enough for the family, in some houses one guest room, in many more no guest room, but a davenport in the livingroom which may serve as a bed.

Labor-saving devices have helped to make it possible for the woman in the ordinary home to do her own housework and, in many instances, her laundry work as well. Electricity, the great emancipator for women, does the washing and ironing easily, the electric sweeper has robbed cleaning day of its terrors, electric table appliances—toasters and percolators and waffle-irons, and grills on which an entire meal may be cooked—are in everyday use by families who would not consider hiring help with the housework. Rugs, taking the place of the heavy, nailed-down carpets of the Victorian era, are clean all the year round by the use of the electric sweeper, instead of one or two days' hard labor beating the life out of them, and using them dusty and soiled at least three-fourths of the year. Gas and electric and oil and gasoline ranges have almost entirely superseded the coal and wood range and cookstove.

Almost every family has a refrigerator, and waste of food has been almost eliminated. Ice is reasonable in price, and many families use electric refrigerators. Electricity has scrapped the old oil lamps, and with them the hated daily job of filling and cleaning lamps and lamp chimneys. On farms which electricity has not reached, many substitutes are used, with reasonable satisfaction. Family washings are as different from those of the Nineteenth Century as though the clothing were worn by a different race of people. Clothing fabrics today are much easier to cleanse than those of an earlier period.

A summer outfit for a woman, in the Victorian era consisted, beginning at the skin, of a chemise of heavy bleached or unbleached muslin, reaching well below the knees; drawers, of the same fabric, with a band buttoned tight around the waist, also reaching below the knees. The heavy corset was covered by a corset cover of the same heavy muslin, fitted by darts and extending several inches below the waistline. These garments were heavily trimmed with lace or embroidery and often with rows and rows of fine, close tucks, making them heavier and warmer, and each time they were laundered were starched stiffly. Petticoats, two or three of them, flounced and embroidered and starched till they rattled as the wearer walked, of heavy bleached muslin, were hard to wash and hard to "do up," but if there was any difference, the muslin for petticoats was heavier than for other undergarments, as there must be no possibility of "seeing through" one's petticoats. No woman could have suffered greater humiliation than to have worn few enough petticoats that she could be "seen through."

Over all of this tight and airless armor might be worn any kind of dress, but the waists of even the alleged cool summer dresses often were heavily stayed. No silk or wool dress ever was made up without stays of heavy boning in each of the six or eight darts in the tight waist, sewed to the inside of the seams formed by the dress material and its heavy lining.

At some periods, added to the skirt lining was another lining of crinoline extending upward half way or more from the bottom of the skirt, which was edged with heavy wool binding. For a few years these bindings took the form of tiny ruffles of wool braid, which came ready-made, and were excellent dust-catchers. At the time large sleeves were an important addition to real style in a woman's dress, the sleeve puffs were distended by crinoline, and many women were three feet across from the outer edge of their big sleeves. Tiny hats were skewered to the head by long or short hatpins, implements of torture. And in the first decade of the present century came the Merry Widow hats, described by an Emporia woman as "gigantic hats of tremendous proportions."

The hands, on almost every occasion, were encased in tight kid gloves, hot in summer and cold in winter. Women brave enough to wear silk gloves in hot weather were looked upon as having not quite the proper idea of what constituted good dressing. Shoes, at some periods, were of the toothpick toe variety, and about the same number of foolish women wore toothpick heels as today. An Emporia woman who always has dressed well says the first pair of five dollar shoes she owned were her wedding shoes, and that it was a long time till she was so extravagant again. Heavy cotton or lighter lisle hose were worn, and it is related that, when an Emporia man failed in business, the neighbors blamed his wife and daughter for his downfall. It was declared indignantly that Mrs. Blank and her daughter never wore anything cheaper than fifty-cent stockings, and how could it be expected that any man could prosper with such extravagance in his family?

In the Emporia Daily Republican in 1887 was advertised, with a cut illustrating it, a combined stool and bustle for women's wear. The skirts, distended at the back from waist to hem, contained ample space for an ordinary kitchen stool of light construction, on which ladies might rest, when shopping, when they no longer could endure the strain of their heavy clothing, and no other seat was available.

The muslin underwear sales, starting probably in the nineties, in the larger dry goods stores in Emporia, were looked forward to as an opportunity to stock up on all kinds of underwear for a year. These sales were instituted, of course, after ready-made garments for women were put on the market, and were almost in the nature of a society event. Prior to that time muslin for underwear was bought by the bolt, and much time was consumed in making and trimming these garments. Yards and yards of home-made lace and tatting adorned them, and making up a "set" of muslin underwear was a job of weeks. Time was when a bride must have "a dozen of everything" in underwear, and often the bride and her mother were worn out with sewing, weeks before work on the wedding gown and other outer garments was begun. There were dozen of dressmakers in Emporia forty years ago to one today. Ready-to-wear clothing was another step in women's emancipation. And furthermore, women who have time, and the least talent for sewing, easily can fashion their own dresses today, so simple are the styles and so plain the directions on the patterns.

The marriage of L. Levy, Guthrie, Oklahoma, to Miss Serena Goodhart, of Emporia, in 1892, was "the most elaborate and brilliant wedding ever chronicled in Emporia," according to the Republican. The ceremony was performed in the Whitley Hotel parlor, a rabbi coming from Kansas City to officiate, and was followed by what would be considered today a dinner so elaborate as not only to be wasteful and unnecessary, but an exhibition of bad taste. The remarkable menu was printed in the Republican, exactly as it appeared on the dinner card, and follows:

Blue points, bouillon in cups, roast turkey, cranberry sauce, roast duck with French peas, ox tongue with Monaco sauce, escalloped oysters, sardines a la imperial, quail, salmon salad, shrimp salad, lobster salad, Saratoga chips, asparagus, celery, radishes, chow-chow, olives, tipsy angel, Roman punch, charlotte russe, wedding cake, ambrosia, angel food cake, kisses, macaroons, bonbons, salted almonds, ice cream, bananas, oranges, Malaga grapes, Edam cheese, water crackers, coffee, tea, champagne, claret and Rhine wine.

The wedding party and the hundred guests sat at the table three hours, after having partaken of the Cup of Happiness, a Jewish marriage custom. The parents of the bride ordered and furnished, in addition to the lavish provisions made by the hotel, the wines and the elaborate flower decorations. After dinner, the dancing lasted all night. Mrs. Sadie Griffith, who lives at 415 West Fourth, was head cook at the Whitley at that time, and had charge of the preparations for the dinner, for which the hotel received three dollars a plate.

EARLY-DAY FUNERALS

Early-day funerals were different from those of to-day. During the first decade of the settlement of this State, and later, caskets were made by carpenters or cabinet makers, or anyone "handy with tools," and hearses were unknown. The death of a baby, which occurred in mid-winter in a neighborhood remote from town is recalled, when snow was drifted over the roads and getting about was difficult. One of the neighbors who "did a little carpentering" along with his farming, made a casket of rough pine boards he happened to have on hand. He had no paint nor varnish, so he covered the casket with black calico, donated by another neighbor who had it in the house. This carpenter-farmer, who also was what old-timers called "a one-horse preacher," conducted the simple funeral services for the baby at the home and at the grave. The tiny casket, draped with a sheet, was hauled to the bleak prairie "graveyard" in the only spring wagon in the settlement. There were no flowers, and the music was "Precious Jewels" and "Shall We Gather At the River?" sung by the assembled neighbors. The spring wagon referred to was a three-seated affair, and for years took the place of a hearse at many funerals in that neighborhood.

Often death came to families who had absolutely no proper apparel in which to lay away their dead, or for other members of the family to wear at the funeral. Two or three women of the neighborhood would work all day, and all night, if necessary, making a shroud for the corpse, and clothes for the family. Homemade coffins—they seldom were called caskets—were the only ones to be had, at first, because no stores carried such supplies. But many families, even after "store" caskets became of common use, could not afford to pay the price asked for them, and buried their dead in home-made coffins.

Dying, and being buried, fifty to seventy-five years ago, was a much less complicated and expensive proposition than it is today. If the family were extremely hard up, the carpenter who made the coffin charged only for the material he used, and nothing for his labor. "Neighbor women" nursed the sick, cooked for the family, cared for small children, often carrying their own food supplies from their homes. After it was all over, the men dug the grave, and all this was done with no thought of pay. The coffin was lowered into the grave with a pair of lines taken from the harness of one of the teams at the cemetery. The men who dug the grave filled it up, the family and friends standing in solemn silence until the last pat with a spade was given the new-made mound.

FLOURSACK DAYS

In the Country Gentleman of February 25, 1922, appeared an article under the above head, a part of which is printed below:

"Every once in so often someone bobs up with a new story about the use of floursacks. Especially has this been true with war prices on muslin the past few years. But the use of floursacks in Kansas for all sorts of household purposes is as old as the State itself. A few years ago a writer in a well-known magazine told the story of an Italian priest and what he did for a ramshackle Pennsylvania village of Italian slate-workers. The Italians worked for a miserable wage, the writer declared, and were desperately poor. . . . . . The writer, speaking of their dire poverty, said, in awe-stricken italics:

" 'Some idea of the petty economies they still practice is suggested by the fact that they buy their flour in cotton sacks—they won't take paper ones—and when the sacks are empty they wash them and save them up till they have six; then they sew them into a sheet!'

. . . . . . "The saving of floursacks, to be made into garments for every member of the family, was practiced by every careful housewife in the early days, and by many in more recent years. 'Factory,' sixty years ago, was as high in price as at any time during the World War, and even scarcer, and what was the use of paying out hard-earned 'butter'n egg money' for muslin, when floursacks answered every practical purpose?—provided there were enough of them.

"All of the children's summer underwear—waists and pants and petticoats for the little girls and shirts for the little boys—was made of floursacks. For handkerchiefs and dishtowels and diapers they were invaluable, and often were used in a pinch for hand-and-face towels, though most housewives preferred grain sacks. The entire layette of more than one Lyon County baby was made of floursacks. When the backs of men's vests wore out they were replaced with floursacks. . . . . . .

"Six floursacks sewed together made a good tablecloth, as well as a good sheet. Also, six floursacks sewed together make excellent comfort tops and linings. Often these were colored with dye made from sumach berries or walnut hulls. Quilt linings were made of six floursacks sewed together, and there are quilts with floursack linings in many Lyon County homes today. . . . . . .

"There is no limit to the uses of the humble floursack. It stands in the history of pioneer days alongside the despised but couldn't-have-get-along-without-it sorghum, the home-made hominy, the sowbelly, the dried wild grapes and plums, and the hard, bitter, sour wild gooseberries, and the corn bread that made the coming of the floursack not half often enough for the pioneer housewife."

In more recent years, many women dye floursacks with commercial dyes in bright, pretty shades, and make them into lovely dresses for their children. It is highly improbable that a floursack ever went to waste in Lyon County.

EMPORIA BANDS

The first band in Emporia was the Hall Brothers' Silver Cornet Band, organized by four early settlers, Samuel, Thomas, James and Joseph Hall, though they were best known as Sam, Tom, Jim and Joe. They came to Emporia in 1858. For years the Halls played on all festive occasions, and their music was much in demand. They ran a music store in Emporia for three or four decades. In 1866 another and more pretentious band was organized, and three of the Hall boys were among its members. The members were George Waite, J. R. Hall, A. R. Bancroft, Thomas Manter, Max Fawcett, Thomas Hall, Samuel Hall, Ezra Trask, Horace Bundrem, John Bay, J. T. Pierson and H. C. Clark.

The Knights Templar Band, sponsored by Emporia Commandery No. 8, Knights Templar, was known all over the United States as one of the leading bands of the country, and kept up its good work for many years. It was generous with its service to the community, and turned out, without money and without price, when the town needed its help. It was organized in the seventies by T. C. Davidson, a member of the Commandery who was interested in band music and knew how to teach it. The Commandery bought the band uniforms and instruments, and paid most of its bills. Mr. Davidson played one of the instruments, and kept all the members up to a high state of efficiency. Charlie Holmes played a tenor horn, and Charlie Hibben the big bass drum. Charles Cleaver recalls young Hibben particularly as he was more than six feet tall and only about six inches thick.

When former President Grant visited Emporia, July 5, 1880, the Emporia Knights Templar, with its band, was asked to head the parade, and its members scoured the country to find black horses enough for the event. Then the Grand Commandery, because General Grant was not a Templar, refused permission for the Emporia Commandery to appear in the parade, as Knights Templar turn out only when the occasion is Masonic in nature. Winking the other eye, Dr. L. D. Jacobs, eminent commander of No. 8, asked permission from the Grand Commandery for No. 8 to hold a picnic and reunion of its members on the fifth of July, and permission was granted.

About the time the Grant parade was forming on Commercial Street, for the review by the General before marching to the Grove, Commandery No. 8, headed by its band, also appeared, ostensibly on the way to its own picnic. But, somehow, the band and the Commandery got in line and the rest of the Grant parade dropped in behind it, and the Knights Templar Band and Commandery No. 8 led the procession.

When the band and the Commandery passed the General's carriage the old war horse arose and stood with uncovered head as they went by. He told one of the men in the carriage with him that he had traveled around the world, that all sorts of honors had been paid him, but this was the first time he had been honored by the Templars. When this was repeated to Emporia Commandery, the members declared they didn't care what might be the outcome of their disobedience.

Later, an official high in the Grand Commandery was sent to Emporia to investigate this act of rank insubordination, and after considerable discussion he informed No. 8 that its officers would be suspended, but that the Grand Commandery felt that the band must go to Chicago to attend the Grand Encampment, so the Emporia Templars were invited to join in with the Topeka Commandery and go as a part of that body. Not a man would go to Chicago under such conditions, and told the high official so, and said if the officers were suspended the members must be also, as all were equally guilty. And they let it be known that they didn't feel so terribly guilty, at that, as they felt they had been justified in honoring the greatest man of his time. They ended with, "If anyone is suspended, all must be."

The result was the Emporia Commandery attended the grand encampment in Chicago, and took the band along. It attracted more attention than any other band, with headquarters at the Palmer House. The band played in the lobby, where a band leader from New York refused to leave while the band was playing, as his companion wished to do, saying, "See here, you go on and tell them I will be there later. You should know me well enough to know that, so long as that band will play, that long will I be here listening. I did not know Kansas could get up anything like that, and I take off my hat to them."

At a meeting following the grand encampment, the Grand Commandery again took up the matter of the Emporia Commandery's disobedience. Finally it was suggested that the whole thing be dropped, and the story of No. 8's insubordination was expunged from the records. No. 8 has grown from its original twelve members to nine hundred.

C. L. Dickerson, piano tuner and band man, was leader of the Emporia band several years immediately preceding M. C. Grady. Dickerson was the promoter of the All-Stars Minstrels, an Emporia organization which played in Emporia and surrounding towns the winter of 1895-1896. Among the Dickerson band men were Harry McConnel, John Craig and Will Keefer, all of whom live in Emporia; Frank Tyler, Hutchinson; Clifford Hillerman, and Ed Malloy, head of the music department of the State Teachers College at Hays. The Dickerson family consisted of Mr. and Mrs. Dickerson and daughter, Freda. They have lived for years in Topeka.

Much of the time during the past thirty years a

municipal band has been maintained, the town providing partially for its support. Sometimes the band has been a regimental organization of the State Militia. Marcellus C. Grady, who came to Emporia in the early nineties, was leader of the Emporia band for years, and probably did more for the advancement of band music than any other one Emporia man. Not only did he manage and teach the regular band, but always he had a "kid" band in training, and he gave much valuable instruction to scores of the boys and young men of the town. As the boys grew up they filled vacancies in the regular band or, if they left town, they were equipped to join a band wherever they might locate. Since Mr. Grady's death[1] the town band has had various leaders. Every Friday night, from May to October, free band concerts are given in the town's two small parks, alternately, and the large crowds that attend attest their popularity.

The town band has been ready at all times to play on public occasions, and has merited the support given by the town and by private citizens. The Emporia Municipal Band of thirty-seven members, Ora G. Rindom, manager, and Dale Stinson, leader, took first place in Class A competition at the Kansas State Fair in Topeka, 1929. The personnel of this band and the One Hundred Sixty-first Field Artillery Band are almost identical, and both receive the benefit of Federal and State support, part of which consists of two weeks' encampment each year, all in addition to the assistance given by the City of Emporia.

In 1907 Ora Rindom, then a student at the State

[1] In November, 1921, Mr. Grady was caught in a moving elevator while in Kansas City with his band attending a convention of the American Legion. His body was so badly crushed that he died a month later.

Normal School, organized a twelve-piece band which played for the pep rallies, football games, and the usual school activities. In 1911 Marcellus Grady, former director of the Emporia Municipal Band, took charge and continued with this work until 1913 when another student, Albert Weatherly—now director of instrumental work at Tulsa, Oklahoma—continued with the band work until 1915 when Dale Stinson, a student, now director of the Emporia Municipal Band, took over the work of Weatherly. In 1916 Mr. Grady again resumed the work with the band and continued with this work until the time of his death. For several years the school was without a band. In 1922 C. W. Janssen was employed to take charge of the band work. In addition to a band an instrumental course was formulated for the purpose of preparing teachers to organize and supervise instrumental work in the city schools. At this time the school purchased a number of instruments and the band uniforms. Mr. Janssen continued with the work until the summer of 1925 when Forrest L. Buchtel, the present band and orchestra director, came to Emporia.

Under Mr. Buchtel's leadership the band has grown to an organization of sixty players, with complete instrumentation. The band rehearses daily and their prime motive is, not to learn a few marches to be played at football games, but to acquaint students with the best band literature. Additional instruments and uniforms have been purchased each year and almost the entire third floor of Music Hall is given over to the instrumental work. Specially constructed rooms care for a large library of band music and the housing of the instruments and uniforms. A rehearsal room extends the full length of the third floor.

Through the superior work done along this line students have been attracted to the Teachers College from many States. The present band numbers students from Wisconsin, Michigan, New Mexico, Oklahoma, Missouri, and Iowa. Many girls are interested in band work and the present band includes fifteen girls.

The band in 1928 accompanied the football team to Kansas City and to Washburn. This year it went to Lawrence for the football game, and to Topeka for the Washburn game.

At the time Sousa's band played in Emporia, Mr. Sousa gave the Teachers College Band high praise and remarked that it was the first time in his career that he had heard an amateur drummer who actually interested him.

Forrest L. Buchtel, the director, played in the band during his high school days and during his four years of college work directed his college band. Before coming to Emporia Mr. Buchtel had charge of the instrumental work at Grand Rapids, Michigan.

IN THE PUBLIC EYE

LYON COUNTY NEWSPAPERS

Emporia's first newspaper, the Kanzas News, its first issue printed June 6, 1857, became the Emporia News in 1859. For many years it was one of the most widely circulated, popular and influential Republican newspapers in the State. Jacob Stotler, after his purchase of the News from its founder, Preston B. Plumb, January 29, 1859, ran it alone until 1870, when J. R. Graham and E. E. Rowland each bought an interest in it. The News became a Daily September 22, 1870, but the Daily was discontinued August 8, 1871. The Weekly became so prosperous and so popular that, in 1878, again a Daily was launched. In 1879 Graham and Rowland sold their interests to Alex Butts and Frank P. MacLennan. In 1884, Butts went to Kansas City and became an editorial writer of power and prominence on the Kansas City Star, working on that paper until his death. MacLennan[1] stayed with the

[1] When Frank MacLennan left the Emporia News he "stood not upon the order of his going," according to a story he related to a group of newspaper people a few years ago. In 1885 the late Col. H. C. Whitley had acquired a controlling interest in the News. The Colonel, in view of the fact that one State educational institution was located in Emporia, felt there was no room for another, so had opposed the founding of the College of Emporia. But the College had been founded without the aid of the Colonel or the support of the News. Frank MacLennan, part owner of the News and its managing editor, had been instructed by the Colonel to run nothing in the News that would be of assistance to the College. The Rev. Robert M. Overstreet who, more than any other one man, was responsible for the location of the College in Em-

News until 1885, when he bought the Topeka State Journal, which ever since he has owned and controlled. A. B. Newcomb then became editor of the News, and in 1889 the News business and plant were sold to the Emporia Republican, and the consolidation of the two papers was effected April 30, 1890.

The Republican, established in 1880 by former Lieut. Gov. C. V. Eskridge, as its editor and owner, had been a morning paper until its consolidation with the News, when it took over the afternoon field. The three-story building on West Sixth, owned by the Carters, was the home of the Republican until after the failure of the First National Bank, in 1898. Then the Republican built the first story of the White Eagle garage building, at Eighth and Commercial.

Following the death of Eskridge in 1900 his son, Edward,[2] and his daughter, Mattie, continued to run the Republican until they sold it a few years later to Albert Strong, who after running the paper a year or

---

poria, one day brought to the News office a long story concerning the College and its needs—and Frank MacLennan ran it in the paper. The result was that MacLennan hastily sold his interest in the News to Colonel Whitley, and found himself out of a job and a business. MacLennan told his troubles to Mr. Overstreet, who assured him the Colonel had done him a favor when he fired him from the News. Mr. Overstreet felt MacLennan could do better in a larger town, and advised him to go to Topeka. He went, bought the State Journal at sheriff's sale, waded into the work, and was successful from the start. Years ago he refused an offer of $500,000.00 for the State Journal. And later, Romance stepped in. MacLennan and the Overstreet young people had been friends in Emporia, and through the years a pleasant acquaintance had been maintained. A few years ago, long after the death of Mrs. Anna Goddard MacLennan, Frank MacLennan was married to a daughter of the Overstreets—Mrs. Madge Overstreet Wright, widow of Lee R. Wright. Mr. and Mrs. MacLennan live happily in Topeka.

[2]Edward Eskridge, the only surviving member of the Eskridge family, lives in Arizona. Mrs. C. V. Eskridge died in Pasadena, Calif., in 1928, surviving by several years her daughters, Clara, Mezzie and Mattie. The old Eskridge home, built in 1878 at a

two, sold it to William Stahl. Finally, the plant was dismantled and the equipment sold in lots to various printing offices.

The Emporia Gazette was founded in 1890 by J. R. Graham, who had been one of the owners of the News, and later had been connected with the Republican. The first issue of the Gazette was printed in August of that year, with Mr. Graham as its editor and H. F. Lincoln, business manager. W. Y. Morgan, of Cottonwood Falls, bought the Gazette from Graham, and in 1895 Morgan passed it on to William Allen White. Mr. White relates the story of his purchase of the Gazette, as follows: He paid $3,000.00, borrowed money, for the paper. He borrowed $1,000.00 from Gov. E. N. Morrill, the same amount from the P. B. Plumb estate, $700.00 from Major Calvin Hood, and $300.00 from George Plumb, all secured by bankable notes. Asked how he came to be on borrowing terms with Governor Morrill he explained that, during a part of Morrill's term as governor, he had been State House reporter for the Kansas City Star. He had become well acquainted with the Governor, who evidently considered him a safe risk.

"I paid off the thousand to the Plumb estate," says Mr. White, "with the profits from my first book, 'The Real Issue,' published in 1896. The Morrill note and the Hood note I met after the publication of 'The Court of Boyville.' The $300.00 I owed George Plumb I paid with Gazette earnings, and most of it was cleaned up by 1900. That year the Gazette moved from rented

---

cost of $13,000.00, one of the handsomest residences in town for many years, with the real estate attached to it, was sold under protest to the State for use of Teachers College. The house was used as classrooms for the music department until the erection of Music Hall, and in 1929 was razed.

quarters on East Sixth to its own building in its present location, next door to the post office, and again I had gone into debt. That has been my policy—to keep in debt, as an incentive to keep at work, to keep down my natural habit of laziness."

The Gazette building has been remodeled and enlarged several times since 1900, and the plant is worth easily a quarter million. Its subscription list in 1895 was 450, today it is 7,300.

The Emporia Times, the oldest newspaper in Emporia, is the lineal descendent of the Allen Tidings, established in 1887 by the late Major Paul. Mr. Paul moved his newspaper to Emporia in 1891, retaining the name Tidings. In 1895 he sold it to P. F. Yearout and Marshall Starr. Yearout had just closed two terms as superintendent of the Greenwood County schools, and Marshall Starr had been for two terms clerk of the court for the Chase-Lyon-Coffey County District, both having been elected to office on the Populist ticket. They changed the name of the paper to the Times, and made of it a straight Democrat paper, the Populist party being on the decline about this time. Within a year, Starr sold his interest to Yearout, and moved to Colorado. In 1900, Yearout bought the Democratic Record from Semper Bucher, and combined the two papers. Yearout ran the Times successfully until 1906, when he sold it to W. T. Dungan, who had been associated with Yearout in the publication of the Times. In 1907, Dungan sold the Times to Harrison Parkman who continued to run it as a Democrat paper. In May, 1920, Parkman sold the paper to P. R. Kellar, of Chicago. Its next owner was H. G. James, of Independence, the next was Keith Fanshier, and the next its present owner and editor, Theodore

Morse. Always it has been the standard bearer for the Democratic party.

The Emporia Sentinel was established by J. A. Hetherington, who sold it in 1882 to J. M. McCown, who changed its name to the Democrat. Mr. McCown ran this paper ten years, part of the time as a Daily, and sold it to E. L. Turner, who sold it to the Republican, which about that time had bought several papers, among them the Dunlap Chief. Semper Bucher ran an Emporia Democrat—in no way related to the Democrat conducted by McCown—a few years. Edgar Martindale, a nephew of the late William Martindale, started the Emporia Daily Journal, which he sold to F. S. Mickey.

The Emporia Ledger was established in 1871 by Judge Robert M. Ruggles, later sold to the Emporia Printing & Publishing Company, composed of J. R. Graham and H. W. McCune. It was Democratic in politics, and supported Greeley for President. The Globe also flourished for a time. The Sun, whose editor was J. M. Davis, and the Greenbacker, by Spangler & Trask, were other newspaper ventures of the seventies. The Tribune was established October 7, 1869, Main & Nixon, editors. The Tribune was absorbed by the News in 1871. The Columbian was a paper printed in the Welsh language for the benefit of the Welsh people who had not yet learned the English language. It ran for several years in the eighties.

Many newspapers have come and gone in Emporia, as in other Kansas towns, most of which of the size of Emporia have had at times three or four dailies. Now, with a larger and more exacting clientele, the people are much more ably served by one daily. An Emporia newspaper directory for 1929 would read about as follows:

College Life, College of Emporia, established 1900, student editors.
Emporia Gazette, 1890, subscriptions 7,300, W. A White, editor.
Emporia Times, 1887, Theodore Morse, editor.
Kansas Farm Journal, subscriptions 22,000, Ralph Snyder, editor.
Kansas Federation Magazine, 1922, subscriptions 14,000.
Kansas State Teachers College Bulletin, 1900, student editors.
Lyon County Farm Bureau News, 1920, Carl Howard, editor.

Lyon County newspapers outside Emporia are the Americus Greeting, founded in 1900, of which D. C. Grinell for many years was the editor. Mr. Grinell's paragraphs were quoted all over Kansas and outside the State, and brought recognition seldom accorded a small country town newspaper. He turned over the paper several years ago to his son, Clarence Grinell, who is its editor and publisher.

The Sentinel was the first newspaper in Americus, started in 1859 by Robert M. Ruggles and T. C. Hill. It ceased publication many years ago.

The Olpe Optimist, founded in 1906, is one of a string of small-town newspapers owned, edited and published by Lawrence M. Shearer. Mr. Shearer's office is in Emporia, from which all of his papers are sent out.

D. S. (Bud) Gilmore, who was born and brought up and learned the printer's trade in Emporia, is editor and owner of the North Lyon County Journal, at Allen, the paper having been founded in 1900. This is the largest and best equipped newspaper office in Lyon County outside Emporia, and the largest paper. It covers the territory for four towns—Allen, Admire, Bushong and Miller—and is an important factor in the northern part of the county.

The Hartford Times has been ably edited and published by A. S. Bernheisel since 1905. It is as much a necessity to Hartford as its school buildings and churches, and admirably fills the needs of the town. The Hartford Call, whose editor was the late W. J. (Billy) Means, was the predecessor of the Times, and was the purveyor of news for Hartford and Elmendaro Township for several years.

The Reading Herald, Leslie Fitts, proprietor, was established June 22, 1908, by Eaton & Halstrom. Eaton continued in the business but a short time, and A. M. Hawks purchased the paper from Halstrom in 1909. Leslie Fitts bought it from Halstrom July 30, 1913. Mr. Fitts relates his first experience in getting out the paper, as follows: "The week's issue was partly printed when I took charge of the paper. I faced the proposition of getting out the paper for the week, finding another location and moving by the next night, so the post office could move, August 1, into the building I vacated. Dr. D. S. Fisher's office was in the building now occupied by the Herald, and he moved from it to the building the post office was vacating. I found temporary quarters for the Herald, moved, then the post office moved, then Doctor Fisher moved, then the Herald moved again. Neither the Herald, the post office, nor Doctor Fisher has moved again."

Mr. Fitts left the Herald and went to work for the Lawrence Journal-World October 1, 1913, and did not return until May, 1919. His father, the late Daley Fitts, his mother and brothers and sisters, got out the Herald each week. "After my return," says Mr. Fitts, "my father continued to be the guiding hand on the Herald until his death in September, 1925. Since then my mother, Mrs. Mary E. Fitts, has taken his place." Mr. Fitts has been postmaster at Reading since January 1, 1922. He owns the Herald Plant and building, and employs one man, James Price, in the shop. Leslie Fitts is a World War veteran.

Reading's first newspaper was the Advance, its first copy appearing May 27, 1893, editor, Samuel Johnson. In 1894 S. H. Stratton was editor and publisher of the Advance, and the paper was discontinued in 1895. The Reading Record was short-lived—February 25-December 30, 1898. The Reading Recorder was established January 13, 1900, by Austin A. Torrance. He ran it in Reading until 1908, then moved the plant to Lebo.

POLITICS AND POLITICIANS

Politically, Lyon County and Emporia have enjoyed variety. The Republican party, usually in the lead, has been compelled on numerous occasions to give way to other parties. In the early seventies, the Greenbackers caused the Republicans much uneasiness, and in 1873 the farmers nominated the only ticket in the field for the county election. For a majority of the offices there were two, and sometimes three nominees. The Union Labor party in the eighties gave the Republicans another bad turn, and when, in the nineties, the Populists elected county officers and members for the legislative and judicial districts, and helped to elect a couple of governors of the State, a United States senator and congressman, the Republicans were convinced that Lyon County had gone to the dogs. The Bull Moosers, the first decade and a half of the present century, again caused the Republicans to squirm, and kept them busy, after several elections, as had the Populists, explaining how and why, in a "county normally Republican," it was possible for any other party to win a victory.

But the real how and why is that Lyon County people exercise their God-given right to vote as they please, to split their tickets at any time they wish to do so, and to bolt their party if they choose. In a "county normally Republican," no doubt it is good for the souls of members of all parties that no party is continuously triumphant, but that each must keep "on its toes" in an effort to escape the criticism of the other. Politics in Lyon County becomes each year more a pleasurable game and less a deadly serious proposition. Because, deep in his consciousness, each voter knows that, in all probability, the candidates of both parties are honest men and women, ready to do their duty by their friends and neighbors if elected to office.

Always the political reform movements and all parties in opposition to the Republicans have had as their leaders some of the strongest men in the county, who have put the best that was in them into the fight. Among the early-day Democrat leaders were Robert M. Ruggles,[1] appointed district judge in July, 1861,

[1] Robert M. Ruggles, attorney, settled first at Americus, where with T. C. Hill as publisher, he started the Americus Sentinel, and as its editor put up a hard but losing fight to retain the county seat at Americus. The Sentinel appeared first September 26, 1859. After the election of 1860, at which time by vote of the people, the county seat contest was decided in favor of Emporia, Judge Ruggles moved his law office to Emporia. Here he formed a partnership with P. B. Plumb, and the firm of Ruggles & Plumb became one of the ablest in the state. On the Ruggles farm, on the east side of the Americus road immediately south of the Ruggles bridge across the Neosho, Judge Ruggles bred registered Durham cattle, and Mrs. Ruggles—who was Susannah Spencer before her marriage—was considered as successful a cattle-raiser and as competent a judge of livestock qualities as was her husband. This farm long was one of the show places of the county. W. S. Ruggles, sr., of Emporia, is a son of Judge and Mrs. Ruggles.

to fill the place of Judge O. A. Learnard, who had enlisted in the Civil War. Ruggles was elected to this position at the general election in the autumn of that year. Perry B. Maxson was a state senator, elected in 1862 without opposition, and again in 1866 with but sixty-eight votes polled against him. He became an ardent Greenbacker in the seventies, and represented that party in the lower house of the State Legislature. When the Populist party grew out of the Farmers Alliance, Mr. Maxson took up that cause with all his old-time fervor. He was an able and conscientious man, firm in his convictions and ready to fight for them as long as he lived.

In 1871 and again in 1876 the Democrats elected E. B. Peyton as district judge, and he was a leading attorney in this county for many years. Levi Dumbauld, of Elmendaro Township, a successful farmer and stock-raiser, became a leader in the Populist uprising, and was elected by that party to the State Senate in 1892. He has lived for many years at Las Animas, Colo. William E. McCreary served the Populist party faithfully and well, without thought of personal reward. M. A. Coppock and J. V. Randolph were wheelhorses in every political reform movement. P. F. Yearout led the Populist party in Lyon County—and his influence extended over the State—from the date of his purchase of the Emporia Times in 1895, and after the dissolution of the Populist party, gave his personal influence and the influence of his paper to the Democrats until he sold the Times, in 1906.

R. T. Snedeker, of Hartford, a highly educated and able man, an adherent of Henry George, preached Single Tax in season and out of season for many years in Lyon County and over the State. He advocated other lines of political reforms, but Single Tax was his hobby. Hartford long was the Single Tax center for Kansas, and was known all over the United States for the devotion of its followers.

William C. Harris, Democrat, served three terms—twelve years—as district judge, having been elected in 1912, and twice reelected. W. M. Price, elected to the State Senate from the Lyon-Greenwood district in 1912, since that time has held the leadership of the Democrat party in this county and judicial district. Lon C. McCarty, who served three terms, 1916-1918-1920, as county attorney, in 1928 was elected district judge by a large majority. Many other Democrats and reform party men and women have held office in Lyon County.

In the Progressive movement of the early part of the present century, W. A. White was national committeeman for the Progressives, and among other leading Lyon County men of this political faith were J. H. Glotfelter and C. A. Stannard.

The foremost Republican of the first three and one-half decades in town and county was Preston B. Plumb who, after serving his community and State in numberless ways, and his country during the Civil War, in 1877 was elected to the United States Senate, holding that high office until his death in 1891. L. D. Bailey was elected an associate justice of the Kansas Supreme Court, one of the group at the first election under the Wyandotte Constitution. He was nominated at Osawatomie, at the convention which met to organize the Republican party in Kansas, to which Oliver Phillips, J. M. Rankin and David Swim were delegates from Lyon County.

Other early-day Republican leaders were Jacob

COLLEGE OF EMPORIA, 1929

Stotler, Charles V. Eskridge and E. P. Bancroft, all of whom represented their districts in both branches of the State Legislature, and Eskridge was elected lieutenant governor in 1868. Gov. Samuel J. Crawford[1] lived in Emporia in the sixties, and took an active part in Republican politics. William Martindale,[2] from the time he was elected a representative to the lower house of the Kansas Legislature in 1865, reelected in 1866, and later elected to the State Senate, for almost half a century was a power in county, district and State politics. Lyman B. Kellogg, following his great service to the State as president of the Normal School, in 1876 was elected a representative to the State Legislature, then served Lyon County three terms as probate judge and before the expiration of the third term, was elected to the State Senate. In 1888 he was elected attorney general of Kansas. I. E. Lambert, for twenty years preceding his death in 1913, was active in County and State politics, and wielded a wide influence. George Plumb has given, for many years, freely and unselfishly and without partisanship, of his time and talents for the good, not of his party, particularly, but of the people whom he served.

E. W. Cunningham in 1903 was appointed by Governor E. W. Stanley to a position on the Supreme Court bench of the State, an additional place in that body

[1]Samuel J. Crawford lived in Emporia at the time of his election as governor of Kansas, in 1865. The Crawford home was at Ninth and Union, the house built by the Crawfords having been for many years the home of the Samuel Hall family.

[2]William Martindale settled in Greenwood County, near Madison, in 1857, where until 1899 he owned the largest farm and cattle ranch in that county. He was interested in banking and milling, as well as in politics and ranching, and was known as one of the shrewdest stockmen and financiers in the State. The Martindales moved to Emporia in 1889, and the youngest son, Chester Martindale, with his family, lives in the home built by his father and mother at 811 Constitution.

having been created by the Legislature. Charles B. Graves, who was elected district judge in 1876, was appointed by Governor Stanley to fill the place made vacant by the death of Judge Cunningham. W. L. Huggins, in 1892 elected county superintendent of public instruction, served the community in this office two consecutive terms, then for twenty-two years practiced law in Emporia uninterruptedly. In 1919 he was appointed a member of the Kansas Public Utilities Commission by Governor Henry J. Allen, and a year later was appointed by Governor Allen as presiding judge of the Kansas Court of Industrial Relations.

James Evans, of Hartford, was one of the keenest-minded leaders of the Republican party in this county. For several decades he was high in its counsels, and his great regret in leaving Lyon County to live in California was that the move compelled him to give up his favorite diversion—politics in Kansas. He was appointed postmaster for Hartford about 1895, and held the office three consecutive terms. The fact that he was blind several years did not interfere with his political activities. He died at his home in Hollywood, Calif., a few years ago. Charles Johnson, of Hartford, was another Republican leader who could be depended upon to "vote 'er straight," or to render any other service in the interests of his party.

ORGANIZATIONS

WOMEN'S CITY CLUB

The Women's City Club of Emporia, with a membership of 1250 women listed in its Year Book for 1929-1930, has demonstrated more conclusively than any other one group or organization of this town, that so large an assemblage can work together harmoniously and effectively, without duplication, without dissension, as a collective body or in small gatherings, when actuated by the spirit of unselfish cooperation which makes possible the activities and the continued growth of this club.

According to the announcements of the Year Book, general meetings are held, as usual, the fourth Tuesday afternoon of each month, and departmental meetings on Mondays, all at the Broadview Hotel, from September until May. Entertaining programs and exhibits are offered by the departments of Art, American Home, and Citizenship. A regular line of study is carried on by the Bible department, which meets the second and fourth Friday afternoons of each month.

A new feature of the club this year is Extension Class Day. It provides a study section for the entire club and is open to all members. Beginning at 10 o'clock in the morning, there are almost continuous one-hour classes, and the member may take her choice or attend as many as she wishes. Music Appreciation, Legislation and International Relations, Child Health and Welfare, Sociology and Applied Psychology, Book Reviews and Literature, Current Topics Forum, Drama, and Travel and History, are featured.

The City Club sponsored, during 1928-1929, its art collection, community programs, maternity loan fund, high school loan fund, milk project, garment making for needy children, purchase of playground equipment, Christmas seal sale, better homes exposition, distribution of magazines, dental clinic, legislative activities, Americanization work, the city beautiful, and many social activities. More than one hundred meetings were held by its various departments in 1928-1929. Five hundred dollars' worth of milk was provided for under nourished school children the second term of the city schools, February to June, 1929.

The City Club was organized in 1918. Mrs. J. H. Wiggam was its first president. Following her were Mrs. H. G. Lull, Miss Laura French, Mrs. W. A. White, Mrs. R. L. Hershberger, Mrs. J. W. Mayberry, Mrs. E. A. Mitchell and Mrs. Harrison Parkman.

The Federation Magazine, authorized organ of the Kansas State Federation of Women's Clubs, is edited, printed and published in Emporia. It reaches every one of the 13,000 to 14,000 federated club women of Kansas, keeping them informed of club work over the entire state. Seven of the study clubs of Emporia are federated and one of the clubs of the Rural Association—Rinker Community Club—is a member of the State and District Federations.

COUNTY ASSOCIATION OF CLUBS

Eighteen individual clubs make up the Lyon County Association of Rural Clubs, with a membership of four hundred thirty. Many of these individual clubs hold a part, or all, if they wish, of their meetings in the Welfare Association Club rooms, and all of the meetings of the directors of the rural clubs are held there. These women have purchased a piano for this room, and extra chairs for seating it. Besides these clubs of the Rural Association are as many others, or more, in Lyon County which are not affiliated with the association, chiefly because of the distance from the place of meeting. A committee from the Rural Association the autumn of 1929 made a survey of these unaffiliated clubs, with a view to securing their membership and arranging for meetings in different parts of the county, which might make for the convenience of clubs at a considerable distance from Emporia.

Officers of the Rural Association, elected in 1929 are Mrs. Walter Ulm, president; Mrs. Homer Wamser, vice president; Miss Alice Watts, secretary; Mrs. William James, treasurer. Representatives from each club meet at the Welfare Club rooms once in two months for a directors' meeting. The 1929 representatives to the meetings of the Board of Directors are Mrs. William Brough, Grandview; Mrs. J. W. Newman, Lakeside Homemakers; Mrs. Edna Nicklin, Central Community; Mrs. Harry Phillips, Badger Creek Sewing Club; Mrs. W. P. Stanley, Swastika; Mrs. Charles Skinner, Rinker Community; Mrs. Martha Mackey, East Sixth Avenue; Mrs. John Butler, Ruggles; Mrs. Ray Hess, Sunshine; Mrs. B. F. Timmerman, Logan Avenue; Mrs. Ira Jones, Sardis; Mrs. S. S. Jenkins, Rosean; Miss Alice Watts, Salem;

Mrs. Ed Sielert, Plymouth; Mrs. Charles Yost, Happy Hour; Mrs. J. W. Jenkins, Lyndon Valley; Mrs. John Gilbert, Zion Community; Mrs. Charles Loomis, Lang.

Seven clubs of the Association meet once each month, the others twice a month. The presidents of the clubs for 1929 are: Mrs. Ray Cooley, Grandview; Mrs. Tom Price, Lakeside Homemakers; Mrs. Earl DeLong, Central Community; Mrs. T. H. Rush, Badger Creek; Mrs. A. B. Whipple, Swastika; Mrs. Earl Hollingsworth, Rinker Community; Mrs. T. E. Maddern, East Sixth Avenue; Mrs. John Butler, Ruggles; Mrs. Floyd Curry, Sunshine; Mrs. Susie Higbee, Plymouth; Mrs. W. R. Rowhuff, Happy Hour; Mrs. George Witteman, Lyndon Valley; Mrs. E. L. Dreasher, Zion Community; Mrs. Harry Phillips, Lang; Mrs. Loren Morgan, Logan Avenue; Mrs. W. H. Thomas, Sardis; Mrs. C. G. Carr, Rosean; Mrs. J. Calvin Rees, Salem.

The rural club women have done much for the betterment of conditions in their neighborhoods. They got the first results in the protest against the lack of modern facilities in the old buildings at the County Farm, and installed electricity for the weak and trembling old people whose only home is this farm, and in whose hands the kerosene lamps were a positive menace. Now, handsome modern buildings house the dwellers at the County Farm.

The rural club women are the social leaders in their communities, and the remarkable progress of these neighborhoods is due in large part to their efforts. They look after the unfortunate, they care for the sick, they teach in the Sunday Schools and many of them are Sunday School superintendents. Whatever need arises, the club women are expected to meet it, they do meet it, and carry it to a successful conclusion. The Rural Clubs Association holds three big meetings each year—a Thanksgiving party, in which their entire families participate, a midsummer picnic and a luncheon in February. These serve to bring about a general acquaintance.

Mrs. Carl Knouse, a member of the Rinker Community Club, was chosen as the outstanding rural club woman in Kansas, in the contest conducted by the Capper publications, the summer of 1929. She was a guest of the Jayhawker tour of the Northwest for two weeks, with all expenses paid. Mrs. Knouse is president of the Farm Bureau Unit in her neighborhood, and a leader in the County Association of Clubs. Mrs. Thomas Marks, also of the Rinker Club, was chosen by the Capper publications as one of the master farm home-makers of Kansas, early in 1929.

THE FIRST STUDY CLUBS

Some of the women's study clubs were established many years ago, and have carried on their work uninterruptedly. The Thesaurus was organized in the autumn of 1883, according to a history of the club written by Miss Mary Herbert, a charter member, a few years before her death. The first meeting was at the D. W. Holderman home, corner Fifth and State, now the W. R. Richards home. Forty persons, men and women, attended this meeting. This number was considered too large for the average home, so two groups were formed, one for either side of Commercial Street. W. C. Simpson, an attorney, was the first president; William Hart, bookkeeper for the Newman Dry Goods Company, was the first secretary. The Chautauqua course of study was decided upon, and the name Study Club adopted. The two groups met every Monday night. Among the members on the west side were Mr. and Mrs. Simpson, Mr. and Mrs. Hart, Mr. and Mrs. Jerry Evans, Miss Lena Weed, Mr. and Mrs. D. W. Eastman, Mr. and Mrs. L. C. Wood, Mrs. R. J. Edwards, Miss Lizzie Holderman, and Miss Mary Herbert. In 1886 the Chautauqua course was discontinued, the men had dropped out of the club, and its name was changed to Thesaurus. Among early members were Mrs. O. D. Swan, Miss Josephine Patty, Mrs. E. N. Evans, Mrs. T. G. Wibley, Mrs. A. R. Taylor, Mrs. Kate Smeed Cross, Miss Julia Hardcastle, Miss Tillie DeCamp, Mrs. J. M. Griffith, Mrs. J. Jay Buck, Mrs. Augusta Berkshire. Mrs. Simpson, of Chicago is, probably, the only living member of this organization at its beginning, and she and Mrs. Swan, of Emporia, and Mrs. A. R. Taylor, Decatur, Illinois, the only ones remaining of those who were members at the time the club became the Thesaurus. Mrs. L. H. Hausam is the president for 1929-1930, and Mrs. A. W. Moore is secretary.

The Literary League was organized in October, 1888. At the celebration of the fortieth anniversary of this club, in 1928, Mrs. A. Pemberton, one of its original members, told the story of the club, as follows: "In the summer of 1888 a group of women who were neighbors were inspired to organize a study club. These women had heard of the Chautauqua Circle and the pioneer women's club, the Sorosis. The call for the first meeting was extended by Mrs. J. E. Evans, Mrs. T. N. Sedgwick, Mrs. D. S. Bill, Mrs. L. D. Jacobs and Mrs. A. Pemberton. By the end of the year there was a permanent membership of ten, and the name of Literary League was chosen. The membership was limited to ten for a number of years, then to twelve, then to fifteen, and now to twenty. From being a neighborhood club of the Second Ward it has expanded and now embraces the entire town. For several years it was without constitution, officers or dues. The club always has met weekly, and in early years the hostess of the day presided at the meeting. The first officers were elected in order that the club might become affiliated with the City Federation of Women's Clubs. . . . . . During the forty years of the club's existence it has touched upon all fields of knowledge. Its members have been a closely knit unit, of one mind and one object: Growth and mutual help. The presidents have served for long periods. The first president was Mrs. J. E. Evans; the second, Mrs. S. B. Warren; the third, Mrs. Pemberton; the fourth, Mrs. J. D. Graham; the fifth, Mrs. Pemberton; the sixth, Mrs. F. M. Arnold, and the seventh, Mrs. F. L. Gilson."

Mrs. Pemberton was elected president emeritus in 1926, and was the honored guest at this celebration. Mrs. Pemberton, Mrs. L. D. Jacobs, of Garnett, and Mrs. J. E. Evans, of Chicago, are the only ones living of the original members. The Literary League is a member of the State Federation of Women's Clubs.

The Junto was organized in 1889. Mrs. C. N. Sterry was the first leader, and Mrs. J. T. Arnett the second. There were no elected officers at first, and leaders for stated periods were selected. Mrs. G. W. Newman is the only living charter member, and three generations of her family now are Junto members—herself, her daughter, Mrs. Joseph Hughes, and her granddaughter, Mrs. Harold Trusler. Mrs. I. D. Fox was one of the Junto's early presidents, and Mrs. E. W.

Barker is the 1929-1930 presiding officer. Mrs. Harold Trusler is secretary.

The Junto, November 14, 1892, federated with the Kansas State Social Science Club, which later became the State Federation of Women's Clubs. The Junto was the first Emporia club to federate. Mrs. L. B. Kellogg and Mrs. J. M. McCown went as delegates from the Junto to Chicago in June, 1893, where was held the first meeting of the General Federation of Women's Clubs, at the time of the World's Columbian Exposition. Mrs. McCown recalls that the meetings lasted through but two days and one evening session, whereas now they continue for two weeks, and then leave unfinished business. Mrs. McCown gave a reading on Kansas Day, "When the Sunflowers Bloom," and D. O. Jones, of Emporia, sang in the Kansas chorus. The Emporia women enjoyed meeting Mrs. Potter Palmer, who was head of all the women's work in the exposition.

The General Federation again met at a World's Fair, the Louisiana Purchase Exposition, in St. Louis, 1904, and again Mrs. Kellogg and Mrs. McCown attended. Mrs. J. F. Kenney, of Emporia, played an organ solo on Kansas Day. Mrs. McCown has attended four General Federation meetings, the others having been at Atlantic City and in New York City. The membership of the Junto in 1893-1894, when it was organized formally and officers elected, was: President, Mrs. J. T. Arnett; secretary, Mrs. T. J. Acheson; treasurer, Mrs. Ida Moore Irwin; directors, Mrs. G. W. Newman, Mrs. L. B. Kellogg, Mrs. I. E. Perley, Mrs. T. H. Dinsmore; Mrs. C. B. Graves, Mrs. Luther Severy, Mrs. Henry Dickson, Mrs. Park Morse, Mrs. Iva J. Keebler, Mrs. A. R. Taylor, Mrs. Ellen Trask, Mrs. I. D. Fox, Mrs. Martha Sauber, Mrs. Ellen Hibbard, Mrs.

O. B. Hardcastle, Mrs. J. N. Wilkinson, Mrs. J. D. Barnett, Mrs. J. M. McCown, Mrs. J. D. Hewitt and Mrs. T. P. Harper.

Other study clubs which have been organized for long terms of years are the Parliament, the Cosmopolitan, the Research, the M. I. P.

BUSINESS AND PROFESSIONAL WOMEN

In Emporia, also, the Business and Professional Women's Club, with a membership of from one hundred sixty to two hundred, does important civic work in addition to its regular program of work for and by its members. It has sponsored the Red Cross and Y. M. C. A.-Y. W. C. A. budget drives, doing all of the soliciting, it has fed the hungry and clothed the naked, it furnished rooms in the hospitals and in the nurses' homes. It maintains a scholarship loan fund for the benefit of needy girls and young women. More important than all this, it has been the means of broadening the lives of hundreds of young women and girls employed in business and professional work. It has put these women "on the map" as no other agency could have done, and as never before had been attempted. This organization is a power in the town.

The Women's Relief Corps and the Ladies of the Grand Army of the Republic have a combined membership of about three hundred, and both do important patriotic and philanthropic work. The Women's Christian Temperance Union long has been a real power in the enforcement of the prohibitory law, and in many other phases of good citizenship activities. And it is interesting to know that, as early as 1859, a lodge of Good Templars was organized in Emporia with a membership of thirty. From Women's Relief Corps No. 70 have been elected a national president,

Mrs. Belle C. Harris, and four department presidents —Mrs. Harris, Mrs. Margaret Griffith, Mrs. Marian S. Nation and Miss Sadie Whitehead.

The American Association of University Women and two chapters of the P. E. O. have strong organizations, with working memberships that add distinctly to the cultural assets of the town.

The work of the garden clubs in Emporia adds much to the beauty and attractiveness of the town. The activities of the club members, added to their shining example, move many other citizens to improve their homes and surroundings. Garden Club exhibits are shown each year, free to the public, in a convenient down-town location. The large crowds that see these shows testify to the interest of the townspeople in flower gardens and lawns.

PATRIOTIC ORGANIZATIONS

The Grand Army of the Republic, Preston B. Plumb Post No. 55, was organized April 26, 1882, with fifty charter members. A few years later a second Post, No. 464, was organized, the membership of No. 55 having grown so large as to be unwieldly. During the past two decades, however, Grand Army membership has dwindled, and of the half dozen or more posts in other Lyon County towns, none remains, and the surviving members, as well as those of Post 464, have placed their memberships in Post 55. The roster now has but twenty-eight names, while in the earlier years of its organization, the names of many hundreds of Civil War veterans who have answered the last roll-call, filled the record books of the posts. J. B. Sullivan is commander of Post 55. Two members of this Post, J. M. Griffith and Charles Harris, served the Grand Army as department commanders.

Women's Relief Corps No. 70 was organized April 25, 1886, and the Ladies of the G. A. R., Garfield Circle No. 22, June 17, 1890, both organizations being auxiliary to the Grand Army. Miss Sadie Whitehead is president of the Woman's Relief Corps, and Mrs. Jennie Larkin heads the Ladies of the G. A. R.

The Sons of Veterans first was organized in the eighties, but this organization lapsed, and the present camp, No. 86, dates from April 30, 1914. L. T. Bang is its commander. General Lyon Camp, No. 51, Sons of Veterans Auxiliary, was organized in 1896. Mrs. Jennie Harvey is president of the Auxiliary.

The Daughters of Union Veterans of the Civil War, Mary J. Perley Tent No. 11, was organized February 26, 1929. It has a charter membership of 150, the largest charter roll of this organization in the United States. Miss Annette Smith is its president.

The Spanish War Veterans, Harry Easter Camp No. 16, W. J. Reynolds, commander, was organized in 1929. Its Women's Auxiliary, No. 26, Mrs. L. M. Shearer, president, was organized September 2, 1929. Both are building up large and interested memberships.

The American Legion, organized in 1919, has a membership of about 350. R. Wilford Reigle is commander of the Legion, and Mrs. L. R. Jones is president of its Women's Auxiliary.

The Daughters of the American Revolution, Mrs. C. A. Stannard, regent, is a flourishing organization in Emporia.

1902. Emporia is No. 1475. In order of membership Emporia is first, with 200 members; Boston, second; Reading, third. Other Granges are at Hartford, Neosho Rapids and Plymouth, the county membership totaling 550. The highest membership, probably, was in 1909, when there were 808 Grangers in Lyon County. Dan James, of the Boston Grange, is state overseer, the second highest state office. A county organization is maintained, and has an enthusiastic membership. C. C. Cogswell, Kingman, is are maintained. A majority of Grange members own their homes and the farms they till, which gives to state master. National and state monthly magazines this organization a stability of membership which adds greatly to its usefulness.

The Farmers Educational and Cooperative Union of America, in the years when Maurice McAuliffe was state president, flourished in Lyon County as never before or since. In 1909 a state meeting was held in Emporia, and soon the six or seven "locals" were increased to fourteen. Stores were established in several Lyon County towns, the store in Emporia having been burned in the Whitley Opera House fire in 1913, and never reestablished. There were cooperative stores at Americus, Bushong and Olpe, and those at Admire and Allen still are doing business. This organization established creameries and elevators, and maintained a jobbing association. C. E. Huff, Salina, is state and national president, and John Scheel, Emporia, always interested in farm organizations, was state conductor and lecturer sixteen years. Among the Farmers Unions now functioning are those at Admire, Summit and Bushong.

The Lyon County Farm Bureau was organized in the spring of 1914, with John Scheel as its first pres-

PLUMB MEMORIAL HALL
Kansas State Teachers College, 1917

ident. J. W. O'Conner was its vice president, and James R. Plumb, secretary. The first county agent was H. L. Popenoe, and others have been Gaylord Hancock, C. L. McFadden, and the past two years Carl L. Howard has held this position. The Farm Bureau News, a monthly, is the county organ of the Farm Bureau.

In 1929 the services of Miss Gertrude Allen, county home demonstration agent, were secured for Lyon County. One of the requirements for securing this agent was that the Farm Bureau have a membership of not less than two hundred women, and this soon was more than met when two hundred seventy-five women became Farm Bureau members. The 4-H Clubs of boys and girls, sponsored by the Farm Bureau, are of much value educationally for farm young people. There are eighteen or twenty 4-H Clubs in Lyon County.

The Farm Bureau does an important work, and its members feel they benefit greatly by cooperation with the county agent. The women expect equal benefit from the work of the county home demonstration agent.

The Farmers Alliance, organized in Lyon County in 1889, was the strongest and most important of the farm organizations in the county. It established stores, warehouses and elevators, and did a thriving business for several years. When the Alliance went into politics and became the Populist party, it elected many county officers and helped to elect many state officials. While its tenets at that time were ridiculed, by all who stuck to the old parties, most of the reforms it advocated have been incorporated in the political platforms of both these parties. The Populist party has been called, fittingly, a voice in the wilderness.

The Farmers' Association was organized in 1906, with William Miller, president; George Plumb, secretary; vice presidents were B. Tolbert, Plymouth; Tom Evans, Hartford; James Plumb, Reading; Willis Clayton, Admire; J. P. Brickley, Americus; John Langley, Olpe. Lecturers from the State Agricultural College at Manhattan addressed the meetings of this association from time to time. Few records of its activities were found.

THE CHAMBER OF COMMERCE

The Emporia Chamber of Commerce, successor to other organizations of like aims and purposes, was organized in 1917. It has a membership of three hundred, and its object is to assist in the development of the life of the town and county—civic, social, economic, agricultural, industrial and commercial. It cooperates with all farm organizations and all town organizations with like purposes. It meets each Monday noon except during July and August.

The Chamber of Commerce has been particularly active in the development of all-weather roads, and many miles of paved, graveled and sanded highways have been sponsored, with more to come. The million dollar concrete pavement from the east line to the west, through Lyon County and Emporia, was the first of these projects. Now, Emporia is "hooked up" by through all-weather highways to the Atlantic on the east, a great part of the way to the Pacific on the west. North and south projects are under way, and a considerable portion of Lyon County, in these directions, is covered. The Chamber of Commerce gets behind every worth-while activity—the Broadview Hotel, St. Mary's Hospital, the Teachers College Students' Union and Stadium, the musical festivals of the two big colleges, Red Cross and Y. M. C. A.-Y. W. C. A. drives, and dozens of other equally important community needs. H. A. McClure is its president and J. C. Gladfelter, secretary. Other presidents have been H. E. Ganse, A. H. Gufler, John E. Martin, O. A. Kirkendall —two terms—W. N. Gunsolly, Ralph Smalley and M. L. Kretsinger.

The Emporia Business Men's Association was organized February 15, 1897, was incorporated and stock issued at $100.00 a share. J. E. Evans was its first president, and Robert L. Jones its first secretary. The Orient Railway project absorbed much of the interest of this organization for several years. It brought natural gas to Emporia, started the street paving program, and brought to the town some short-lived factories, among them the Rex Fluid Company and a shirt factory.

The reorganization of the Business Men's Association as the Lyon County Commercial Club followed, and records of the Young Men's Commerce Club show that in 1917 these organizations were merged. In October of that year the Commercial Club issued invitations to a "Greater Emporia" dinner, to be given November 6 in the Masonic Temple, as a part of a membership campaign for the newly-organized Chamber of Commerce. L. C. Boyle, a former attorney general of Kansas, was the principal speaker. I. E. Lambert, jr., was president of the Young Men's Commerce Club, and A. L. Oliger and Fred Bowers, jr., its secretaries.

THE RETAILERS' ASSOCIATION

The Lyon County Retailers' Association with propriety may be called the watchdog of the business interests of Emporia and Lyon County. It is an incorporated institution, with a membership of one hundred, and E. H. Wade is its competent secretary. It looks carefully after the interests of its members, secures information as to the credit of newcomers or other customers who have not established credit, and saves its members thousands of dollars annually, as well as endless trouble. Calls for information come to the Emporia office from every State in the Union, and advices are received from the same area. The Emporia Association is a member of the State and National Associations, which have large memberships. In 1912 there were but fifteen or twenty retailers' associations in the United States, now there are more than two thousand.

SOME OF THE SCHOOLS

TEACHERS COLLEGE CHRONOLOGY

The name of the Kansas State Normal School was changed to Teachers College February 20, 1923, for the reason that the name normal school designates an institution which gives a two-year course, whereas the school at Emporia long had maintained a four-year course. In other words, it was a college. There are two hundred state teacher training institutions in the United States. More than one hundred of these give a four-year course of training and are called teachers colleges. The two-year schools remaining still are called normal schools, or junior teachers colleges.

The Kansas State Normal School was opened February 15, 1865, in the Old Stone Schoolhouse, located on the northeast corner of the Senior High School grounds. The Normal occupied the second floor of this building, the quarters being lent by Lyon County School District No. 1 until a state building could be provided.

The first building on the present campus was erected on the site of the present flagpole, in 1867, at a cost of $10,000.00. It was 40x60 feet in size, two stories, basement and cupola, and the assembly room on the second floor would seat 120 persons. This building, of stone, afterward was used for a time as the president's residence.

The second building was on the site of the present sunken garden. It was built in 1873, and was burned in 1878. The City of Emporia had borne one-sixth of the cost of this building, which was $50,000.00. It was rebuilt after the fire at a cost of $25,000.00, and returned to service in 1880. In 1888 a $25,000.00 addition to this building was erected on the west. In 1895 this structure was still further enlarged by the addition of Albert Taylor Hall on the east end of the building, and the final addition came in 1902, when a gymnasium was annexed to the north side.

Kellogg Library was built in 1892; the Training School, now being converted into a junior-senior high school, 1905. The old power house, formerly located at the southwest corner of Plumb Hall, was erected in 1905.

The building now used as a hospital and a building which had been used as the residence of the superintendent of buildings and grounds were purchased in 1905 when the site for Norton Science Hall was bought. These buildings were moved about three hundred feet north of their original locations, and remained at a place immediately south of the old power house until 1917, when they were moved to their present location.

Norton Science Hall was erected in 1907, and the Physical Training Building in 1910. The old Eskridge residence, a brick building used until recently as a music hall, was purchased in 1910, and razed in 1929.

Plumb Hall, the administration building, was erected in 1917, the cafeteria in 1919. Morse Hall, a dormitory for women, was built in 1924, and the steel and concrete stand on the west side of Stadium Field, in 1925.

The site for the present Music Hall was purchased in 1927—formerly the Richard Thomas residence. This building now is located north of the power house, and serves as an annex to the women's dormitory. Music Hall was erected in 1928.

The addition, or recreation hall of the Student Union building was erected in 1929, and the Training School also was built in 1929.

The campus has been increased from its original twenty-acre tract to forty acres.

"We are proud of the many new buildings and other important improvements which have been made on the campus of the State Teachers College within the past few years," says President Thomas W. Butcher, "but the biggest thing is the recognition, by standardizing agencies, of our higher standards of scholarship. In 1928 we were admitted to the college and university list of the North Central Association of Colleges and Secondary Schools. Of about two hundred schools, Emporia is one of twelve in the first list."

The Peabody Journal of Education, Nashville, Tennessee, published in 1928 under "Outstanding State Teachers Colleges," a list checked by men high in educational work, from institutions of learning in all sections of this country, who gave twelve schools three hundred fifteen votes out of six hundred forty, the list including seventy-seven schools. Emporia came second in this list of twelve.

Presidents of the Normal School:
Lyman B. Kellogg, 1865-1871.
George W. Hoss, 1871-1874.
C. R. Pomeroy, 1874-1879.
Rudolph B. Welch, 1879-1882.
Albert R. Taylor, 1882-1901.
Jasper N. Wilkinson, 1901-1906.
Joseph H. Hill, 1906-1913.
Thomas W. Butcher, 1913-

EMPORIA BUSINESS COLLEGE

The Emporia Business College was established in 1880 or 1881, by O. W. Miller, who was its proprietor until 1895 or 1896. C. E. D. Parker in 1896 acquired Mr. Miller's interests, and with him for a time was associated a Mr. Gould.

C. D. Long taught classes in the Business College for Mr. Parker the winter of 1905, and took over the school in February, 1906. It was located at that time in the third story of the old Peters hardware store, Fifth and Commercial, and was moved to the second story of the Watson-Ballweg Lumber Company's building, Sixth and Mechanic, September, 1906.

Mr. Miller opened the school in the second story of the building now occupied by the Hughes-Todd Jewelry Company, formerly the D. D. Williams jewelry store. This building had been occupied previously by classes from the Emporia City Schools. The Business College was moved next to the second story of the Racket store, 615-617 Commercial, and later was established in the second story of the present Roberts-Blue funeral home, on Merchant Street, and again in the second story of the Palace Clothing Company's store. It was moved from this location by C. E. D. Parker to the Peters building. O. M. Wilhite says he attended the Emporia Business College in 1880 or 1881, Mason McCarty was a student in 1885 or 1886, and Bert Johnson attended it in 1894.

C. D. Long was head of the Emporia Business College from 1906 until 1923, and built up a strong and growing institution. Its graduates are well equipped for business life, and have no difficulty in securing jobs. The school is a distinct asset to the town and community. J. E. Hawkins, a former mayor of Emporia, has been its president since 1923, and C. C. Hawkins is business manager. Its location at 724 1-2 Commercial, the second floor of the Burnap Brothers' plumbing establishment, into which it moved in 1928, is roomy, convenient and well equipped.

A Mrs. Geer taught a night school on the south side of Sixth Avenue, east of Commercial Street, for two three-month terms in the eighties. This school was in no way connected with the Emporia Business College.

THE DISTRICT SCHOOLS

¹Lyon County has 116 school districts in which 243 teachers are employed. The enrollment is 3,430, of which 1,994 are in the 102 one-room schools of Lyon County. Six of the schools have Superior Classification with the State, and nineteen are Standard.

A new classification has been evolved by the State Board of Education this year—that of Accepted Schools. Accepted Schools meet every requirement of Standard Schools except that they have crossed light instead of unilateral lighting.

Lyon County has a valuation of $68,435,190.00, with the estimated value of school property at $1,649,200.00.

The average salary of men teachers in the county (one-room schools) is $87.50, and of women, $96.00 per month. Salaries of men teachers in grade schools average $125.00 per month, and of women, $111.44. High school teachers' salaries average, for men $183.05, and for women, $156.53. The cost of tuition, based on enrollment, is: One-room schools, $7.75; two or more rooms, $21.06; and high schools, $29.71. The cost of tuition based on average daily attendance is: One-room schools, $10.16; two or more rooms, $24.76; and high school, $33.40.

Eighty-three boys and eighty-nine girls were graduated from the rural eighth grade, and thirty-six boys and forty-three girls were graduated from the eighth grade in the grade schools in the spring of 1929. Twenty rural and one grade teacher are teaching for the first time this year.

There are 9,828 volumes in the libraries of the elementary grades in the county, 800 of which were added this year. The State library law, which requires every district in the State to purchase annually at least $5.00 worth of approved books per teacher per school, was complied with by all but eight schools of the county in 1929.

All teachers outside of Emporia, including those in the seven rural high schools, the one consolidated high school and the one parochial high school, are under the supervision of the county superintendent's office.

The high schools are visited also, biennially, by the State high school supervisor. The Standard and Superior Schools are visited annually by the State rural school supervisor. The law requires that the county superintendent visit each teacher outside the first and second-class cities at least one hour each term.

Twenty-three rural schools have music supervision from one to four times per month. The school board members of the county organized the Lyon County School Board Association in September, 1927, and five semi-annual meetings have been held since that time. Three hundred forty-eight board members govern the 116 schools of the county.

The Lyon County Teachers' Association was organized in 1922 and meets the last Saturday in each month during the school year.

High School superintendents, exclusive of Emporia, are:

Hartford, D. E. Flower.
Neosho Rapids, Lawrence Gardner.
Reading, J. H. Richard.
Miller, Paul B. Cooper.
Bushong, J. K. Moore.
Americus, E. R. Sheldon.
Admire, H. C. Bryan.
Allen, H. C. Jent.
Olpe, Sister Clementia.

'Exclusive of Emporia.

TOWN AND COUNTY TODAY

CITY WATER SYSTEM

[1]Dan Dryer, commissioner of public utilities of Emporia for six years, with the cooperation of the other members of the commission, solved the water problem for Emporia. In 1920 the Neosho River probably never had been so low, and the scarcity of water was the concern of every citizen. Mr. Dryer, with a gang of workmen, ditched the dry bed of the Neosho for thirty miles, across the northwestern part of Lyon County and into Morris County. With dynamite they blasted out the rocky bed, forming a channel by which the water might flow from shallow pool to shallow pool. Work on the dry and frozen river bed was extremely difficult. The men established a camp, moving from one location to another as the work progressed. Much of the rocky, frozen bed was picked and hammered out with hand tools. Often the temperature was below zero, and the men suffered from the cold.

All along the river the men opened springs, connecting them with the channel. The Ruggles dam and the Correll dam were raised and these, with the dam at the waterworks, provided three high dams. A new

---

[1]Dan Dryer died September 13, 1924. The naming of the municipal park at the waterworks in his honor was an expression of the City Commission's appreciation of his work in securing the town's water supply. Ed Mitchell was appointed to fill the unexpired term of Mr. Dryer.

filter plant was built at the waterworks, a new reservoir and a larger distributing system were installed, also a new booster tank. The three dams furnish storage capacity for 252 million gallons of water. The value of the entire water system of Emporia is $900,-000.00. This includes the entire property—the land and all appurtenances of the plant, the dams and distributing system.

In 1879 the city voted $50,000.00 bonds for the installation of a waterworks system connecting with the Cottonwood, and the plant was established at the foot of Congress Street. In 1885 W. T. Soden applied to the courts for an injunction to prevent the city from obtaining water from the Cottonwood, as it interfered with the work of his gristmill, which was operated by water power, only a short distance below the waterworks plant. Rather than enter into what might have been prolonged litigation, the city decided to abandon the Cottonwood.

Bonds for $162,000.00, for the construction of a waterworks plant on the Neosho River, were voted by the city in 1886, and were sold for $158,000.00. A site for the new location was condemned, W. S. Jay, Van R. Holmes and F. E. Smith having been appointed appraisers. Dr. Thomas Armor was paid $13,500.00 for his mill site, including the dam and all water rights. Lewis Labron received $1,200.00 for his forty acres adjoining the mill property, and other adjacent landowners were paid in $525.00. A dam and two reservoirs were built, and by 1889 the city had incurred a waterworks indebtedness of $227,000.00. In 1896, the city began furnishing water to the Santa Fe and, had the supply been sufficient for the needs of both town and railroad, this arrangement would have aided materially in meeting the indebtedness. But again and again the water supply was low.

In 1891, fourteen miles of sewers and laterals had been constructed, and ten miles of water mains. The dam was raised ten feet in 1901, increasing the storage capacity from 80 millions to 110 million gallons of water. In 1929, there were fifty-two miles of water mains, in the distributing system inside the city limits, and two and one-half miles of flow line between the pumping plant at the river and the filter plant and the city limits. There are thirty-eight miles of sewer mains and laterals, and thirteen miles of storm sewers.

After many vicissitudes, many seasons of water shortage and the outlay of many large sums of money, without lasting result, and sometimes with no benefit whatever, Emporia's waterworks plant furnishes an abundant supply of water, kept pure and sanitary by chemical processes, approved by the State Board of Health. Water is sold at a reasonable rate, and in dry seasons there is no excuse for householders allowing their lawns and gardens to burn up. With this plentiful supply of water, Emporia grows yearly in the beauty of trees and shrubs and flowers and lawns.

EMPORIA'S PHYSICAL GROWTH

Annexed to the original town site of Emporia are between one hundred fifty and one hundred sixty additions, varying in size from a few blocks to large acreages, the city now covering two and one-half square miles. In spite of the vicissitudes of the first decade in the life of the town, records show that additions, the Ruggles and Copley, were made as early as 1867. H. E. Norton, Robert and Susannah Ruggles,

J. V. Randolph, Mrs. J. H. Slocum, W. H. Skinner, J. C. Fraker, Andrew Hinshaw and others, brought territory into the city in 1869 and 1870. Mrs. Sarah W. Lewis's addition, described as the northeast quarter of the southeast quarter of section 9, on either side of Grove Avenue, was admitted to the city May 12, 1870.

Later additions, among them being Goodrich's of thirty-nine acres, came in in 1875, but afterward was vacated, as were numerous other additions of that and later periods. In the eighties the additions came thick and fast, a few of them being the Normal addition, in 1881; Cottonwood place, by I. E. Perley, 1885; the H. C. Cross addition, 1885; Factoryville, 1883; McCandliss, 1885; Woodland Park Association, two additions, 1887, the association officers having been J. M. Steele, president, and J. D. Holden, secretary; the Jacobs and Borton additions were brought in in 1887, several by L. T. Heritage in the eighties, Highland Place, Perley, 1889; University Place, R. S. Lawrence, 1889; College Hill, 1884.

Among later additions were Lakeview Heights, 1905; Kretsinger-Hardcastle, 1910; Mason McCarty, 1914; Country Club 1916 and Country Club Court, 1917; West View, Widick, 1921; Washington Heights, Stannard, 1923; the Hallberg additions.

J. J. Morris, within the past few years, has developed and brought into the city two additions, the first a ten-acre tract, the second five acres, immediately south of the Newman Memorial County Hospital. The lots have been sold and on them have been built comfortable homes, which are well cared for and the grounds improved with trees and shrubs and grass and flowers. These additions will become, with the care given them, one of the highly desirable sections of the town. Besides the additions, Mr. Morris has bought lots and built houses in almost every section of the town. He owns about sixty residence buildings.

The Graystone Addition, twenty acres on the north side of Sixth Avenue running west from Garfield Avenue, was brought into the city by Frank J. Dale, in 1923. Another twenty acres to the north of the first twenty, a part of the original tract, was added to the city by Mr. Dale in 1925. All of the first addition except the old Taylor residence on Garfield Avenue has been sold as home sites, and on most of them have been built comfortable homes. A considerable portion of the later addition has been disposed of, and the new grade school building, the Mary Herbert School, is located in it. The large number of new homes, added to those already in this school area, make this an ideal school site.

This forty acres was a part of the original homestead of the late David Plumb, the abstract showing the transfer from the Town Company to him. Later, the land came into the possession of Preston B. Plumb, David Plumb's son, who sold it in the early eighties to the late Col. David Taylor. Colonel Taylor in 1885 enlarged and built around the story-and-a-half brick house which had been built by the Plumbs, and made of it the large residence which ever after was the home of the Taylor family.

In the winter of 1926 Calvin Lambert, a son of the late I. E. Lambert, long a leading Emporia lawyer, purchased and consolidated three tracts of land adjoining Emporia on the northwest. Fifteen acres of land was included in the deal, and the tract was platted for a new residential district. It was Emporia's first restricted subdivision and was platted with curved streets, center parks, odd-shaped lots and other inno-

PRESTON B. PLUMB
1857

vations in city planning. The district was named Berkeley Hills, Mr. Lambert choosing the name from Berkeley, California, where he was a student at the University of California.

The area which formed Berkeley Hills had several interesting landmarks. Jay's pond, a small lake formerly owned by W. S. Jay, was in the northeast corner of the land. The site of the old Born slaughterhouse was on top of a hill, near the intersection of Berkeley Road and Sheridan Court. On the west side of the addition was an old concrete barn, used as a dairy in 1910 and 1911 by the College of Emporia students.

In 1929 Mr. Lambert extended his district by purchasing ten acres to the northeast. Part of this ground was for many years the home of the Baxter Hainline family, and the little farm was noted for its grapes and strawberries. At one time a deer park was located in this tract.

In all, Mr. Lambert has developed twenty-five acres, with a total of one hundred twelve lots and four parks. Four new streets, Sherwood Way, Berkeley Road, Sheridan Court and Mayfair Street were staked out. The Berkeley Hills addition was the first accepted by the city under the supervision of the zoning commission. Mayor O. T. Atherton signed the plat of the first addition, and Mayor C. A. Bishop's name heads the commissioners who signed the plat for a continuation of the district.

Washington Park Addition consists of land set aside for a park in platting the original town site—the half block on the east side of Commercial Street between Eighth and Ninth, running east to the alley between Commercial and Mechanic, and a similar half block on the west side of Commercial between Eighth and Ninth, running west to the alley between Commercial and Merchant. This was planned as a town beauty spot, to be landscaped and otherwise improved. Little was done by the city, however, and in 1870 it was cancelled as a park and brought into the city to be placed on sale for business or residence uses. This was low, boggy ground, deep in mud in rainy weather, and considered at that time as of little value. It is said the sites for the First Presbyterian and the Episcopal Churches, in this block on the east side of Commercial, were purchased for an extremely small consideration. Regret has been expressed by early settlers, and others, that the city did not retain this ground for its original purpose.

PUBLIC HEALTH SERVICE

The Lyon County Health Unit is composed of the Red Cross, the United States Public Health Service, Lyon County and the City of Emporia, all cooperating in an effort to control and eradicate disease from this town and county. Much has been accomplished, but the fight is not ended. Keeping down disease is a matter of eternal vigilance, says Dr. J. S. Fulton, head of the Lyon County Health Unit.

Doctor Fulton came to Emporia in September, 1923. With the aid of his assistants, individual members of the Unit, the two hospitals of the town, the many physicians, the teachers and pupils of the schools, and the parents and other citizens, disease has been greatly reduced. In 1924 there were one hundred three cases of smallpox in the county, in 1928 but twenty-four; thirty-two cases of diphtheria in 1924, in 1928 but four; in 1924, thirty cases of typhoid, in 1928 only seven. Health and sanitation are taught regularly in the schools, and children learn to conserve their health, or to improve it if below the standard. Examinations are given by doctor and nurses, and all infectious cases are isolated promptly. No typhoid has appeared among Lyon County school children in the past three years.

Doctor Fulton's assistants in the county are Miss Elsie Henery and Miss Esther Latimer, nurses, and Miss Una Mae Crumb, office. The County Unit has the cooperation of the county superintendent of schools, Miss Jean Cowan, and of the city schools nurse, Miss Stella Klein. The City Schools and the Colleges maintain vigilant health programs, and few children or older students are out of school because of illness.

The city's health program is largely one of prevention. Alleys are clean, garbage cans are covered to keep out flies, and an effective garbage disposal system has been established. With the proper precautions expected of each householder, disease-carrying flies have been almost completely banished. City water is tested regularly, and its quality entitles the city to maintain "Safe Water" signs at entrances to the town. No water stagnates in streets or alleys to breed mosquitoes, there is so little filth exposed that insect pests find little encouragement to locate in Emporia. The average grade of health in Emporia and Lyon County has increased from 67 in 1923 to 85 in 1929.

ROADS AND BRIDGES

In the late summer of 1929 the City of Emporia had to her credit thirty miles of concrete pavement, and five of graveled streets. In the county, outside Emporia, are eighty-one and one-half miles of all-weather roads—twenty-eight and one-half miles of concrete, thirty-six miles of graveled roads, sixteen and one-half miles of sanded roads, and half a mile of brick paving. Twelve more miles of graveled road will have been completed before 1930. This does not include the many miles of graveled streets in the smaller towns of Lyon County.

Many county roads for years have been well graded, and are dragged following rains, keeping them in as good condition as is possible for dirt roads. Township roads are linking up with all-weather County and State roads with stretches of gravel, five miles of such roads having been constructed in Emporia Township in 1929.

At the general election of 1867 the people of Lyon County voted on the erection of three bridges—one across the Cottonwood at Emporia, the Soden Bridge; across the Neosho at Emporia, the Merchant Street Bridge; and across the Neosho at Neosho Rapids. The vote stood 596 for the bridges, 399 against the proposition. These were the first permanent bridges built in Lyon County. For many years bridges have spanned almost all of the crossings on well-traveled roads, and fording a stream is an unusual experience. Many of the earlier bridges have been and are being replaced by modern structures, and all of the later bridges are built to accommodate two-way traffic.

The first road in Lyon County was the Santa Fe Trail, entering from Osage County a few miles north of the town of Miller, and crossing Lyon County in an approximately east-and-west direction two and one-half to three and one-half miles north of the towns of Admire, Allen and Bushong. In March, 1825, Congress passed an act authorizing the President of the United States—John Quincy Adams—to cause a road to be marked from the western frontier of Missouri to New Mexico, and to appoint three commissioners to carry out this act and to gain the consent of the Indians to do so. These commissioners, Benjamin Reeves, George C. Sibley and Thomas Mather, left St. Louis in June, 1825, and August 10, 1825, met the chiefs of the Great and Little Osage Nations at Council Grove on the Neo Zho. The Osage Indians were paid $800.00 for the right of way through their territory for this road to New Mexico. The treaty took place under Council Oak, an historic landmark of Council Grove.

Six days later the commissioners went to Turkey Creek, McPherson County, and held a similar treaty with the Kaw Indians. In 1906 the Daughters of the American Revolution and the State of Kansas began marking the Santa Fe Trail across the State with substantial granite markers. Highway No. 50 North follows the general direction of the Trail, on which were located the old Allen post office, at Withington's, three and one-half miles northeast of the present town of Allen. Trail and Agnes City post offices, further west on the Trail, became the Bushong postoffice. The exact route of the Old Trail may be followed many miles today by the deeply washed wheel ruts which mark its course.

The Burlingame Road was the first officially established highway coming into Emporia. It was laid out by Government authority, but laying it out was about all the Government did for it. The first wheel tracks over this route were made by Oliver Phillips[1] when,

[1] Oliver Phillips was Lyon County's second settler, having taken a claim on 142 Creek in April, 1855. He moved to Duck Creek in 1857, and was this county's first assessor. Mr. and Mrs. Phillips

in February, 1857, he drove diagonally across the prairie from his claim on Duck Creek to help stake out the new town site of Emporia. The road crossed the Neosho near the Rinker ford, which later was named for Royal Rinker, who settled on the north bank of the river, immediately east of the ford—the farm now occupied by the Jack Tallon family. A stage station, at which horses were changed, was established at the Phillips place, and there was much travel on this road.

In 1874 it was resurfaced, staked eighty feet wide, and designated as the Lawrence-Emporia State Road.

---

reared a family of seven sons and daughters. Frank Phillips, of the third generation, is a bridge foreman in the employ of Lyon County. Irvin Phillips, another grandson, is trustee of Reading Township. Among other settlers who ante-dated the founding of Emporia were Jefferson S. Pigman, who opened a store in Columbia in 1855, and was that town's first postmaster; in 1856 R. P. Snow was the Columbia blacksmith; the Fowlers, mentioned elsewhere; Charles Johnson and James H. Phenis, who settled on the Cottonwood southwest of Emporia in May, 1855. Also in 1855 came David VanGundy and his family and John Rosenquist, who took claims at the Junction, and the Rev. Thomas J. Addis and family also settled at the Junction. Lorenzo Dow and R. H. Abraham in 1855 took land north of town—Dow Creek got its name from this original settler.

Others who came prior to 1857 were Joseph Hadley and Joel Haworth, southwest of town on the Cottonwood, 1854, and William Eikenberry in 1855 in that neighborhood; also, to the west and southwest came Charles N. Linck, James and Elihu Newlin, D. Roth, Solomon Phenis—for whom Phenis Creek was named— N. Lockerman and Patrick Manning, 1856. South of town were the Curtis Hiatt and the Milton Chamness families, immediately to the east the Andrew Hinshaws, down the Cottonwood below the Fowler claims the Gunkels and Brendels, in 1856; Robert Best, William Grimsley, the Richard Millers, and Thomas Shockley to the north. Isaac Wright and family settled west of Americus in 1856, Joseph Moon in Pike Township in 1855, M. O. Abraham, Fremont, 1855, L. H. Johnson, 1855, E. M. and S. T. Hiatt, 1856 and H. T. Payne, 1856.

At the election of delegates to Congress, held at Columbia October 9, 1855, twenty votes were polled. This was the only voting precinct in the county.

Up and down the Big and Little Eagle Creeks, before Emporia was staked out, the Priest and the Williams families had taken

It was the principal highway to the northeast until the paved and sanded road was built in recent years, touching only a few rods of this road on its route to Admire. With the graveling of the Burlingame Road, however, it probably will regain its popularity. When claims were taken along this highway their boundaries followed the lines of the "cata-cornered" road, and farm lines still are subject to these boundaries.

The Rinker ford[2] was considered the only safe and reliable crossing—before the stream was dammed for waterworks purposes—on the Neosho in this neighborhood. Frequently, owing to heavy rains, it was neither safe nor reliable, and often could not be forded. The late Peter Bishop—Mayor C. A. Bishop is his son—established a ferry[1] above the ford, and ran it there for a year or two. He sold his ferryboat to the late W. O. Ferguson,[2] who moved it up the river to a

---

claims near the Olpe town site; Mrs. Morgan Yager and her children came in 1856 and took up land between the two creeks, two or three miles further east. In this neighborhood Simon Bucher, who put up perhaps the hardest fight of anyone for the retention of old Madison County, in 1856 was starting on his land what became the largest peach orchard in the county. Further down, near the junction of the streams, Henry Stratton, a brother of Mrs. Yager, and County Commissioner J. L. Stratton's father, was raising cattle and farming. The John Mahaffeys and the Cooleys had claims in this neighborhood, and along the creeks were the Jones, the Graham, the Quimby, and the Shockley families. Mr. Graham was a territorial judge appointed by President Buchanan, and presided over sessions of court held in Elmendaro. A man named Harper settled what for many years, later, was the farm and cattle ranch of N. W. Brewer, and for him Harper Creek was named.

[2] A ford higher up on the Neosho, known as the Holmes ford, was just below the Country Club dam. Jack Holmes, from whom it got its name, was one of John Brown's men at Osawatomie.

[1] A ferry also was used at the Lockerman ford on the Cottonwood, southwest of town—now the Lockerman bridge—when high water made fording impossible.

[2] Mrs. W. O. Ferguson and her daughter, Miss Lu Ferguson, principal of the Walnut School in Emporia, live at 718 Constitution, which has been the family home many years.

point immediately below the Fawcett & Britton sawmill, below the confluence of Allen Creek and the Neosho. The stage often crossed on the ferryboat, but could not pull its passengers up the steep bank of the river. Instead, the passengers walked, and helped to push the stage up the bank. Wagonloads of corn, brought to market from north of the Neosho, were carried up the steep bank by the sackful on the shoulders of the driver. A fee of 25 cents was charged for a man, team and wagon. Stage drivers who used the ferry were John and Will Walker and Lee Glenn. The Walkers had a claim on the Burlingame Road— the R. S. Spiker farm.

When the David Plumb family came to Emporia, in June, 1857, they directed their course by a compass, with a view to finding a location at or near which a town was to be started. When the teams reached the north bank of the Neosho, David Plumb stopped at the cabin of Dr. and Mrs. Thomas Armor to inquire where he could find a crossing. Mrs. Armor was at home, and she told him of a place a short distance down the river where she had known of teams crossing, but she warned him that he must drive in carefully, and then drive upstream along the north side of the river bed, and so gradually ascend the south bank. Near that place the Rinker ford afterward was established.

Stage lines were established from Topeka and Lawrence, running to Leavenworth, over the Burlingame Road. The stage line from Emporia to Eureka, through Madison, carried mail and passengers from the time it was started in the sixties until the Howard Branch was built in 1879. The old stage barn on the hill three miles northwest of Madison, stood until recent years, when it was wrecked by a high wind, and was an interesting landmark. The old store building on the same site, minus its square front, still stands, overlooking a long stretch, down the river and up both the North and South Branches, of the beautiful Verdigris Valley.

On the high prairie away from the streams, numerous roads were made by the simple expedient of driving wherever the way seemed smoothest, with few straight lines followed and hence few square corners to turn. When the wheel tracks became rutted by use and washed by rain, it was an easy matter to turn out of them and make new tracks. Often as many as ten or a dozen tracks followed approximately the same course, and when mudholes in the "draws"[1] got too deep for safe or comfortable crossing—Lyon County mud is sticky, and wagons often were mired—again it was an easy matter to change the place of crossing to a better one a little further up, or down, the draw. Meadows and fields, fenced in later years, long carried the scars of these roads, made without regard, indeed without knowledge of section lines.

The roads being crooked and unfenced, often travelers were lost on the prairie on dark nights. In many windows lamps were set to guide members of the family or others who might be wandering on the prairie, as "lost on the prairie" might mean that the bewildered person had lost all sense of direction. People who ordinarily could mark their course by the direction of the wind, even when the sky was overcast and not a star in sight, had to give up when the wind changed. This happened frequently, and the traveler did not immediately observe the change and continued on his way, to find later the wind had played a bad

---

[1] The word draw is quoted in deference to readers who may not be familiar with the Kansas language. Its meaning is entirely plain to the real prairie man or woman.

joke on him. Sometimes people wandered most of the night within a few rods of their home, moving in a circle and getting nowhere.

A man and his wife, lost on their way home from Emporia to their prairie claim, traveled until late at night, then unhitched the horses and tied them to the wagon wheels, while they slept in the wagon. They awoke at dawn in sight of their home, not a quarter of a mile distant. Many horses, "given their heads," would take their owners home, but at times the horses, as well as humans, seemed to become confused.

The Cottonwood is a crooked, treacherous stream, and many lives were lost in it in the early days. Below some of the fords were deep holes, and such crossings were dangerous. People who knew the river could negotiate them safely, but strangers might, not knowing of the holes, drive a few feet below the safety zone of the ford, and drop off into deep water. Most fords were located at riffles, which made them comparatively safe, and the old Rocky Ford on the Cottonwood was filled with tons and tons of stone, many years before the bridge was built. The Neosho was less dangerous but it, too, has its record of drownings before bridges were built.

Tiny creeks, running little water ordinarily and in dry seasons none at all, might become raging torrents following a heavy rain. The stones or pieces of plank or rails which had been laid down in the crossing to "keep vehicles from going clear to the bottom" were washed out, and deep holes, running water enough to swim a horse, sometimes caught unsuspecting travelers, and there were occasional drownings in the most harmless appearing creeks.

OUTSTANDING CITIZENS

PRESTON B. PLUMB

The most useful and distinguished citizen of Emporia and Lyon County from the time the town was founded until his death in 1891 was Preston B. Plumb, United States senator from Kansas. He was an unusually versatile man which, combined with his extraordinary ability and his tremendous capacity for work, made his life one of much more than ordinary attainment. To the facts and figures concerning his accomplishments, should be added what may be termed by-products of his brain and heart and hands. He loved his State, his community, his home and family with the sincerest devotion, and labored incessantly for their benefit.

Preston B. Plumb was born in Delaware County, Ohio, October 12, 1837. His parents, David and Hannah Bierce Plumb, moved with their family to Marysville, in Union County, in 1846. Preston Plumb attended the village school in which, by 1849, he had made all the progress possible. Arrangements were made for him to go to Kenyon College, an Episcopal institution, Gambier, Ohio, a department of which, Milnor Hall for boys, seemed to suit young Plumb's requirements. This college maintained a paper, the Western Episcopalian, which printed the catalogue and other school publications. Preston Plumb worked in this printing office to pay his way through school, beginning in 1849 when he was not quite twelve years old. He did not stay long enough to secure a degree, but it was a sufficient time to acquire a love for the sights and smells of a printing office. He was there about three years.

Plumb, on his return to Marysville, went to work on the Tribune. Another newspaper office in Marysville, owned by Joseph Cassell, failed in business, and Plumb and another printer, J. W. Dumble, were considering buying the plant, which was for sale at a bargain, and reviving the defunct newspaper. Their employer, C. S. Hamilton, naturally did not want the paper started again, and offered the boys $100.00 on the purchase price if they would buy the plant and take it to another county to start their paper. They had no money, and Plumb appealed to his parents. He was sure he could succeed, and his mother favored the plan. The David Plumbs mortgaged their home to obtain the money to pay for the plant. The boys moved it to Xenia, Ohio, and established the Xenia News. The first issue of their paper was February 24, 1854, Plumb being only a few months past sixteen. This was the manner and these the reasons for Plumb learning the printer's trade, which stood him in such good stead when he came to Kanzas Territory in 1856.

When the Kanzas fever struck him, as it struck many young men of that day, he started at once for the new Territory, leaving the paper in the hands of his partner. He traveled over much of Kanzas Territory on foot, and at about the site of Salina he and others laid out a town, which they called Mariposa. There was no work, and little to eat, and the party almost starved to death. Plumb went to Lawrence, where he got a job on the Herald of Freedom, and became acquainted with the men who were making up a town company for the founding of Emporia. He became a member of the town company and helped to select the site. He returned to Ohio in March, 1857, sold his interest in the Xenia News, and induced several other young men, among them Jacob Stotler, to come to Kansas. From this time on, much of Plumb's activities have been related in other parts of this book.[1]

Soon, Stotler bought a half interest in the Kanzas News, which had been established in June, 1857, and in 1859 Plumb quit the newspaper business, selling his entire interest to Stotler. Plumb studied law in Cleveland, Ohio, two winters, returned to Emporia in 1861 and opened a law office. In 1862 he recruited two companies for the Eleventh Kansas Cavalry, in the Civil War. He was successively promoted to captain, major and lieutenant colonel, and was mustered out of the service September 30, 1865. In 1867 he formed a law partnership with Judge Robert M. Ruggles, the firm practicing under the title of Ruggles & Plumb until 1872. In January, 1872, Plumb was elected president of the Emporia National Bank, which he, chiefly, had been instrumental in organizing.

Plumb held the following official positions: Member of the Leavenworth Constitutional Convention, 1858; reporter for the Supreme Court, from which position he resigned, 1861; representative to the State Legislature, 1862; representative and speaker, 1867; representative, 1868; elected United State senator in 1877, reelected in 1883 and in 1889, and was serving

[1]For a detailed account of the life and public and military services of Plumb, see William E. Connelley's Life of Preston B Plumb.

his third term at the time of his death, in Washington, D. C., December 20, 1891.

Mr. Plumb was married to Miss Caroline Southwick, of Ashtabula, Ohio, March 8, 1867. Of their six children Thomas, the third, died in 1872. The eldest son, A. H. Plumb, lives in Emporia; two daughters, Miss Mary Plumb and Mrs. Caroline Plumb Griffith, live in Kansas City; Preston Plumb, jr., and Mrs. Ruth Plumb Brewster live in Pasadena, California. Mrs. Plumb died in 1919.

OTHER DISTINGUISHED CITIZENS

The most distinguished citizen of Emporia and Lyon County in the Twentieth Century is William Allen White, whose political editorial, "What's the Matter With Kansas?" in 1898, attracted national attention, was quoted all over the United States, and was used as a campaign document by the Republican National Committee. Since that time Mr. White has become an international figure. While in Paris during the World War, engaged in writing for an American newspaper syndicate, he was appointed by President Wilson as United States delegate to a peace conference with Russia, at Prinkalpo, an island in the Sea of Marmora, off Constantinople. This proposed conference did not materialize, France withdrawing after all plans had been made, and the French conferee not appearing.

Mr. White has written more than a dozen books, which have had a most satisfactory sale. Always his work is in demand by high-class magazines, and a great deal of his writing consists of magazine and newspaper articles. The Emporia Gazette, of which he has been editor and owner since 1895, is one of the most widely quoted newspapers in the Middle West. In 1924, as a protest against what he believed the domination of the Republican party by the Ku Klux Klan, he announced himself as an independent candidate for governor of Kansas. He spoke to large audiences in almost every county in the State, traveling in an automobile driven by his son and accompanied by Mrs. White. He polled votes enough that Ku Kluxers have since found it convenient to keep out of Kansas politics—which was Mr. White's object, as he had and has no desire to hold public office. He merely voiced his protest, and that of thousands of other voters, against Klan domination in Kansas politics.

George Plumb, who came with his parents, Mr. and Mrs. David Plumb, a boy of 13, to Emporia in April, 1857, long has been one of this town and county's most useful citizens. He enlisted in Company H, Eighth Kansas Cavalry, formed November 13, 1861, for service in the Civil War. This was the first company to leave Emporia for three years, or the duration of the war. He was transferred to the Second Kansas Cavalry, and later to Company B, Ninth Kansas Cavalry. He took part in many engagements, and in 1862 crossed the plains with Company B, escort to Governor Hardy, appointed by President Lincoln as governor of Utah. There was much fighting with Indians along the way, and many thrilling incidents.

After the war, Mr. Plumb went into the farming and stock-raising business, northeast of Emporia, and became one of the leading sheep and cattle breeders of the State. He was married August 21, 1867, to Miss Ellen Cowles, of the Rinker neighborhood. He had the contract for grading a mile of Santa Fe roadbed in 1870, he served on the Badger Creek school board and in the Sunday School as superintendent and teacher, and helped materially in the erection and support of the Lang Methodist Church, of which he is a member. In 1904 he was elected secretary of the Kansas Livestock Association, continuing in that office until 1910, when he resigned to become a member of the Kansas Railroad Commission. He was elected a member of the Kansas House of Representatives—1905 and 1907. He was one of the foremost champions of the direct primary law, of the 2-cent railway fare law, of the anti-discrimination law, and of the maximum freight rate law. He was the author of the railroad law permitting the commissioners of other States to demand lower rates in common territory.

For six years, 1915-1921, Mr. Plumb served the City of Emporia as commissioner of finance. He is a director in the Commercial National Bank, a member and a former commander of Preston B. Plumb Post, Grand Army of the Republic. Mr. and Mrs. Plumb in August, 1929, celebrated the sixty-second anniversary of their marriage. For six decades they have been among the most honored, useful and popular citizens of Lyon County.

William Smith Culbertson, son of Dr. and Mrs. George Culbertson, long honored citizens of Emporia, was graduated from the College of Emporia, in 1907, then took a degree at Yale. He was appointed to a place on the Federal Trade Commission, which he held several years, then was appointed ambassador to Rumania. He resigned this post in 1928 on receiving an appointment as minister to Chile, to which country he moved, with his family. A press dispatch dated Lima, Peru, October 30, 1929, says of Mr. Culbertson:

"William S. Culbertson of Emporia, Kan., special

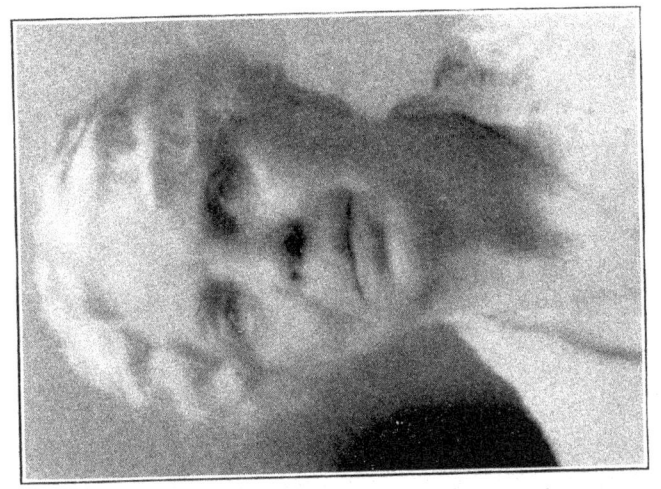

MR. AND MRS. GEORGE PLUMB, 1857-1859

ambassador of the United States for the inauguration of President Leguia, was decorated with the grand cross of the order of the sun before sailing for New York on the steamer Santa Maria this afternoon. His daughter, June, accompanied him on the voyage."

E. W. Cunningham and Charles B. Graves, Emporia attorneys, were honored by appointment as associate justices of the Kansas Supreme Court, where they upheld the high standards of their community and did most creditable work.

The Murdocks—the Rev. Thomas Murdock and his wife, Catherine, and their sons and daughters, Marshall, Thomas Benton and Roland, and Levera and Ella, came to Lyon County in 1858. Originally they were from Virginia, but had tarried in Iowa for a time before reaching Kansas. The Murdock family throughout each decade has made its influence felt all over the State and, by some individuals, nationally. In Emporia, Mr. and Mrs. Thomas Murdock lived to a ripe old age, dispensing the garnered wisdom of their well-spent lives. Their sons eventually became residents of place and power in Wichita and ElDorado, and their daughters married in Emporia. Levera became the wife of Jacob Stotler, one of the early newspaper men of the town, and Ella married Albert Pemberton. Mrs. Pemberton, who lives in Emporia, is the only surviving member of the family of her generation. She was a little girl when the family came to Emporia, but so vivid were the impressions of the new environment on her plastic mind that she recalls many details of the early days in Emporia that might otherwise have been lost.

LYON COUNTY OFFICIALS—1929

Judge District Court, Lon C. McCarty.
Clerk District Court, Mrs. Laura E. Miller.
Sheriff, Tom Owens.
Attorney, O. R. Stites.
Clerk, W. J. Hanna.
Treasurer, J. H. Glotfelter.
Probate Judge, Wilford Reigle.
Register of Deeds, Mrs. Frances Parrington.
Superintendent Public Instruction, Jean Cowan.
Engineer, O. D. Henry.
Physician, Dr. J. S. Fulton.
Nurse, Elsie Henery.
Superintendent County Farm, Henry Brott.

Board of County Commissioners, First District, Fred Fowler, chairman; Second District, William Schultz; Third District, J. L. Stratton.

EMPORIA CITY OFFICIALS—1929

Mayor, C. A. Bishop.
Commisisioner Finance, J. F. Kenney.
Commissioner Public Utilities, W. J. Reynolds.
Clerk, E. T. Mendel.
Attorney, O. L. Isaacs.
Treasurer, E. H. Wade.
Chief of Police, D. P. Cowan.
Chief Fire Department, Charles Stinson.
Water Superintendent, Morris Dunsworth.
Engineer, Fred Humes.

WALT MASON

Walt Mason who lived in Emporia from 1907 till 1920, has written miles of verse with an appeal that gets under the skins of more persons, it is safe to assert, than the verse of any other American writer; and while one is about it, one might as well add, than any other versifier, foreign or domestic. Walt Mason started writing prose poems for the Emporia Gazette in 1907, and soon they were used by so many newspapers that he had them copyrighted. For years he has sold them through a syndicate to several hundred newspapers in the United States, Canada and Great Britain, including London, Dublin and Belfast —the Irish like 'em—Edinburgh, and Bombay, India. He has probably a dozen books to his credit, among which are Rippling Rhymes, Business Prose Poems, Terse Verse, and Walt Mason—His Book. Perhaps the most popular verse he has written is Little Green Tents, printed in thousands of newspapers each year on Memorial Day.

Mr. and Mrs. Mason moved to La Jolla, California, in 1920, but always Kansas, and especially Emporia, will claim Walt Mason for their own.

THE HONOR ROLL

Emporia and Lyon County are happy that some of the original settlers still are numbered among their citizens. Among these, who came previous to 1860, and the years of their arrival in Lyon County, are:

Mrs. Phebe Haworth Roth, 1854.
Mrs. Phebe Schoeck, 1855.
Mrs. Annie Dukes, 1855.
J. H. Studebaker, 1855.
Mrs. Letha Fowler Stack, 1855.
Mrs. Will Wayman, 1855.
Dorris Fowler, 1855.
Gulia E. Hinshaw, 1856.
M. M. Snow, 1856.
Mrs. Nancy Serviss, 1856.
Mrs. Margaret Gilmore, 1856.
Henry Gunkel, 1856.
Mrs. John J. Rees, 1857.
William Hammond, 1857.
Mrs. Nellie Storrs Newman, 1857.
Mrs. Eli Fowler, 1857.
Mrs. Elizabeth Logan Conner, 1857.
Mrs. Matilda Kirkendall Pickett, 1857.
Miss Sarah Kirkendall, 1857.
George Plumb, 1857.
Mrs. Jennie Clark, 1857.
Mrs. Ellen Gregory, 1857.
Mrs. Ella Pemberton, 1858.
Charles Hallberg, 1858.
Mrs. Mary E. Schwartz, 1853.
Mrs. J. J. D. Lewis, 1858.
Stephen Hinshaw, 1858.
Mark Sutherland, 1859.
Mrs. George Plumb, 1859.
Calvin Moon, 1859.
T. D. Little, 1859.
Mrs. Ruth Childers, 1859.
William P. Stanley, 1859.

CITIZENS BANK CHANGES HANDS

F. C. Newman, president of the Citizens National Bank, because of failing health, in 1929 started negotiations for the sale of the Newman interests—the controlling interests—in this bank. A sale was consummated November 20, and William T. Kemper, of Kansas City, and M. A. Limbocker, of Burlington, became the owners of the Newman interests. Mr. Limbocker succeeds Mr. Newman as president of the bank.

Mr. Newman died November 27, 1929.

www.ingramcontent.com/pod-product-compliance
Lightning Source LLC
Chambersburg PA
CBHW051038160426
43193CB00010B/982